BEING IN RELATION

BEING IN RELATION

Indigenous Peoples, the Land, and
Texas Christian University, 1873–2023

Edited by
THERESA STROUTH GAUL
SCOTT M. LANGSTON
C. ANNETTE ANDERSON

TCU
Press

Fort Worth, Texas

Library of Congress Cataloging-in-Publication Data

Names: Gaul, Theresa Strouth author | Langston, Scott M. author | Anderson,
  C. Annette, 1957- author
Title: Being in relation : indigenous peoples, the land, and Texas
  Christian University, 1873-2023 / by Theresa Strouth Gaul, Scott M.
  Langston, and C. Annette Anderson.
Description: Fort Worth, Texas : TCU Press, 2025. | Includes
  bibliographical references and index. | Summary: "Combining historical
  scholarship and first-person interviews and essays by Indigenous
  contributors, Being in Relation: Indigenous Peoples, the Land, and Texas
  Christian University, 1873-2023 centers Indigenous perspectives to
  examine the relations of an institution of higher education with Native
  communities and peoples across its history. What might healthy,
  respectful relations between Native peoples and institutions of higher
  education look like? How do the Indigenous lands upon which TCU resides
  teach important lessons? How does TCU's 150-year history with Indigenous
  peoples and the land in North Texas affect prospects for its present and
  future relationships with them?"-- Provided by publisher.
Identifiers: LCCN 2025002053 (print) | LCCN 2025002054 (ebook) | ISBN
  9780875659176 paperback | ISBN 9780875659268 ebook
Subjects: LCSH: Texas Christian University--History. | Indian land
  transfers--Texas--Fort Worth--History. | Indians of North
  America--Education (Higher)--Texas--History. | Community and
  college--Texas--Fort Worth--History.
Classification: LCC LD5311.T382 G38 2025 (print) | LCC LD5311.T382
  (ebook) | DDC 378.764/5315--dc23/eng/20250402
LC record available at https://lccn.loc.gov/2025002053
LC ebook record available at https://lccn.loc.gov/2025002054

TCU
Press

TCU Box 298300
Fort Worth, Texas 76129
www.tcupress.com

Design by Adrienne Martinez

Cover photo: Haylee Chiariello speaking at TCU's Reconciliation Day, April 24,
2021. *TCU Marketing and Communication, photo by Amy Peterson.*

CONTENTS

DEDICATION

Many books offer a dedication page in remembrance of those who contributed to the making of the book or to the lives of the people who are its focus. The editors have struggled to find words that could adequately express the painful stories we have absorbed and experienced on a cognitive level as a result of preparing this collection of essays.

This book focuses only on the 150-year history of the relationship of Texas Christian University (TCU) with Native peoples and the perceptions of the Native people who have worked with the university as students, employees, or community contributors. We did not find evidence of a TCU person directly responsible for the deaths of the Native people on the land now owned by TCU. But federal and military policy resulted in land that did not belong to TCU being exchanged or purchased by the university. The research conducted and documented by Dr. Scott Langston into how TCU and its benefactors obtained the land may appear as a story of passive and possibly accidental recipients, but we want readers to understand the ramifications to the Native people who call Fort Worth home, including those who are no longer allowed to live there.

The idea for this book began to take shape during one of the most devastating health crises this nation ever faced, COVID-19. This is ironic because, from a Native perspective, destruction began as a result of first contact with the Spaniards on the Gulf Coast during the early 1500s that was eventually responsible for multiple and repeated pandemics (smallpox, measles, flu and more), resulting in the deaths of as many as 90 to 95 percent of Texas Native populations.

We want the readers to know that the painful stories of destruction to this land and its people began with these early Spanish contacts five hundred years ago. We hope this book will help the broader community embrace the next step. How should we reflect on the illness, targeted violence, and cultural destruction experienced by the First Peoples of Texas? How can we support local Native communities and Nations in the region that successfully survived the policy of annihilation and removal and are documenting and protecting thousand-year-old ceremonial sites, natural resources, and ecological knowledge to help preserve this land for the next seven generations?

We hope this book helps readers reflect on today and tomorrow. We must step outside of history and support the peoples who continue to maintain their ties to this land, who feel it is their spiritual obligation to protect it and its people. The research that was done to prepare for this book brought to light a violent, inhumane history of treatment toward all Native people who are descendants of the survivors and who still call this land home. This painful past resulted in Native lands being gifted to strangers without the blessing or permission of their original stewards.

It is sad that it has taken so many years to recognize the treatment of the peoples original to this land and to finally make attempts to build a strong and lasting alliance with the current day Native communities. There is no book, journal, or other recording that will fully represent the destruction and devastation of the Nations who called the land where TCU is built home. We know that this book does not fully express the level of loss that transpired and does not solve anything. We admit that we cannot undo the pain that has already passed.

Despite the forced relocation of the survivors of the federal and military policies of annihilation, Native homelands remain home regardless of where the people are living now. It is an attachment that remains precious even if they never get to return. This land will always be home to the Wichita and Affiliated Tribes as well as the Native peoples who came before and after them, and to them we dedicate this book.

"This ancient land, for all our relations."

We respectfully acknowledge all Native American peoples who have lived on this land since time immemorial. TCU especially acknowledges and pays respect to the Wichita and Affiliated Tribes upon whose historical homeland our university is located.

October 1, 2018

tiʔi hiraːrʔa hiraːwis hakitataːriraːrkweːekih

TCU LAND ACKNOWLEDGMENT

As a university, we acknowledge the many benefits we have of being in this place. It is a space we share with all living beings, human and nonhuman. It is an ancient space where others have lived before us. The monument created jointly by TCU and the Wichita and Affiliated Tribes reminds us of our benefits, responsibilities, and relationships. We pause to reflect on its words:

This ancient land, for all our relations.

We respectfully acknowledge all Native American peoples who have lived on this land since time immemorial. TCU especially acknowledges and pays respect to the Wichita and Affiliated Tribes, upon whose historical homeland our university is located.

EDITORIAL NOTES

Editorial Method

The coeditors invited each contributor to choose whether they preferred to write their chapter or be interviewed. Those who selected oral history interviews had their conversation recorded and transcribed. An editing process followed, in which the contributors had several opportunities to compare the edited version to the original transcription and review changes. Some elected to make substantial written revisions. Each contributor indicated final approval of the finished chapter.

The editing of the interviews was based on the following principles and methods:

- Retain the unique style of speech and expression of each contributor while ensuring the interview is easily readable.
- Eliminate repetitions of words that frequently sneak into speech, like "so" or "actually" or "like," omit verbal sounds like "umm," and correct minor grammar errors that are common in speech but can be distracting in writing.
- Divide speech, which tends to flow along at length without discernible breaks, into sentences and paragraphs.

- Reorder ideas so that ideas connect and events follow a roughly chronological order.
- Correct names of organizations or other information when necessary.
- Add explanatory information in brackets when a reader would benefit from clarification.
- Rarely, cut material in order to stay within our length limits.

We have capitalized *Indigenous* throughout the book, following practices established in Native and Indigenous studies. We have chosen to capitalize *White* in order to mark its status as a racialized identity (rather than an unmarked norm) alongside our capitalization of *Indigenous* and *Black*. Recognizing the many terms used to refer to Indigenous peoples, we respected the choices made by each contributor and retained their word preferences.

This book represents TCU's activities through 2023, the year of TCU's 150th anniversary and when the manuscript was completed. It does not reflect changes in higher education practices nationally or at TCU after 2023.[1]

Cover Photo

TCU student and contributor to this volume Haylee Chiariello (Cherokee) appears on the book's cover. In 2020, TCU launched the Race and Reconciliation Initiative to investigate and document the university's relationship with slavery, racism, and the Confederacy. The initiative held its first Reconciliation Day on April 24, 2021, and Chiariello, dressed in her regalia, read as a land acknowledgment a portion of the text inscribed on TCU's Native American monument. She exhorted the crowd to "remember the learning at TCU happens in the context of a more ancient and successful, sustainable connection to this land." Behind her is a statue of Addison and Randolph Clark, TCU's founders, which Chancellor Emeritus William E. Tucker and his wife, Jean Jones Tucker, donated in 1993. The symbolism of this dynamic young Native leader at TCU—

standing in front of and with her back turned to the founders' statue and the history it represents while looking into the present and future—encapsulates the vision of this book.

Coeditors' Backgrounds and Positioning

The three coeditors bring various backgrounds, expertise, and motivations to this project. We share the following to acknowledge our relationships with the material presented in this volume and the people who have contributed to it and to be transparent about the ways our own identities and experiences shape our participation as coeditors.

C. Annette Anderson: I grew up in the eastern part of Indian Territory, what is now known as Eastern Oklahoma. My family's story was greatly impacted by treaties signed with the Chickasaw and Cherokee Nations, congressional laws, and the drive toward Oklahoma statehood, all of which sought to violate and interfere in tribal sovereignty. The impact on my father and aunt fueled my interest in understanding their identity struggles as well as the struggles of other children who were alienated from their Native Nations due to political decisions and "Christian" morals.

My father grew up reading everything he could get his hands on. He was a wealth of knowledge. He had two master's degrees in engineering, which I realize somehow reflected his persistent questioning of what he learned from books. He spent time talking with his Native friends and the elders, trying to put books, especially about our culture, into context. That method of learning was passed on to me. We should try to read everything we can about our culture but verify that knowledge through oral history in the Native community.

In the 1960s and 1970s, Tulsa Public Schools incorporated Oklahoma Native Nations into our history, geography, and literature lessons. I feel very fortunate to have that foundation. When I entered my master's program in social work at the University of Oklahoma (OU), my culture was reinforced by Native American instructors and mentors. I received specialized training in the Indian Child Welfare Act (ICWA) and Native worldviews, which also helped open doors into the Texas Native American community.

Growing up in Tulsa, I had Native teachers and Native people from multiple Nations around me every day at school and in the community. I spent my summers in the rural areas of Eastern Oklahoma with both sets of grandparents, enjoying the outdoors and all that you learn from being on the Oklahoma lakes and camping in the woods. My father built my connections in the Oklahoma Native community. I took all that for granted.

We moved to Plano, Texas, in 1985, where we raised my two daughters. It was so different and difficult raising Native children in Plano. From the time they were in preschool, I realized my children would have no Native identity if I didn't build those relationships in the DFW community, but Native people were hard to find. Building a family through helping local Native organizations was my first step in this direction, along with my work with the Indigenous Institute of the Americas (IIA). I assisted on some ICWA training for Child Protective Services. I cochaired the first IIA powwow in 2007 with Tosawi Pena and was nominated to be on the IIA Council when they moved headquarters from New Mexico and formed a Texas nonprofit in 2014. Serving on that council and chairing one of the largest intertribal events in North Texas helped me walk down many wonderful roads and meet some of the amazing authors highlighted in this book. As we worked on this volume, in Fall 2023, the Texas Education Agency approved the first ever American Indian/Native Studies Innovative Course for high school students in tenth through twelfth grades. This book highlights some of the knowledge keepers who helped collaborate on the content for the course.

This beautiful community of Native people in Texas has been healing for my family. Learning about the violence, displacement, and failures of what is now known as the State of Texas toward

Native people makes me even more grateful to have grown up in Oklahoma at a time when our Nations' issues were talked about openly and candidly. The current climate in Oklahoma is quite different, as the governor openly tries to attack the sovereignty of the many Nations. I hope this book provides a thoughtful reflection on our past and it helps us pivot toward a more truthful history and positive future for Texas Native Nations and the DFW community.

Scott M. Langston: From the beginning of my life, Euro-American Christian colonization has shaped how I relate to the world, even though I was, for a long time, largely unaware of how it was molding me. My family's story has been shaped by colonization, as well. Its various branches, coming from England and other European countries at least as early as the eighteenth century, have ever since resided, often as poor farmers, on lands inhabited for millennia by Native Nations. In each place they lived, mainly in what we now call the southern United States, my family helped displace Native peoples from their ancestral homes, taking advantage of policies and actions put in motion by much more powerful people and institutions as they sought to live their modest lives. My ancestors' trek through what was renamed as the Carolinas, Georgia, Alabama, Tennessee, Kentucky, Mississippi, Louisiana, Arkansas, and Oklahoma eventually brought them to Texas.

All of my Texas family benefited from forceful and violent removals of Native peoples that made it possible for them to raise families where Native peoples had previously raised theirs. I and my parents and children were born in the historical homeland of the Wichita and Affiliated Tribes, more commonly known by names given by colonizers. My paternal great grandfather had come in the late nineteenth century to the area where Montague, Jack, and Clay Counties meet each other, just over a decade after the last local conflicts between Native Americans and White colonizers. My dad grew up in a small farming community in this area (to the northwest of Fort Worth) during the Great Depression without electricity or running water and had a long career as an air traffic controller. My mom grew up in Fort Worth, the daughter of a Fort Worth fireman who had come from central Texas to the city in the 1910s. That side of the family began its colonizing movements into Texas in the 1850s.

I was born in Fort Worth but grew up during the 1960s–70s in a small southeast Texas town located in the Big Thicket near the San Jacinto River, where the Bidai and Akokisa have lived for thousands of years. There, I absorbed colonization's various tenets, living them out in political, educational, economic, gendered, racial, Christian, and other ways. I saw the world through the lens of Christian Manifest Destiny, rarely giving a thought to the colonizing forces and processes that had created my privileged life. I was well into my forties and long past my formal education before I ever had any personal interactions with Native and Indigenous people, although I do vaguely remember a childhood visit to the nearby Alabama-Coushatta Tribe of Texas reservation. Through nearly two decades of growing relationships with Native people, I have begun to understand the realities of colonization while also learning positive, constructive ways of living in relation to the land and all living beings, human and nonhuman. Wynema Morris, Omaha tribal elder and faculty member at Nebraska Indian Community College, first taught me to learn from, rather than about, Native peoples. This has been transformative, and I owe a great debt to the Native and Indigenous people and communities who have generously and graciously shared these ways with me. Thank you, truly.

Theresa Strouth Gaul: I am of German descent and grew up in Minnesota on Nakota Land that became available to my farming ancestors through the Homestead Act after the US-Dakota War of 1862, a history of which I was entirely ignorant growing up. My ability to study literature as a first-generation college student came about because of the prosperity my family cultivated from that land. I spent years being educated on Nakota and, later, Dakota and Ho-Chunk land. I first became curious about local Native histories when I saw a marker on the University of Wisconsin campus commemorating the route of Sauk leader Mahkatêwe-meshi-kêhkêhkwa (Black Hawk) during the Black Hawk War in the 1830s.

My dissertation and subsequent research career, carried out on the ancestral homelands of the Wichita and Affiliated Tribes, has been devoted to recovering nineteenth-century histories of people who have been forgotten, ignored, suppressed, or marginalized in dominant narratives of US literature. In my teaching, I strive to uphold what I see as an ethical obligation to bring students into encounters with the perspectives, stories, and writings of Native people to help the students recognize the diversity and complexity of US history and culture.

My work in supporting TCU's Native American and Indigenous Peoples Initiative as one who seeks to be a non-Native ally is motivated by a desire to build relationships in a local context. As a literary scholar who has studied how editors of the past presented Native speakers' and writers' words, I recognize that my participation in this book bears legacies of editorial violence and a responsibility to do better. I have learned so much in the process of working with the essays and interviews in this book, and this knowledge has moved and challenged me. I am grateful to my coeditors and each contributor in this volume for what they have shared in their chapters and their trust in me as I worked with their words.

Acknowledgments

Together as coeditors, we wish to thank Dr. Sonja Watson, dean of the TCU AddRan College of Liberal Arts, Dr. Sharon Weltman, chair of the Department of English, and TCU Press for financial support of this project.

HOW TO READ FOR HOPE, SUPPORT, AND HEALING

Guided by Anderson's experience as a social worker, we are aware that
the content of this book represents the multigenerational trauma of the
Native people who lived on the land where TCU is now located as well
as the current trauma experiences of students, faculty, staff, and administrators. It is hard trying to navigate the emotional stress that is created
when we try to be sensitive, kind people. It causes us hurt that can lodge
itself in a place deep in our hearts. Once there it can be hard to shake.

We hope that you will pace yourself while reading this book. Take
your time and monitor how it is affecting you. We encourage the readers to reach out to trusted friends or professionals for support should
reading this text reactivate your own trauma or result in secondary
trauma. Our intention is not to cause distress but to bring awareness.

If the book does not touch you in any way, it may mean that it's
hard for you to identify with the stories and the authors. We ask you to
search a little deeper to touch the part of you that can sympathize with
the impact of loss, relocation, family disintegration, and other themes
that have impacted the Native Nations on this continent.

We hope that reading this book will help all of us find a narrative
that can result in preventing future historical traumas to groups of people and instead build hope, support, and healing for future generations.

FOREWORD
What Words We Breathe upon the Land
by Dr. Patrisia Gonzales

Dr. Patrisia Gonzales (Kickapoo/Comanche/Macehual descendant) is an award-winning scholar, journalist, and promotora-investigadora, *or community health promoter-researcher. She grew up in Fort Worth on the banks of the Trinity River not far from the TCU campus. Her family was the last Indigenous family residing on the bluffs of the river, living in a house whose foundations dated to the erection of the military fort that gave the city its name. Gonzales is recognized as a gifted teacher and practitioner of Indigenous knowledge systems, medicine, and community healing from a hemispheric perspective. She recently retired after a distinguished career as a professor at the University of Arizona. Her books include* The Mud People *(2003),* Red Medicine: Traditional Indigenous Rites of Birthing and Healing *(2012), and* Traditional Indian Medicine: American Indian Wellness *(2016). She was the keynote speaker for TCU's Native American and Indigenous Peoples Day Symposium in 2019.*

Speaking to the above and the below, and all around: we place these words before you as we seek to acknowledge those who came before us and all that has been before us and endures within these lands where Texas Christian University now stands. For many Indigenous peoples, when we enter into someone else's territory, home or homelands, or when we enter into the spiritual territory of the natural world, we ask for permission to enter, agreeing to respect the accords that structure and govern those worlds and places and both human and nonhuman community. We are acknowledging our own responsibility to act respectfully and with reciprocity and humility toward generative relationality. We often offer gifts to honor these relationships, to make relations, and to strengthen relationships and kinship. And, as C. Annette Anderson (Chickasaw and Cherokee) notes, in land acknowledgment we seek to acknowledge and honor the ancestors with the words spoken upon our breath in reverence and respect.

Fort Worth is the homelands of the peoples who comprise today's Kirikir?i:s, or the Wichita and Affiliated Tribes. It is also a place where many of our Indigenous relations camped and lived, following the water and the hunt. Many tribal peoples camped, set up homes, birthed babies, made allies and relations, fought to defend their peoples, and left their footprints upon these lands that became known as Fort Worth, Texas.

My relatives also referred to this region as part of the Comancheria, an area occupied by my Comanche ancestors. I speak as someone whose umbilical cord is buried in the land of Fort Worth. I am literally part of the land. I was raised near the banks of the Trinity River, where my family served as the last caretakers who lived on its bluff and were forced off the land when the City of Fort Worth claimed eminent domain to develop a park.

In 2019, I was the featured speaker at TCU's fourth annual Native American and Indigenous Peoples Day Symposium. Standing not far away from the teepee erected on the Campus Commons, I was joyful and amazed at the visual Land Acknowledgment set in a monument and written "in Indian" as the elders might say, or rather in a Native language, that now is inscribed upon the landscape.

This ancient land, for all our relations.
ti?i hira:r?a hira:wis hakitata:rira:rkwe?ekih

We respectfully acknowledge all Native American peoples who have lived on this land since time immemorial. TCU especially acknowledges and pays respect to the Wichita and Affiliated Tribes, upon whose historical homeland our university is located.

The monument and Land Acknowledgment reflect traditional Indigenous thought regarding our relationships to the land, and the TCU resources accompanying the Land Acknowledgment recognize events that harmed the Original Peoples during the wars against Indians in Texas. With the Native and Indigenous Student Association, TCU

members, faculty, and leadership consulted, developed, and collaborated
with the Kirikir?i:s, the Original Peoples of this land base, to establish a
land acknowledgment. The land acknowledgment is set within a circle,
signifying the circle of life, the sacred hoop holding interconnected experience. All living beings are within the circle, the four sacred elements of
life, the water, the plant nations, and animal nations who hold their own
peoplehood. The sacred hoop, as my Mescalero Lipan Apache Brother
Gregory Gomez (a founder of the Indigenous Institute of the Americas)
has often spoken of, conveys the value of mutuality, mutual respect, and
consideration.[1]

The physical monument embronzed on the TCU campus emplaces
upon the land a reminder of truth, for people to visit amid trees and the
natural world. The Land Acknowledgment, monumentalized in a Native
language on a bronze marker on granite that is Indigenous to the region,
breaks through many ruptures, breaking open multiple landscapes of
meaning. It makes visible the Indigenous knowledge of the Original
Peoples of this land, and the Kirikir?i:s language rearranges space
and perception. The language, when sounded, is returned to the land,
changing the resonance of this land base.

TCU's engagement with Indigenous peoples to develop the Land
Acknowledgment and physical monument in consultation with the
Kirikir?i:s demonstrated respect for the Original Peoples' tribal sovereignty. The Kirikir?i:s survived the exterminating forces of Texas. The
Land Acknowledgment is extraordinary, particularly because of the
history of TCU and of Fort Worth as a fort that was created to protect
the settlers from "the Indians." And because of the state's campaigns to
secure President Mirabeau B. Lamar's 1838 call to the Texas Congress
for the "total extinction or total expulsion" of Native Nations, tribes, and
bands from Texas.[2]

Over some sixty-six solar rounds of my life, I recall elders' stories of
hanging trees, raids, and massacres, how my ancestors traveled by night
to avoid being captured and either killed or forced onto reservations,
and what life was like in the 1800s for my grandparents, great-grand-
parents, and great aunts and uncles and great-great grandparents, many
of whom lived into their nineties and even beyond the centenary. My
Kickapoo and Comanche grandmothers and great-grandmothers and
great-great grandmothers left us ways and instructions to remember the

strength of our peoples, and of Native women. Listening to my elders' rememberings, it was as if I was breathing in the atmosphere of time and memory of a dangerous, pivotal period of the 1800s for Indigenous peoples, before Texas was a state or a republic. They also spoke of how they walked freely and rode horses in and out of territories that, at different times, were claimed by Spain and Mexico and the Republic of Texas. My American Indian ancestors intermarried with peoples of the Chichimeca and Huesteca Indigenous regions of Mexico, with Macehual peoples and Mexicans as Indians. The stories were told while porch sittin', visitin' at kitchen tables—and before being retold, it was remembered that they were first heard amid grandma and grandpa stories of Geronimo, Indian camps, the Alamo, and sometimes in between some fiddlin' or bringing out the guitars, or as part of the times when stories are told for a reason. I am their descendent and the inheritor of these stories.

When I was growing up in Cowtown, the master narrative of Texas was that of the vanquished Indian. This "eradicated Indian" false story led to a Native American Indigenous Studies Association conference panel in Austin in 2014 to address "Ain't No Indians in Texas" narratives. The Cowtown/Texas narrative is not about "Cowboys and Indians" but about the Cowboy—and a land—without Indians, a supposed razing so complete it is no longer acknowledged. Despite this narrative, there's been a resurgence of tribal recognition, self-determination, and sovereignty and the reconstituting and strengthening of tribal authority in Texas. We are here; we remain.[3]

This collection acknowledges not only the benefits of TCU today but how TCU benefited from the violences upon Indigenous lands. This courageous collection of essays and interviews, oral tradition, and testimonies speaks to the actions that must accompany land acknowledgments, so that they are not merely performed as a ritualized statement, a gesture losing meaning with perfunctory repetition. There is no book like this from another university in Texas.

This book should accompany the layered context available as part of TCU's Land Acknowledgment resources. The full-length explanation of TCU's Land Acknowledgment on TCU's Center for Connection Culture website also acknowledges forced relocations and displacements, with prompts for discussion and reflection. It states, *"As a university, we*

acknowledge the many benefits we have of being in this place. It is a space we share
with all living beings, human and nonhuman. It is an ancient space where others have
lived before us. The monument created jointly by TCU and the Wichita and Affiliated
Tribes reminds us of our benefits, responsibilities, and relationships."

Ideally, traditional land acknowledgments remind us to take action, to be mindful of how we walk and of the words we speak. They also situate us as to our own position within a territory, a place, and the sacred circle honored in TCU's Land Acknowledgment. As institutions have begun to adopt land acknowledgment practices, they must consider: How did we get here? How did we come to be here? What are our roles and responsibilities? How do those in the present benefit from harm? Few Texans are taught the history of the Indian Country that Texas occupies, or of the more than six hundred tribes that were recorded as existing in Texas from 1500 to 1900 in the 1976 Texas Handbook.[4] Or of the vast Southern Buffalo herds in Texas that were nearly decimated. Where did they go?

The idea of the Vanquished Indian in Texas occurred through erasure of Native histories and colonizing acts rarely taught in Texas schoolbooks, acts of annihilation, ethnic cleansing, displacement, forced relocations, and statistical erasure. Indigenous peoples also enacted survival strategies, such as hiding or camouflaging as Mexican—disappearing within the Mexican identity—or passing as White, or simply not naming their Indigeneity outside of protected, relational networks.

◆

TCU alum Lauran Denham notes that her determined efforts to institutionalize the TCU Land Acknowledgment were an effort to acknowledge and educate the TCU community on a "dark and flawed" history that provided the context for its success.

Dr. Scott Langston's chapter documents the harsh history that must be spoken, that must be contextualized to understand how wealth was accumulated through the ongoing persecutions against Indigenous peoples to solidify the creation of Texas through both state-sanctioned and extrajudicial acts of extermination and expulsion. TCU was established and flourished within this context. Relatedly, *High Country News* documented how expropriation and genocide are the colonial foundations of "land grab universities" in its March 2020 reportage on land grant university systems, and how their properties, endowments, and success resulted from these institutions' profiting from Indigenous dispossession.[5]

Langston reminds us of the role of Christian doctrine and theology in repressing and dispossessing Indigenous authority over their lands, lifeways, and souls. Recently, the Catholic Church repudiated the Doctrine of Discovery, which was used to justify claims on Indigenous land and life. In a March 30, 2023, bulletin from the Holy See, the Catholic Church recognized that this colonial history "demands an acknowledgment of the human weakness and failings of Christ's disciples in every generation."[6] The "Joint Statement of the Dicasteries for Culture and Education and for Promoting Integral Human Development on the 'Doctrine of Discovery'" continues on to say that the faithful members and institutions must find new ways of conduct and actions aimed at respecting Indigenous rights: "As Pope Francis has emphasized, their sufferings constitute a powerful summons to abandon the colonizing mentality and to walk with them side by side, in mutual respect and dialogue, recognizing the rights and cultural values of all individuals and peoples. In this regard, the Church is committed to accompany indigenous peoples and to foster efforts aimed at promoting reconciliation and healing." Langston details the discomforting truths that most students are not exposed to in history books, in order to move the TCU community toward a "constructive acknowledgment."

Dr. Pablo Montes (Chichimeca Guamares and P'urépecha peoples) asks readers to consider what it means to be guests on this land. What does it mean to acknowledge the land and the history that has occurred, and what are its effects on the Indigenous present? What are the implications, when instructors acknowledge in a classroom that "you are learning on stolen land"? Truth-telling can bring confusion, dissonance, and rile up guilt and anger when settlers realize they are the *uninvited* guests, as Quechua Indigenous education scholar Dr. Sandy Grande notes.[7]

This collection of stories, essays, and interviews also helps us to imagine an Indigenous future, the possibilities of change and opportunity, restoration and renewal. We hear from Haylee Chiariello, a Cherokee baton twirler advocating for awareness on Missing and Murdered Indigenous Women, an Oneida game designer and professor, and a Comanche-Kiowa textile design artist. They remind us of the everyday lives of Indigenous peoples as they join the Frogtones or work to address MMIW or Missing and Murdered Indigenous Relatives (MMIR), or how the whole tribe gathered and organized to bring a student to the school. They are on scholarships and on basketball teams. They are Christians and traditionalists. They are distinct, not exotic. Embedded in these stories is resilience in the face of loneliness, amid stereotyping and cultural fatigue, as the lone Indians who must address stereotypes and misinformation. These frank accounts also lay bare the Native reality, such as when Albert Nungaray (Tewa) is reported as carrying a weapon—a traditional Tewa flute. Yet, he remained committed to singing with the Frogtones. As Nungaray states, he is a loyal Horned Frog, but he also found part of his experience "exhausting."[8]

Tabitha Tan, a TCU alum and former member of TCU's Native American Advisory Circle, who attended a high school on the Navajo Nation that housed a legendary girls' basketball team, enjoys a good game of B-ball with the TCU community. She developed trusted friendships with other Frogs, in new spaces of belonging.

And there is loneliness and cultural fatigue, "exhausting" and excruciating efforts for faculty, students, and staff in being the only one, the one who must speak up, the one who is asked to contribute their emotional and physical labor, and in a variety of ways, the one who is gazed upon as representing all of Indianness, as if there was some generalizable totality of more than 574 federally recognized tribes and thousands more Nations that are the original inheritors of what is today known as the Americas, each with distinct philosophies, structures of governance, sciences, and ceremonies.

Where do they draw strength? From the land itself, from going into prayer. We read of the power of blessings and ceremonies, the whole community offering prayers for the one that would go off the reservation and into the White man's world, blessings of their apartments, the fanning of smoke and prayers for protection, and for good things to emerge.

Indigenous students persist, they endure, they continue to dare to learn within White spaces. The students persist in their knowledge seeking, often far from their own traditional lands and families, and frequently as first-generation college students. And yet, student and alumni contributors, such as Tan, "bleed purple."[9]

Lauren Denham (Unangan) documents her dedicated effort as a member of the Student Government Association in getting SGA to pass a resolution requesting all faculty to include TCU's Land Acknowledgment on their syllabi. She recounts valiant efforts to have the Land Acknowledgment adopted by the faculty, yet, as she notes, the effort failed because of concerns regarding control over syllabi and adding a burden on the faculty. She then wrote legislation to codify the Land Acknowledgment as part of the student government code, which was adopted by the SGA. Notable is her disappointment when the Land Acknowledgment was not read at her TCU graduation; also striking is her agency in making phone calls to TCU leadership afterward to ensure the Land Acknowledgment would endure as more than a forgotten or overlooked statement.

The chapter by Jodi Voice Yellowfish, Nino Testa, and Theresa Strouth Gaul, focused on MMIW, unpacks the complexity of addressing ongoing violences from the perspective of pedagogy and Indigenous advocacy. These writers ask for key terms to be acknowledged, such as sacredness, sacred data, and kinship, suggesting tools that could be incorporated into classroom teaching. At its conclusion, this conversation turns its gaze toward the advocates and recommends how they may interact with non-Natives interested in supporting the work to combat this epidemic. Like much of the book, it breaks several conventions, such as providing a dialogue as opposed to a theoretical article, making this an accessible and nonconventional approach to educating learners on this topic.

They engage in a discussion regarding "how non-Native communities and educational institutions should ethically and intentionally learn from and support the efforts." This is a key question that the contributors address, and this is the undergirding point of "why a land acknowledgment?" The truth stirs up the distorted muck of history. Throughout this collection, the contributors raise the question of the instructor's responsibility and scope. What is needed or useful? In fact, those who work with Indigenous knowledge must demonstrate accountability to the lineages of Indigenous knowledges as part of acknowledgments.[10]

Dr. Wendi Sierra (Oneida Nation) speaks of the well-intentioned conversations and exchanges she has with students and the TCU community that result from Native peoples being a footnote in history and monoliths in the Western imagination. Here, we see a dynamic professor, a Native gamer, teaching students to learn through an Oneida imagining of the future. In this way, the future organizes experience in the present, that "we're still here," as Sierra notes. She describes the burden of Native faculty who must find a delicate balance between truth-telling and not creating, or replicating, a victim story.

Anderson contextualizes the urban Indian experience in the Dallas–Fort Worth region, as well as the endeavors of the Indigenous Institute of the Americas, which has organized significant intertribal events that include Indigenous peoples from Abya Yala, the Guna name for this continent—"land in its full maturity." Despite relocations, forced migrations, and dislocations both from our physical lands and often from our membership within tribes, there remains the Indigenous resurgence as distinct peoples and Indigenous reemergence as decolonial acts. Anderson describes the challenges to survive as distinct peoples, including transcending borders to include and collaborate with Indigenous relatives migrating from the Southern hemisphere and relocating in the DFW area. Recognizing Indigenous peoples by their nations, such as K'iche' Maya or Q'eqchi' Maya or Itzaes from the Mayapan region, rather than the nation-states of Guatemala or Mexico, and building relations based on this recognition, is a form of territorial acknowledgment.

Texas has the fifth largest American Indian population and the second highest population of Indigenous peoples from south of the US-Mexico border, based on US Census 2020 data.[11] Indigenous Texas will continue to grow with the recent migrations of Indigenous peoples, of which 20 percent speak a Native language, according to a 2019 report submitted to the United Nations by the Indigenous Alliance without Borders and the International Mayan League, who collected their own data from shelters in Tucson, Arizona.[12]

Anderson also discusses the efforts of people wanting to honor land acknowledgments and develop protocols based on these accords and the various efforts by numerous Native organizations and nonprofits to build community in the Indian country of the urban Dallas–Fort Worth region. She offers an excellent template for a land acknowledgment that comes from the heart, which could easily become the first lesson in many courses at TCU, to center people's responsibilities and teach them to situate themselves within an Indigenous memory/truth speaking.

Sarah Tonemah (Comanche and Kiowa), a former employee in costume design in TCU's Theatre Department and former member of TCU's Native American Advisory Circle, recounts how the theatre department incorporated a land acknowledgment, yet did not consult her as someone who is a living Native person within the department, referring to the "difficult conversations" that many Indigenous peoples must engage with to surmount misguided efforts, however well intentioned. Consultation with Indigenous peoples and representatives is at the center of recognizing tribal sovereignty, particularly amid White/institutional privilege. She and others discussed the power of coming together through campus and community Native organizations—the power of the collective. She calls on TCU leadership to understand that each student embodies a nation with traditions and histories, and for the institution to understand why expanded services and outreach are needed, with more in-depth conversations and a deeper register of commitment and interaction.

These accounts show the potential for shifts, particularly when allies take a stand and walk alongside Indigenous peoples. Much gratitude to the Indigenous leadership that persisted in the endeavor, and to Dr. Langston for his fierce stance as an ally. This book should be required reading for all faculty, staff, and university students. In fact, it should be distributed to all TCU constituents as part of the Land Acknowledgment efforts. It may provide a starting point for deeper conversations aimed at deliberate institutional change.

Throughout this collection, we see ways in which an Indigenized pedagogy could be used as a required text for many courses at TCU. Each chapter provides key recommendations that can move TCU toward meaningful actions that go beyond the Land Acknowledgment—engaging and developing integrated approaches that range from scholarships, mentoring programs, and changes and expansions in curriculum to include Indigenous knowledges.

The contributors, members of TCU's community, offer solutions: create a Native American cultural center, establish a community of practice of Native and non-Native allies, a required course on Native Americans, courses on Native feminisms and histories, full scholarships for the Original Peoples of this landbase, more scholarships for Indigenous students in general, mentoring, and support for Native students, faculty and staff. Tonemah calls for ongoing commitments and concerted actions for the larger TCU community to "shift their minds collectively."

TCU's Land Acknowledgment shows the minimum foundation that institutions of higher learning must construct to become accountable to the present and the future. Montes asks readers to consider what it means to be good guests. To be a guest means to relinquish entitlement. To be in relationship, to build relations with the land, requires concerted efforts. He asks how far will the commitment go to be in good relations? The Land Acknowledgment is only the beginning, the preamble; what will be amplified? What will be relinquished? How can the power and weight of TCU as an institution be redirected to honoring the land and the sovereignty of the Original Peoples of these lands?

There are many kinds of acknowledgments that occur within Indigenous relations. In ceremonial time, we stand in both the present and the future, holding the past in acknowledgment. The land pulls from us, the land absorbs, the land holds stories, the land is the ancestors who were returned to the earth. Our spiritual teachings upon the land return us to our center, despite interruptions and ruptures. Even if we no longer live in our original homelands, we may return to them in ceremony. We carry our original places in bundles, songs, and prayers.

In developing this foreword, I had to ask myself, how am I to write this? As an Indigenous scholar? As an ancestor to the Future? Land acknowledgments clear our minds so that we may act with respect. The intention is so that we honor the lineages upon the land and so that we may act with goodness in our hearts. In our traditional ways, our ceremonies guide these acknowledgments, the sacred guides us. It was the sacred that was targeted as part of colonization, our traditional, customary practices, knowledge systems, and philosophies of how we understood life and the universe and how they guided our daily lives. In many ways, we are in a ceremony of return.

When I returned to Fort Worth to deliver a keynote at TCU's Native American and Indigenous Peoples Day Symposium in 2019, with my family there, a Comanche drum, and many Native peoples in attendance, I felt as if the circle had been completed. That we should all be there at this time. The seers and the voice hearers connecting with the Unseen World speak of the Spirit People that come when we pray, remember them, call them in. They have waited for us to gather as Indigenous peoples in Texas, to take our place, to stand in strength and wisdom. The seers say that the ancestors and Spirit Beings come to stand with us when we stop to pray and go into ceremony. That is the unseen world of the land acknowledgment, the ancestor world, the spirit world, the up and the down worlds, the all-around worlds. As Anderson explores in her own heart-based land acknowledgment, the land and territory of the Original Peoples is "sacred ground that carries their memories."

The land holds stories and memory, waiting to be told. As Lipan Apache elder Emma Ortega taught me long ago when we were part of a Turtle Island storykeepers' circle in San Antonio, Texas, "The story has a reason for wanting to be told."[13] Many Native languages are verb-based—in keeping with a verbing of Indigenous languages, this collection comprises what Santa Clara Pueblo scholar Gregory Cajete calls "storying" in his book *Native Science: Natural Laws of Interdependence*.[14] These stories are therefore "truthing" the experience of Indigenous peoples in the space occupied by TCU.

How can we be changed by the stories? How can we do things differently? What will we commit to? What responsibilities do people hold to the land that they have occupied within the circle of life? The answers are contiguous and contingent, multiple, and relational in our place within the Sacred Hoop. It requires us to think from our hearts, to let our minds and intellect to sit in the wallows of deeper wisdom.

TCU's Land Acknowledgment is in the Wichita language. Our languages come from the land, from how we, as Indigenous peoples, evolved and emerged from the depths of the earth and our particular place within the sacred circle. That language is the land speaking to us, it is the birds and the water, the winds, the stones speaking through human form. Those words come from the land, in the past, in the present, and what may emerge in the future. How will you show your respect?

"ti?i hira:r?a hira:wis hakitata:rira:rkwe?ekih"

INTRODUCTION

by Theresa Strouth Gaul, Scott M. Langston, and C. Annette Anderson

*Being in Relation: Indigenous Peoples, the Land, and Texas Christian University,
1873–2023* uses Texas Christian University's 150th anniversary in 2023
to examine the relationships between TCU, Native Americans, and the
lands the university has inhabited throughout its history and into the
future. TCU's Land Acknowledgment, adopted in 2021, reminds us
that the university exists in relationship with the land, the nonhuman
beings residing on it, and the Indigenous peoples who have inhabited
it. The essays and interviews collected in this volume critically and
candidly examine TCU's relationships with Native peoples and the land
across its history.

   Being in Relation presents essays and interviews by TCU students,
alumnae, staff, and faculty as well as Native community members
who have significantly engaged with TCU since it commenced a
series of initiatives, which have come to be called the TCU Native
American and Indigenous Peoples Initiative (NAIPI), in 2015.
In sharing their experiences, perspectives, concerns, and ideas
for change, the contributors tell a collective story of TCU's past,
present, and future that is characterized by pain, resilience, and
hope. In this moment when many universities are reckoning with
the racism and discrimination in their histories, the centering of

Native and Indigenous perspectives in *Being in Relation* is a necessary entry into higher education discussions on how past damage must be acknowledged. It explores what it might look like to build new and healthier relationships between universities and the groups they have oppressed, profited from, excluded, and marginalized. The book's authors go beyond articulating the need for measures to address past harm to point out positive possibilities that arise from respectful and balanced relationships between institutions of higher education, Native and Indigenous Nations and communities, and the land. In short, colleges and universities are more effective and can provide stronger education to their students when they partner with the Native and Indigenous peoples who have developed thriving, sustainable, and sophisticated relationships with each other and the land over thousands of years. These institutions can learn much if they will listen.

All who have contributed to this volume share the hope that their stories will move members of TCU's community toward change and action in addressing the issues discussed. We also hope this book may reach readers in higher education who are grappling with similar questions about their university's relations with Indigenous peoples or wondering how to better acknowledge, support, and collaborate with Native members of their own and surrounding communities. Finally, and most importantly, we hope that, in keeping with a valuing of reciprocity, the stories conveyed in these pages may be valuable to the DFW Native community in documenting the experiences of its ancestors and current members.

Being in Relation, whose title was inspired by Dr. Pablo Montes's essay on being in relation with the land, takes a distinctive hybrid and collaborative form, poised between oral and written, academic and nonacademic audiences. Centering Indigenous voices and perspectives on TCU, the collection presents oral history interviews and essays by members of TCU's community and the DFW Native community and original historical research on TCU's history of relationships with Indigenous peoples and Indigenous lands. *Being in*

Relation thus stands as the first documented record of TCU's history given through an Indigenous lens, describing the experiences and perspectives of Native members of its community before they came to TCU and while they worked, studied, or collaborated here. It also provides testimony to the work undertaken from 2015-2023 comprising TCU's NAIPI. Finally, the book challenges TCU's administration and faculty and administrators at other universities to continue moving their institutions toward healthy and respectful relationships with Native and Indigenous peoples and communities.

The Beginnings of TCU's Native American and Indigenous Peoples Initiative

The context for this book is shaped by the collaborative efforts, beginning in 2015, of individuals from several Native Nations and a small group of non-Native TCU faculty that would grow into serious engagements supported and facilitated by the university. While a few faculty were addressing Native American topics in their courses at the time, there were no broader, institutionalized initiatives trying to create mutually respectful and reciprocal relationships. In fact, it is safe to say that throughout most of its history, the university gave little thought or respect to the original stewards of the lands on which it has resided (see Scott Langston's essay on this history).[1]

The leadership, patience, and kindness of skilled, highly knowledgeable individuals from diverse Indigenous cultures cannot be underestimated in sparking and guiding the transformation occurring at TCU. The university's Native American and Indigenous Peoples Initiative began with Chebon Kernell, citizen of the Seminole Nation of Oklahoma, Mekko (traditional ceremonial leader) of the Helvpe ceremonial grounds (Muscogee [Creek]), and at the time, executive secretary for Native American and Indigenous ministries of the General Board of Global Ministries for the United Methodist Church. Starting in spring 2015, he spoke every semester in religion courses and to broader university audiences until COVID stopped on-campus gatherings in 2020. He also expanded the circle of connections by bringing other Native American speakers with him to address a variety of topics, providing introductions to others, and giving important guidance. As faculty began opening their classrooms to these speakers, the desire to learn from those representing multiple Native Nations, perspectives, and experiences increased and gained momentum across campus.

Learning from, rather than about, the hundreds of unique Native Nations and cultures has been a foundational attitude and ethic shaping TCU's initiative. The simple act of respectfully listening and being open to diverse Native knowledge and perspectives has guided activities and strategies. After multiple sessions in university courses in Fall 2015 addressing contemporary issues related to Native American and Indigenous spirituality and Native American and Indigenous women, Kernell and co-panelist Edyka Chilomé, an orator, writer, and spiritual activist of diasporic Indigenous descent (Salvadorian and Mexican), raised the possibility of doing something bigger at TCU. Dr. Theresa Gaul, a professor in the English Department and then director of Women and Gender Studies, also made similar suggestions after witnessing Kernell's and Chilomé's powerful engagement with students.

These conversations led to TCU's first Indigenous Peoples Day Symposium (later renamed Native American and Indigenous Peoples Day Symposium), held on October 3, 2016. Money to fund the event the first year came from a TCU Instructional Development Grant, aimed at enhancing learning in certain courses that semester (including Gaul's Native American Literatures), and generous contributions by the AddRan College of Liberal Arts. In consultation with Kernell, the symposium chose Indigenous perspectives on the observance of Columbus Day and the ramifications of Western colonization and assimilation of Native peoples and lands as its inaugural theme. Joining Kernell and Chilomé as keynote speakers were two prominent leaders in the Dallas Native community, Peggy Larney (Choctaw), and her son, Brian (Choctaw and Seminole). Both Larneys played a pivotal role in the 2013 Texas legislature's decision to designate the last Friday in September as

American Indian Heritage Day in Texas.

The four keynote speakers spoke in numerous classes in various disciplines throughout the day. Carl Kurtz, member of the Citizen Potawatomi Nation and TCU class of 2014, set up his tipi (lodge) in the heart of the university on the Campus Commons near Frog Fountain, talking with individuals and meeting with classes to explain his Nation's history and culture. The university's Mary Couts Burnett Library created a small exhibit featuring the Indigenous peoples of Texas. In addition to the estimated four hundred people who took part in the day's events, six hundred people attended an evening keynote session that included the four speakers, a drum known as Comanche Thunder composed of Head Singer James Yellowfish and several male singers, and dancers from Tribal Traditions Arts & Education from Dallas. Several university programs and TCU faculty either required or offered extra credit to their students for attending the symposium, an essential act helping ensure the event's attendance success. From the outset, many TCU faculty and staff have provided vital support for TCU's Native American and Indigenous activities by encouraging and incentivizing students to attend. This has been a key component in the growth and success of the initiative.[2]

The level of campus and community interest in the first symposium propelled the initiative's work to much higher visibility and participation. Shortly after the symposium, a small group of students organized the Native and Indigenous Student Association (NISA), receiving university approval in November 2016. As its constitution states, "The purpose of this association is to form a coalition of resilient individuals, to build a community, and create a space for and by Native and Indigenous peoples and allies to share their cultures, heritages, traditions, languages, and customs in a respectful manner." The group has always been small and not all Native students have participated, but it offers Native and non-Native students a way to build connections, support each other, educate the campus, and participate in Native community activities outside of the university. For example, in 2021, NISA organized and led an on-campus drive in support

Carl Kurtz teaching at his tipi (lodge) on the Campus Commons during TCU's sixth annual Native American and Indigenous Peoples Day Symposium, October 3, 2022. *TCU Marketing and Communication, photo by James Anger.*

of the Wichita and Affiliated Tribes' effort to create an Indigenous library. Through NISA's leadership, members of TCU's community purchased and sent Indigenous-authored books to the Tribe.

The symposium has since been held annually, with TCU's chancellor Victor J. Boschini Jr. designating, in 2017, the first Monday in October as Native American and Indigenous Peoples Day at TCU. Administrative recognition and willingness to support efforts in increasingly significant ways has been another important element in the initiative's survival and growth, not only elevating the work's prominence but also opening doors within the university that allowed it to flourish. Former TCU provost Nowell Donovan gave enthusiastic encouragement in the early days, especially needed in the initial period of establishment and when participants began to realize the possibility of doing something more than a one-off program. The symposium has now become the center of growing efforts to build relationships with Native American peoples and communities, while also educating the campus.

Student luncheon at TCU's first annual Indigenous Peoples Day Symposium, October 3, 2016. First row (left to right): Edyka Chilomé, Peggy Larney, Brian Larney, and Chebon Kernell. Second row (left to right): Theresa Gaul, Tabitha Tan, Jordan Baird, Franciso Marcano-Santos, Morgan John, Scott Langston. Third row (left to right): Albert Nungaray, Keith Whitworth, Carl Kurtz, Scott Stafford, Lawrence Grubbe, Kendra Hall.

TCU's Context and Goals for the Native American and Indigenous Peoples Initiative

From the outset, TCU's Native American and Indigenous Peoples Initiative has had these goals:

1. To raise awareness of and respect for Native American and Indigenous peoples, cultures, and perspectives
2. To learn from and respectfully engage Native American and Indigenous knowledge(s) throughout all levels of the campus community
3. To create a welcoming, informed, and respectful environment on campus for Native American and Indigenous students, faculty, staff, and visitors
4. To build healthy, respectful, and mutually beneficial relationships with Native American and Indigenous peoples and communities

The model for our work has been based on two principles:

- Respectfully learning from, rather than about, Native American and Indigenous peoples, thus avoiding the "scholar-as-expert" model
- Working with individual faculty, departments, and programs at TCU to develop Native American and Indigenous-led programming and relationships that are relevant to their specific needs, rather than siloing campus efforts in a single department or program

Recognizing and understanding the factors pertinent to TCU's specific situation has shaped how the initiative has developed. First, unlike some universities, TCU is not surrounded by relatively large tribal populations, nor does it have significant numbers of Native people on campus. Native Nations that inhabited north Texas were largely removed from Texas to Oklahoma during the nineteenth century (see Scott Langston's essay in this volume). Currently, there are only three federally recognized Tribes in Texas, with the closest to TCU being the Alabama-Coushatta Tribe of Texas, located approximately two hundred fifty-five miles southeast of the university in Livingston. The Wichita and Affiliated Tribes, upon whose ancestral homelands TCU is located, is headquartered in Anadarko, Oklahoma, approximately two hundred fifteen miles from TCU. There are also non–federally recognized Tribes that have resided in Texas for long periods. The contemporary Native community in the Dallas–Fort Worth metroplex is an urban community, having grown from the United States government's Indian Relocation program when an office was opened in Dallas in 1957. The Native community in and around Dallas, located thirty or more miles away from its Fort Worth counterpart, is larger and has formed more institutions and organizations, including Texas Native Health (formerly the Urban Inter-Tribal Center of Texas), the only urban Indian health clinic in Texas, American Indian Heritage Day in Texas, Indigenous Institute of the Americas (IIA), MMIW Texas Rematriate, Dallas Indian Mission United Methodist Church, and more. Texas Native Health reports, "According to 2020 census data, the State of Texas is home to approximately 800,000 American Indians and Alaska Natives (AI/AN), with over 220,000 of them residing in the Dallas/ Fort Worth Metroplex, comprising 2.7% of the state's population and 3.3% of the DFW population."[3]

TCU, therefore, must develop relationships with Native Nations located hundreds of miles away, as well as with a diverse local Native urban population and organizations made up of individuals from many tribal Nations across the United States. Like other universities and colleges, TCU has in its one hundred fifty years of history promulgated the myth of the extinction of Native peoples, advanced research on them as objects of study existing only in the past, and dismissed, neglected, and shown disrespect toward Indigenous peoples and communities. These factors have contributed to creating a university that is overwhelmingly non-Native. With few Native people on campus, building respectful and mutually beneficial relationships between the university and specific Native

Nations, local organizations, and individuals from numerous Native cultures and experiences becomes a wide-ranging effort. These relationships need to be developed not only with the university as a whole but also with specific faculty, departments, and programs representing a wide array of disciplines and interests.

The vision for the initiative, then, has been to seek to create a significant network of relationships across campus that will grow and be nurtured by a large number of people, rather than being focused primarily in and led by one department or program. Sustaining these relationships becomes the desire and responsibility of many people, rather than a relatively few. The resultant relationships are individually tailored to the specific environments in which they arise. While some have advocated for immediately establishing a Native American studies program or minor, this has seemed premature given current insufficient commitment and staffing across campus to sustain necessary course offerings and insufficient relationships between the university's departments and programs and Native communities. Given the current context, the initiative has focused on establishing numerous relationships relevant in ways specific to the campus's many programs.

A Relational and Indigenous Knowledge-Centered Approach

Like most colleges and universities, TCU confronts an urgent need to educate all members of its community, and especially students, regarding Native American peoples and perspectives beyond basic cultural awareness. A large-scale lack of knowledge pervades all levels of the university, and the low Native American literacy rate of the campus is informed by misinformation and stereotypes. As a predominantly White institution that is almost completely non-Native, the university prepares a large number of non-Native students who will work in fields and communities where having respectful and knowledgeable understandings of Native peoples is essential, if often overlooked. Even if a Native studies program or minor existed, its offerings would not reach most students. Native American perspectives, however, are relevant to virtually every discipline on campus. Fortunately, there is an openness and even a hunger to learn in many parts of the TCU community that goes beyond the traditional academic desire to harvest information for writing books and articles.

How then can we reach students and provide them with the knowledge and skills necessary to work effectively with Native American individuals and communities? One example will serve to illustrate the potential of a Native relational and knowledge-centered approach to disciplinary or professional training. Tribes often make significant economic impacts in the areas where they are located. According to a study from 2022, "In 2019, the total economic impact that tribes made in Oklahoma was $15.6 billion." Understanding how to work with Tribes who are "major drivers" of economies is important for students in an array of fields.[4] How then, for example, might students going into the field of real estate be better prepared and make greater future contributions in their industry by encountering Native American understandings and experiences with the land? How can real estate developers be successful in a capitalistic system while acknowledging and respecting the history and needs of the lands they are buying, selling, and developing? These are difficult questions to answer, but dialoguing with Native American communities can help develop reasonable and responsible solutions. Students could, for instance, develop a set of best practices for real estate developers that considers the needs and experiences of the land, Native communities, and the industry. Helping students develop a self-practice that understands the land and Native peoples where they live and work from a noncolonized perspective will make them more effective in their respective fields.

Creating partnerships with Native Americans that are rooted in and tailored to enhance learning in specific disciplines is, therefore, one way to effectively reach large numbers of students.

Faculty and staff from a wide array of disciplines who respectfully work with and learn from Native people and communities will provide a better education to their students. Indeed, we have a vision that perhaps one day TCU's graduates will be known for their understanding of and abilities to respectfully work with Native American people and communities. As TCU places greater value on such endeavors and develops accompanying supportive infrastructures, a Native American studies program or minor would certainly be an important addition to the overall efforts.

The university's administration did not initiate or recommend this approach focused on building an extensive network of respectful and mutually reciprocal relationships with Native American people and communities. Rather, it arose at the grassroots level through those involved in the earliest efforts and was shaped by a conviction that Western theories and knowledge and the centering of power in those who had mastered such knowledge (such as Western-trained academics) needs to be balanced by Indigenous knowledge. TCU's NAIPI holds that Indigenous knowledge is powerful and relevant to the contemporary world and that the ultimate understanding and control of such knowledge resides in Indigenous communities. Teaching about Indigenous peoples only through the lens of Western theories, models, and goals is an act of ongoing colonization. In other words, we at TCU have much to learn, and we will not be able to learn it by adhering to Western ways rooted in Euro-American Christian colonization. Furthermore, we must respect the sovereignty of Indigenous knowledge and not violate it. Failing to do so parallels the actions that prepared the way for TCU's founding, when the Republic of Texas and General Edward H. Tarrant violated tribal sovereignty by taking lands that were not theirs and upon which TCU now resides (see Langston's essay). We must not take knowledge that is not ours and use it in ways that distort and disrespect it and the communities who created and care for it.

Supporting Native and Indigenous Members of TCU's Community

As a predominantly White institution, TCU has very low numbers of Native American faculty, upper-level administrators, and trustees. The latest available data shows that in Fall 2022, they comprised only 9 out of 709 full-time faculty, far below any other group tracked by the university (Asian, Black/African American, Hispanic/Latino, and White). Nor to our current knowledge have there been any Native trustees or upper-level administrators other than Larry Adams, a member of the Shawnee Tribe who served as associate vice chancellor for academic affairs. In other words, Native Americans are not being included in positions of power at TCU. Often, there are uninformed explanations for this fact, which essentially blame Native Americans: there are not many qualified Native Americans, Native applicants cannot be found, there is no need to have many Native faculty because TCU does not have many Native students, these small numbers are in proportion to the overall Native population in the United States (which fails to recognize the impact of genocide on Native populations), and so on. Such thinking debilitates TCU, especially its students who are deprived of significant skills and knowledge that Native Americans can teach. It also shuts the door to potential Native students, faculty, staff, administrators, and trustees. Educating individuals, departments, and programs is, therefore, paramount. It is an ongoing task that must be constantly addressed. To assist with this, TCU's Native American Advisory Circle produced and made widely available *A Guide to Recruiting Native American Employees and Students at TCU*.[5] One stellar example of a positive attempt was a recent faculty search led by Dr. Darren Middleton in which the job opening was posted in multiple Native American academic publications and websites, as well as distributed to all 574 federally recognized Tribes. Nonetheless, much work needs to be done to attract and retain Native American students, faculty, staff, and administrators, including developing more supporting and empowering infrastructures.

Just as important as increasing Native presence on campus through hiring and retaining Native faculty, staff, and administrators is increasing and supporting the Native student population. One way TCU has addressed this is through the Four Directions Scholars Program, which began accepting students for the 2024–25 academic year. Former TCU provost Teresa Abi-Nader Dahlberg initiated a conversation about a possible scholarship for Native students. Months of discussions resulted in a scholarship and mentorship program. TCU will annually award two four-year scholarships, consisting of fully funded tuition and room and board. Open to first-year undergraduate students, recipients must be a citizen of a federally recognized Tribe. Recognizing the need to provide more than just financial support, TCU will provide a mentoring program for recipients with monthly meetings each semester with a Native American mentor. Additionally, recipients will meet once a semester with their academic advisor and participate in Native American-related events and programming at TCU or locally for a minimum of ten hours per semester. TCU's Native American Advisory Circle played a major role in developing this program.[6]

A robust slate of paid Native American–led programming through campus-wide, departmental, and individual course activities is also helping address the lack of Native presence and leadership. Native people from the local community, as well as various tribal representatives and individuals from across the country, have addressed a wide array of topics, including the Dakota Access pipeline, boarding schools, the destructive legacy of Euro-American Christianity, tribal sovereignty, language revitalization, missing and murdered Indigenous women, Native American women, health, and spirituality, Native identities, contemporary Native cultures, food sovereignty, and more. Such programming grows from concerns expressed to us by Native and Indigenous people, rather than the decision-making of non-Native academics. Relationships established between individual faculty members and programs and Native individuals and organizations have made significant contributions. For example, during the Spring 2022 semester, Harris College of

President Terri Parton (2012-2024), Wichita and Affiliated Tribes, at TCU's Native American monument, October 3, 2023. *TCU Marketing and Communication, photo by Amy Peterson.*

Wichita and Affiliated Tribes drum group performing at the dedication of TCU's Native American monument, October 15, 2018. Left to right: James Marquez, Brenton Chaddlesone, Jimmy Reeder, Kody McAdams, Silas Reeder, Kevin Marquez, and Gary McAdams. *TCU Marketing and Communication, photo by Amy Peterson.*

Gary McAdams, cultural program planner and former Tribal president of the Wichita and Affiliated Tribes, speaking at the dedication of TCU's Native American monument, October 15, 2018. *TCU Marketing and Communication, photo by Amy Peterson.*

Nursing Professor Marie Stark led Public Health Clinical Nursing students in a service-learning project and educational event held at the Urban Inter-Tribal Center of Texas (now, Texas Native Health) in Dallas on culturally relevant maternal and infant safety, health, and well-being. After consulting with this book's coeditor, C. Annette Anderson (Chickasaw and Cherokee), a local leader who is a licensed clinical social worker, students developed and staged the event. In Fall 2022, TCU's Neeley School of Business hosted a Chickasaw Nation expo, organized by Chickasaw Nation citizen and Neeley faculty member Layne Bradley. Several representatives from the Chickasaw Nation gave historical and cultural presentations and Chickasaw businesses set up informational booths. This was a first step in exposing business students to the Nation and helping them learn how to work with Native and tribal-owned businesses.

Another example of how partnering with Native communities is shaping curriculum and programming while also attempting to support Native peoples in meaningful ways is a series of efforts beginning in 2019 focused specifically on Missing and Murdered Indigenous Women (MMIW) that continue through the present (discussed more extensively in an essay in this volume). During Spring 2019, TCU held a workshop on "Partnering with Native American Communities," which was led by three Native leaders, Jodi Voice Yellowfish (Cherokee, Muscogee [Creek], Oglala Lakota), Shara Kanerahtiiostha Francis-Herne (Mohawk), and Kernell. During this session, the idea emerged that TCU might consider creating a scholarship to honor MMIW and support Native students. As Kernell pointed out, an Indigenous presence is not visible on many campuses and, therefore, TCU must commit to being intentional about Native Americans and their presence here and then put resources behind this commitment. That fall, the university began annually awarding a $5000 Missing and Murdered Indigenous Women's scholarship. It honors missing and murdered Indigenous women, raises awareness about this issue, educates future leaders who will address this and other Native American issues, and provides financial support

Chebon Kernell speaking at the dedication of TCU's Native American monument, October 15, 2018. *Photo by Cristian ArguetaSoto.*

Gifts of sage and sweetgrass presented by TCU to the Wichita and Affiliated Tribes drum group at the dedication of the Native American monument, October 15, 2018. *Photo by Cristian ArguetaSoto.*

to undergraduate students at TCU who demonstrate commitment
to these issues. Two of this volume's contributors, Haylee Chiariello
(Cherokee) and Lauren Denham (Unangan), have been recipients.

Following upon this initial session, TCU has sustained discussion of the MMIW issue, in partnership with a Dallas-based group,
MMIW TX Rematriate (previously called MMIW-Texas, when it
was housed under the American Indian Heritage Day organization),
in these ways:

- Had an informational table on MMIW staffed by local
  Native American leaders at the Native American Health
  and Wellness Fair conducted as part of the 2019 Native
  American and Indigenous Peoples Day Symposium
- Held a MMIW pedagogy workshop led by local Native
  leaders in association with the 2019 symposium
- Focused on the issue in the 2021 Native American and
  Indigenous Peoples Day Symposium, whose theme was
  "Missing and Murdered Indigenous Women, Girls, and
  Two-Spirit People: From Awareness to Action." Keynote
  speaker Annita Lucchesi (Cheyenne), executive director
  of Sovereign Bodies Institute, addressed the crisis and her
  organization's work
- Held a MMIW workshop led by local Native leaders for
  faculty who planned to address it in their Fall 2021 classes
  in conjunction with the symposium
- Held a panel discussion between members of MMIW TX
  Rematriate and TCU faculty and students with the title
  "Reflecting on TCU's Missing and Murdered Indigenous
  Women's Initiatives" as part of the 2023 Native American
  and Indigenous Peoples Day Symposium
- Addressed the issue in several courses from a variety of
  disciplines
- Developed a webpage with information, resources, and videos of presentations on MMIWG2S (https://sis.tcu.edu/
  wgst/initiatives/mmiw/)

In Fall 2020, TCU took another step to create stronger Native presence and influence when it established both a Native American Nations and Communities Liaison and a Native American Advisory Circle, consisting of eight or nine Native individuals from within and outside of TCU. The advisory circle includes official representatives from the Wichita and Affiliated Tribes, the Alabama-Coushatta Tribe of Texas, and the Chickasaw Nation. It has offered essential input on a host of issues and efforts and become a respected voice on campus. The liaison works with the advisory circle, builds trust and mutually respectful and reciprocal relationships with Native people and communities, creates structures at TCU that support and empower Native Americans, and educates the campus by raising its knowledge and respect for Native peoples. The liaison also spends time in Native communities, learning about, assisting, and supporting their various initiatives, and building relationships with local organizations such as American Indian Heritage Day in Texas, the Indigenous Institute of the Americas, MMIW TX Rematriate, Texas Native Health, and more. Increasingly, non-Native organizations in the Dallas–Fort Worth metroplex reach out to TCU for assistance as they consider their own relationships to Native peoples. These actions, combined with individual faculty, departments, and programs establishing and developing their own healthy relationships with Native American people and communities, will help Native presence and influence at TCU grow stronger as we go forward.

In addition to enhancing curriculum and programming through relationships with a diverse array of Native individuals and communities, TCU has also sought to make Native American presence more visible in its physical spaces. This, in turn, raises the consciousness of the university, while also creating welcoming spaces for Native people. This effort began in October 2018 when TCU dedicated a monument acknowledging all Native peoples who have lived on this land, especially the Wichita and Affiliated Tribes. Made of a bronze, circular plaque mounted in rustic mahogany granite, it is located in a high-traffic area between the two oldest buildings on campus, Reed and Jarvis Halls. The idea first arose in 2014 and discussions with the Wichita and

Affiliated Tribes began in 2016. TCU asked the Tribe for its permission to erect the monument and invited them to participate as equal partners in its design and installation. On February 7, 2017, the Tribe's executive committee voted unanimously to work with TCU, and twenty months later, the monument was installed and dedicated. The Tribe participated in the dedication, sending representatives and a drum group, and several university officials and individuals representing various Native Nations and cultures from the Dallas–Fort Worth community and Oklahoma participated in the dedication. After the dedication, TCU provided a meal for the Wichita delegation, program participants, and members of the local Native community. TCU paid all expenses related to the monument's design, installation, and dedication.[7]

Initially, the monument's text served as an unofficial land acknowledgment used by some at a few campus events. As one of its first actions, however, the Native American Advisory Circle suggested in Fall 2020 that the university develop an official land acknowledgment. The advisory circle then composed and recommended an acknowledgment, which after several months of administrative consideration was accepted without change by the chancellor's cabinet in April 2021. The official university Land Acknowledgment incorporates the text of the monument. Simultaneously, TCU developed the Native American and Indigenous Peoples Initiative webpage to explain the TCU Land Acknowledgment and how to use it, as well as supply resources to the campus on a variety of topics. Since then, the Land Acknowledgment's use at official university functions, on syllabi and webpages, and in office spaces has increased. Furthermore, a document and accompanying faculty workshop, "Teaching with TCU's Land Acknowledgment and Native American Monument," help faculty and staff understand and transmit the values contained in the Land Acknowledgment and monument. A visual representation of the Land Acknowledgment using a traditional medicine wheel to emphasize the need for interconnected, interdependent, balanced relationships between TCU and the land, all living beings, all Native Americans, and the Wichita and Affiliated Tribes has been developed as a teaching tool. The essays in this volume by Patrisia Gonzales (Kickapoo, Comanche, and Macehual), Anderson, and Pablo Montes (Chichimeca Guamares and P'urhépecha) continue the efforts to develop our campus's understanding by providing powerful commentary and insight on the monument and Land Acknowledgment.[8]

Through the leadership of Denham, whose interview appears in this volume, TCU's Student Government Association (SGA) overwhelmingly passed a resolution in February 2022 encouraging faculty to include the Land Acknowledgement on their syllabi. Unfortunately, as Denham powerfully narrates, a TCU faculty senate committee declined to act on this resolution. Nonetheless, a growing number of faculty are seeing what the committee failed to: the extraordinary importance, power, and educational opportunities of including the Land Acknowledgment on syllabi. SGA passed a second resolution adding the Land Acknowledgment to the Student Government Code. Other campus units have taken positive actions such as TCU's Housing and Residence Life requesting in summer 2023 Land Acknowledgment training for all hall directors and cultural connectors (undergraduate students who among other things work toward creating an inclusive residential experience), as well as posting the acknowledgment in front lobby areas of all of TCU's residence halls. This, in turn, has led to developing a training module that is offered to any program on campus. For example, some instructors teaching the course "Introduction to University Life," a one-hour course for first-semester students to help them successfully transition into TCU's academic community, have requested this training for their classes. TCU's faculty development workshop, *Finding Ourselves in Community*, designed to help create an inclusive classroom culture, likewise has requested the training. The Land Acknowledgment has become a powerful tool to raise the university's consciousness, create a more welcoming environment for Native peoples, and educate and bring about change. It is more than a mere performative exercise, functioning as a seed planted across the university's diverse spaces that grows and nourishes powerful conversations and actions.

The university slowly but steadily continues to incorporate visible expressions of Native American presence into its physical spaces. TCU purchased two works of art, "Based on Quanah Parker" and "Based on Mrs. Jack Treetop-Standing Rock 1908," by contemporary Comanche/Kiowa artist J. NiCole Hatfield (Nahmi-A-Piah), displaying them on the first floor of the new administration building, the Harrison. Sarah Tonemah (Comanche and Kiowa), whose interview appears in this volume, led the effort in finding, researching, and recommending Native American artists and artwork for this project to TCU's chancellor, who ultimately chose Hatfield. Hatfield then composed the Quanah Parker piece specifically for TCU, while the Mrs. Jack Treetop painting had been completed previously. Hanging in the center of the university's administrative power, the art stands as a reminder of TCU's administrators' relationships and responsibilities to Native American peoples. A set of posters by photographer Matika Wilbur (Swinomish and Tulalip) depicting contemporary Native people, along with posters from every symposium, hang in the Mary Couts Burnett Library in a lounge on the third floor, near the music library. Wilbur was the keynote speaker at TCU's second annual Native American and Indigenous Peoples Day Symposium in 2017.[9] During the 2022–23 academic year, TCU's Native and Indigenous Student Association created the Native American Nations Flags Project to recognize and honor the diverse Native presence at TCU. Installed in front of the central stairs on the second floor of the Mary Couts Burnett Library, nine flags represent:

- The Wichita and Affiliated Tribes, on whose historical homeland our university is located
- The Pawnee Nation, honoring the first identifiable Native American student at TCU, Bert Peters, who attended TCU in 1929
- The Navajo Nation, honoring four Navajo students, Julius Charlie, Michael Charlie, Robyn Mitchell, and Tabitha Tan, who in the 1990s were instrumental in organizing TCU's first Native student organization

Native American Nations Flags Project, created by TCU's Native and Indigenous Student Association, on permanent display in the Mary Couts Burnett Library, August 22, 2023. *TCU Marketing and Communication, photo by James Anger.*

President Terri Parton (2012-2024), Wichita and Affiliated Tribes, and President Daniel Pullin, Texas Christian University, at a reception for Native American and Indigenous leaders, October 2, 2023. *TCU Marketing and Communication, photo by James Anger.*

- Nations representing some of the Native American students attending TCU in 2022–23 (displayed in alphabetical order): Blackfeet Nation, Cherokee Nation, Chickasaw Nation, Choctaw Nation of Oklahoma, Pueblo of Isleta, and Sault Ste. Marie Tribe of Chippewa Indians

Ongoing Challenges and the Future

The contrast between TCU before and after 2015 is astounding. The university's seventh annual Native American and Indigenous Peoples Day Symposium in 2023, which coincided with the university's 150th anniversary, perhaps represents how TCU has grown in its relationships with Native Americans. Connecting with the sesquicentennial observances, the symposium planning committee chose the theme "TCU and Native American and Indigenous Relationships: Exploring the Past, Embracing the Present, Impacting the Future," and the university, in turn, highlighted it as part of a year's worth of activities. Past, present, and future relationships anchored discussions and presentations during the day, culminating in a historic dialogue between President Terri Parton of the Wichita and Affiliated Tribes and a senior university leader, Dr. Jonathan Benjamin-Alvarado, TCU's chief inclusion officer and senior advisor to the chancellor. The conversation also included Kernell and Anderson. Prior to this evening keynote session, TCU president Daniel Pullin hosted a reception in the Chancellor's Dining Room for the speakers and several local Native leaders. Never in TCU's history have Native leaders been welcomed by and engaged in dialogue with senior university leadership. These actions stand in stark contrast to the actions of former TCU president Edward McShane Waits who, in 1928, "wore the feathers and the blanket that made him chief of the tribe" as part of the university's "Indian Spring Festival" (see Langston's essay).

Nonetheless, TCU still faces many challenges that could threaten the health and even survival of the NAIPI. Some of these challenges have been mentioned, such as low levels of Native American presence and leadership and the campus's widespread lack of accurate and detailed knowledge regarding Native American people and Nations, which in turn can lead to problematic or even harmful decision making. TCU's use of a self-identification process that limits Indigenous people to only choose a single identity category can contribute to Indigenous invisibility. Some Indigenous people, for instance, may be classified as Hispanic/Latino in TCU's demographic information. This is especially true for Indigenous people who come from communities in Mexico and further south. The ability to communicate information with the entire campus is a pressing need because many are not even aware of the university's Native American and Indigenous Peoples Initiative. Some members of TCU's community range from apathetic to resistant, either not seeing the need for this work or insisting that Indigenous knowledge and perspectives only be understood through Western theories and standards. Some refuse to recognize the skill and exper-

Reception for Native American and Indigenous leaders during TCU's seventh annual Native American and Indigenous Peoples Day Symposium, October 2, 2023. Left to right: Amanda Smith (president, Native American Business Association), Terri Parton (president (2012-2024), Wichita and Affiliated Tribes), Daniel Pullin (president, TCU), Derek Ross (Wichita and Affiliated Tribes member), Chebon Kernell (Mekko, Helvpe ceremonial grounds, Hanna, OK), and Nita Battise (tribal council vice-chair, Alabama-Coushatta Tribe of Texas). *TCU Marketing and Communication, photo by James Anger.*

tise of Indigenous knowledge keepers unless validated with a Western academic degree or subordinated to Western knowledge. Some rely on outdated history about Native people and are not informed of the current global initiatives seeking Indigenous peoples' assistance regarding land knowledge and lifeways to repair damage to our environments. Occasionally, such attitudes manifest themselves in direct confrontation and opposition. Addressing systemic colonization remains a perpetual challenge. Colonization's goals and values continue to underpin and inform many policies, procedures, activities, and attitudes.

Allocating sufficient resources to recognize the NAIPI as a university priority, thus ensuring the initiative's survival and growth, is an urgent need. As the initiative seeks to assist the university in educating students in mutually respectful and reciprocal partnerships with Native communities and people, investing resources is a positive way for TCU to carry out its responsibilities toward Native Americans in return for all the benefits the university has received through the violent removal of Native people from the lands TCU inhabits. This includes, but is not limited to, creating sufficient support and a reasonable workload for the liaison position.

Despite these challenges, there is reason for hope, primarily because of the kind hearts, good will, and determined persistence of Native and non-Native people within and outside TCU. Any positive changes that have transpired have not been the work of one person. Native individuals and Nations from within and beyond Texas stimulated and led the change. Individuals at all levels of the university have used their varying degrees of power to open doors in courses, departments, programs, and administrative units so these relationships can take root and grow. Informed, compassionate, respectful people will overcome any challenges TCU faces in creating and maintaining respectful relationships with the land, all living beings, all Native Americans, and the Wichita and Affiliated Tribes. In her essay in this volume, Anderson points the way forward, writing, "Study your Land Acknowledgement and follow your heart with its meaning. Take it to heart; don't consider it a history lesson . . . if you study that Land Acknowledgement and think about it and absorb it, it sensitizes you."

PART I:

BEING IN RELATION WITH THE LAND
AND INDIGENOUS PEOPLES

WHAT THE PRAIRIES AND RIVERS CAN TEACH US:

Learning from and Being Accountable to Land at Texas Christian University

by Pablo Montes

Dr. Pablo Montes, who is descended from the Chichimeca Guamares and P'urhépecha peoples, joined TCU as a faculty member in the College of Education in 2022 after completing their doctorate at the University of Texas at Austin. In addition to their scholarship and teaching in queer settler colonialism, Indigeneity, and Land education, Pablo engages in community-based work supporting youth. In their essay, they recount their experiences as a first-year faculty member at TCU, the measures the university must take to actualize its Land Acknowledgment, and a powerful challenge to all members of TCU and institutions of higher education more broadly to live in "good relation" to the Land and Indigenous peoples by being "good guests."

Protocol and Introduction

As my elders have taught me, I first introduce myself. My name is Pablo Montes, and my family comes from a small rancho of about twelve hundred people by the name of *La Luz* at the foot of a beautiful mountain called e*l cerro de Culiacán* in the southeastern part of Guanajuato, Mexico. We are descendants of the Chichimeca Guamares and the P'urhépecha people, who are the original caretakers of the valley that forms much of my rancho, the nearby ranchos, and the pueblo (town) *Salvatierra*. The entire valley is called Guatzindeo, closely translated as "the place of beautiful vegetation," and this is the valley that has taken care of my family for so many generations.[1] Although our language and certain aspects of our communities were stolen from us, much of our cultural practices, our stories, and our ancestral memories remain deeply embedded within the fabric of who we are. The Land has taken care of so many generations of my family, and the relationship we have with our homelands is sacred, real, and intergenerational.[2] My dad once told my sisters and me to never sell the land that has fed us once his earthly departure arrives. He explained, "Esa tierra nos ha dado de comer . . . y por eso no se vende" (that Land has given us to eat, and that is why it cannot be sold). Although I am no longer physically present on my homelands, I live with and through the Land as a relation because that is the gift and knowledge that my parents have afforded me. As such, that is the theoretical foundation that guides my ethics in Land relations. I, we, cannot sell the Land that is a part of us because we are indeed the Land itself.

I write to you all from the Lands of the Kirikirʔiːs (Wichita), including the Wichita, Waco, Tawakoni, Kichai (Keechi), Iscani, and Taovaya, among other affiliated tribes and peoples. I, first and foremost, share that I am humbled and honored to currently reside on these beautiful prairies and bountiful forests filled with pecans, oaks, and junipers. I give thanks to the Trinity River and its tributaries, which give abundance and relief amid the intensity of the sun as they make their way to the Gulf of Mexico. As I finish my third year as an assistant professor here at TCU, I am appreciative of all the Indigenous community elders, leaders, and people whom I have had the honor to learn from and be in relation with.

Indigenous scholars have shared their pressing concerns about land acknowledgments because they are often devoid of material accountability, reparative considerations, and spiritual importance. As Stewart-Ambo and Yang suggest, "indeed, sometimes acknowledging Native nations is conveniently understood to be the action in and of itself, as if recognition is itself a decolonizing act. It is not. It is a first step. The question that those of us in institutions with or without formal acknowledgments face is, why practice them at all?"[3] Thus, I reiterate what Stewart-Ambo and Yang share both as a reminder for myself to continuously be in good relation with the Lands and Indigenous people and as an invitation for TCU faculty, staff, students, and the institution itself to continuously work toward becoming *guests* on these ancestral territories. Stewart-Ambo and Yang draw on the Tongva word *Kuuyam* as shared by Acjachemen/Tongva scholar Charles Sepulveda to describe the differences between being a visitor and becoming a proper guest.[4] As they describe, "What would it mean for a settler speaker of a land acknowledgment to say, 'I am a visitor, and I hope to become a proper guest'? To be a good guest is to be in good relation to the land — to learn from and to be accountable to the land."[5] It is with this understanding that I will highlight how being in relation with the Land and Indigenous people is not merely a moment of acknowledgment, but a profound commitment and responsibility to center, amplify, and be of service to Indigenous struggles.

Being Guests on Stolen Land

TCU's Native American and Indigenous Peoples Initiative, along with the Native American Advisory Circle that includes many Indigenous elders and community members, has demonstrated the possibilities of what institutions can do in working toward honoring Indigenous people and Land. Some of the collaborations, which my colleague Scott Langston highlights in far more depth in his contribution to this book, have resulted in very significant outcomes. For example, our university's Land Acknowledgment was created and formally introduced in 2021 by NAIPI, and Indigenous people themselves helped craft the statement for the university to display. Through concerted efforts, NAIPI was able to accomplish this exciting feat, and a monument was established on campus as a physical way for students, faculty, and staff to see the acknowledgment. Other examples of collaborations are the Native American and Indigenous Peoples Day Symposium, a scholarship for Indigenous students, and hosting multiple workshops centering Indigenous issues. This could not have been successfully carried out had it not been for the continuous commitment from NAIPI and the local Indigenous community. Indigenous presence on campus is crucial to any university because nearly all colleges and universities in the United States are built on sacred Land that has been stolen. For the Kirikir?i:s, that includes many parts of North and East Texas, which house many different higher education institutions. Thus, crafting a Land acknowledgment with the Indigenous people themselves is an initial step that is not only necessary but long overdue for our university.

However, as stated earlier, Land acknowledgments are not the destination of Indigenous relationships but a preliminary step, a moment for the university to reflect and critically assess their history while actively desiring to sustain Indigenous Land, life, and people. The fact remains that TCU benefited from the forceful removal of Kirikir?i:s people, as shared by TCU's Land Acknowledgment website.[6] That means that the basis of the relationship between TCU and the Kirikir?i:s (and other Indigenous communities) is understood through dispossession, forceful removal, and violence. The Land bears the marks of these relationships as well, as can be seen in the reshaping of the Trinity River, the continued hyperdevelopment, and the way that the city is racially and economically segregated. TCU occupies a segment of Fort Worth that is associated with a mostly affluent and predominantly White neighborhood, yet when one crosses the train tracks on Berry Street to the "other side of the tracks" it becomes "Scary Berry." The communities that live on "Scary Berry" are mostly migrants from Latin America, Latinx families, and other racialized communities of color. These narratives are fueled and perpetuated by colonial logics and Whiteness and are the unfortunate and real circumstances of both the city of Fort Worth and TCU.

When harm is inflicted, acknowledging that harm is not enough for a genuine and reparative relationship. What if we reframed our position? What if instead of asking, what does it mean for TCU to reside on Kirikir?i:s Lands, we asked, what do the Lands and Kirikir?i:s need TCU to understand and what are the commitments needed to become guests in good relation? This reframing decenters the institution as the primary entity of interest and instead points our focus toward the *necessity* for TCU (and any institution) to listen intently to what Indigenous people have been actively voicing. The reframed questions I have proposed urge us to consider Land as a relation that must be understood, respected, and validated. TCU's relationship with Land, thus, is just as imperative as their relationship with Kirikir?i:s because ultimately Land and people are an inseparable relation. Does TCU love the Land the way that the Land deserves? Does TCU take into account the agency of Land by reflecting on the potential risks of new infrastructure, the irrigation systems, the continuous planting of purple and white flowers, and the disturbance of the homes of animal kin who have lived here far before the existence of TCU, among other risks? Loving Land as a relation would encourage a different answer to these ponderings, and this chapter is as much about purposeful introspection as it is about the destruction of systems and structures that actively go against the futurity of Land, people, and life.

Additionally, the responsibility is not on Indigenous people to do the work of telling the university what should be done if they are uncommitted to listening with the intent to enact meaningful change. It is TCU's duty to seek possibilities of genuine reciprocity and educate themselves on how to work collaboratively with Indigenous communities. I am hesitant to list examples of what "good relation" might look like because this ask is often inculcated within settler guilt. Meaning, the continuous asking of "what do we need to do" is continuous labor for Indigenous people, and rarely are the suggestions and requests Indigenous people propose taken seriously because they require settlers to confront the reality that they are inheritors of imperial benefits. As Tuck and Yang argue, there is a desire for "settler moves to innocence" that works to absolve settlers from guilt while not having to relinquish Land, power, or resources.[7] Is TCU ready for the demands of a decolonial future? Of an abolitionist project?[8] If TCU is not ready to envision these futures, then continuously asking Indigenous people and communities to share "what can be done" is a fraught ask, at best, and an active derailment to Indigenous futurities at worst.[9]

I share what I would personally see as *minimal* asks, but these should not be confused with acts of being in good relation because one must work toward becoming a good guest. I believe *all* incoming students who are Kirikirʔiːs and from other affiliated tribes should receive full tuition, room and housing, and other miscellaneous expenses. If we are "acknowledging" that TCU is on Kirikirʔiːs Land, the least that a university can do is provide a free education to all communities whose Land TCU occupies. Secondly, center and sustain Kirikirʔiːs leadership in different aspects of the university to help shape what an honorable relationship can be with the Lands and the people. Without Kirikirʔiːs guidance, attempts to move in good relation will exclude the very voices and communities that TCU wishes to have a relationship with. Thirdly, create a major in Native American and Indigenous studies, with classes specifically addressing Kirikirʔiːs history, culture, and people. With this also comes the responsibility to hire Kirikirʔiːs faculty, and faculty from other affiliated tribes, to teach classes, provide mentorship, and contribute to programming for Native and Indigenous students. Lastly, create a

Native American and Indigenous cultural center on campus where the history and culture of Kirikir?i:s and other Indigenous communities can be highlighted and amplified. The center would also be a place of gathering, where Indigenous and non-Indigenous people can meet, center Indigenous spirituality and cultural practices, and provide a central place of community for Indigenous faculty, staff, and students.

The minimal asks I have shared here are exactly that: they are *minimal at best*. In other words, what I propose should not be confused with the act itself of being in active and good relation with Indigenous communities, because these are requests that should have *already* been taken up.[10] Additionally, accomplishing all this can in no way atone for and undo the violence and harm that has been inflicted on Kirikir?i:s Land, people, and other Indigenous communities. Holding both of these truths is imperative: one, that Indigenous people at minimum deserve basic material reparations and, two, that Kirikir?i:s communities and other Indigenous people must be central to any conversation on the commitments of being a guest on Kirikir?i:s Land and what those *responsibilities* entail. That is why providing examples to the question "what can TCU do" from the standpoint of the university and settlers is a question that seeks incomplete answers, often with little to no utility. If relationship is at the core of how TCU must enact an honest journey toward becoming a guest on Kirikir?i:s Land, this question cannot be the inception of the journey. What are your commitments with and to the Land? With and to Kirikir?i:s self-determination, sovereignty, and futurities? When you are asked to forgo power and privilege, what will your response be? If one has not thought of these invitations before, they require a radical shift in the way one thinks and comes to know. But they are necessary. They are necessary because that is where attempts to establish and sustain a relationship can emerge. I urge TCU to consider where they see themselves positioned—to do the work of disentangling the complexities of those answers before asking Indigenous communities what they can do.

Furthermore, Leigh Patel provides an opportunity to think with what I have proposed as she writes, "If colonization is about ownership and territoriality for some at the expense of others, anticolonial stances must imagine still being in relation with each other but for survivance: in order to grow and to thrive from lived agency."[11] Thus, the centrality of what Patel urges everyone to consider is that relationality is vital to the journey of addressing the continued impacts of (settler) colonialism. Importantly, relationality must envision that which must exist, an afterward of abundance, survivance, and Indigenous futurity. Unangax̂ scholar Eve Tuck and Ngāti Awa and Ngāti Porou scholar Linda Tuhiwai Smith illustrate the importance of Indigenous people in anticolonial and decolonial work. As they suggest, "Indigenous educators pragmatically enact decolonizing work while settler scholars can only imagine decolonization as philosophical and theoretical. Indigenous educators carry forward Indigenous teachings and carry forward the relations—circling back to the teaching-as-relation and self-as-relation—that is the heart of Indigenous futurity."[12] Ultimately, both Patel and Tuck and Smith highlight how "good intention" work is a fallacy if the desire to be in relation with Indigenous people and Land are not at the core of what one hopes to accomplish.

Lessons and Invitations from my First Year as Faculty at TCU (2022–2023)

I now take some time to reflect on my experiences at TCU as a faculty member who is deeply committed to Indigenous studies, communities, and desires. As a descendant of the Chichimeca Guamares and P'urepecha people who is now living on the past and present territories of the Kirikir?i:s, I will speak about both the rewarding experiences I have been gifted here so far and the obstacles I have encountered. In general, I was pleasantly surprised to know that at a university with a religious affiliation in the name, there were symposia, panels, and initiatives dedicated to Indigenous communities, both local and more broadly. I have been able to be a part of these efforts by bringing my own traditions onto campus and aligning them to my course in Spring 2023, Indigenous and Decolonizing Studies in Education. Through the support of the Office of Diversity & Inclusion and the College of Education, we were able to host an event called "Indigenous Pedagogy through Dance and Movement," where I was able to bring the group Mitotiliztli Yaoyollohtli, in which I am an active dancer. Mitotiliztli Yaoyollohtli is an Indigenous group that practices the tradition of Danza Mexica (Aztec Dance), and I asked our group to share a formal presentation on how our tradition is rooted in ancestral pedagogies and curriculum. We then concluded our event by showing a demonstration of our dance to the TCU community.

This event was an encouraging moment for me as a junior faculty because, as many scholars have already shared, the academy is not a benign place and is often a place of hostility and harm. Centering the community that I am a part of was a vulnerable experience because I hold my relations dearly and am protective of the spaces that are imperative to my spiritual well-being. Overall, I was excited to see that many students approached us afterward and shared with us that they have witnessed these dances in their hometowns or in other spaces, and that they had always wanted to reconnect to this tradition. The concluding moments of our event gave me hope knowing that the sound of the drum, the heartbeat of our dance, called some of these students back home. Afterward, I was excited at the prospects of continuing Indigenous-based programming and learning at TCU and to continue envisioning robust opportunities for faculty, staff, and students.

Although I have had fruitful experiences at TCU, I would be dishonest if I said there have been no arduous obstacles during my first year at an overwhelming non-Indigenous, White space. A strenuous challenge has been the saturation of White faculty who are not committed to or concerned with Indigenous issues, struggles, and futures. There have been many instances in my one year here where faculty openly say that they are not concerned with issues of diversity and inclusion (understanding also that diversity, equity, and inclusion work has many contentious aspects). These are faculty who often, at face value, are fluent in the language of the academy and say they are excited to have new colleagues pushing the boundaries of academia, yet behind closed doors are quick to dismiss the ongoing struggles of TCU's campus. Many other colleagues, including myself, have shared how we are encouraged to be our authentic selves and to teach the content we are trained in because it is imperative, yet we are often met with hostility in the classroom. Many times students come from a place of never being exposed to or learning about certain histories and truths, and once we begin to uncover some of those realities, we are consistently positioned as biased, against White people, and angry. I enjoy engaging in pedagogy and teaching, but there is a certain level of exhaustion that comes from always being expected to address capitalism, racism, anti-Blackness, cisheteropatriachy, xenophobia, etc., when White faculty are often not expected to do the same.

I cannot be the solution to all the ills of academia because that would require the entirety of my being, and I, along with other Black, Indigenous, and other faculty of color should not have to assume the full responsibility of "fixing" a system that was designed for our exclusion. As I completed my first year as faculty, I constantly felt that I must address all the concerns on campus because in many ways my presence creates that assumption. However, I have realized that I cannot be of service to our Black, Indigenous, and communities of color if I exhaust myself. Many of my undergraduate students did not know about the TCU Land Acknowledgment monument or the Race and Reconciliation plaque and the efforts that went into creating both. As faculty, there *has* to be shared responsibility in elucidating the importance of these initiatives, and I once again urge faculty who may not see the connection between structures of power and their content to invest time into mapping out how everything that we teach is already embedded in the inner machinations of these structures.

Dreaming of Relational Worlds

I conclude this chapter by circling back to how we began: What is your relationship with Kirikir?i:s, Land, people, and lifeways? Do you think the Land acknowledges you? Sees you as a guest? Invites you to be in relation? As mentioned, these questions are epistemological, ontological, and axiological in nature because they demand a different answer beyond saying, "What can I do to help?" We must reorient and center these relationships because it is through these ways of being and understanding that aspirations to be good guests will emerge. I have done my best in explaining what I mean by striving to become guests, to take accountability, and to envision Indigenous futurities at TCU and beyond the limits of its campus. It is a continuous process that must be taken care of and that requires diligence. If being a guest is a practice that one must consistently enact, then we must move away from wanting solutions to a reality that requires a much more profound desire.

As someone who is not ancestrally from these beautiful plains, I must wake up every day and remind myself that I am honored to be here and to always remember that these Lands hold so many stories, knowledges, and ways of existing far beyond what I can ever come to know. That is both the beauty and the lesson of this understanding. Although I have shared my concerns and have addressed them candidly, I do believe that the work done by the Native American and Indigenous communities at TCU and in the broader Dallas–Fort Worth area demonstrates a potential to transform and create worlds better fit for our relations. It is my hope that one day the Land here can earnestly say that it is in relation with us. Until then, we must continue onward toward repairing, transforming, and dreaming of otherwise worlds where being guests is not just a proclamation but describes the relations that one must be committed to.

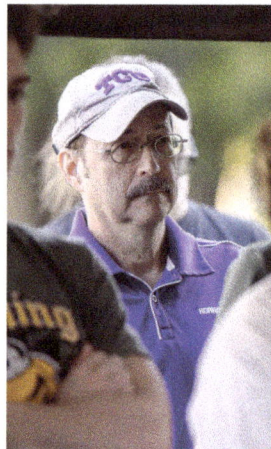

TCU'S RELATIONSHIPS WITH NATIVE AMERICANS AND THE LAND, 1838–2014

by Scott M. Langston

Dr. Scott M. Langston descends from Euro-Americans who, though largely poor, helped displace Native peoples from their ancestral homelands primarily in what became the southern United States. He taught at TCU for nearly twenty years before retiring in 2023 as an instructor in the Religion Department. He served from 2020–2024 as the inaugural TCU Native American Nations and Communities Liaison. The Helvpe Ceremonial Grounds of the Muscogee (Creek) Nation in Oklahoma, where Chebon Kernell serves as Mekko (traditional ceremonial leader), took him in as a member in 2018. TCU's Native American and Indigenous Peoples Initiative grew out of relationships with Native community members that arose while he was teaching courses on US history and interactions between Native Americans and Euro-American Christians. In his essay, Langston presents original historical research on the early history of TCU and demonstrates the university's complicity in the colonization of Native peoples over the 150 years of its existence.

In 2023, Texas Christian University celebrated its one hundred fiftieth anniversary.[1] Throughout the year, there were many celebrations of the university's considerable achievements, but there also was time for institutional introspection. Even though this can be difficult and contentious, it can also be positive and constructive. This essay is part of that process, as it seeks to uncover, acknowledge, and respond to TCU's relationships with Native Americans and the lands it has resided on.[2] It also provides context for the essays and interviews contained in this volume.

Admittedly, Native and non-Native readers may find what follows to be a hard read for different reasons, and some undoubtedly will disagree with its conclusions. It deals with disturbing actions, painful language, and at times, a shameful past. There is the temptation to be defensive and to respond with, "Yes, but . . . ," rather than hear what the past is saying to us. We cannot change the past, but we must individually and institutionally acknowledge and deal with the present realities that the past has created. TCU's Land Acknowledgment can help guide the process of introspection and change. The word "acknowledge" appears three times in the language of TCU's acknowledgment.[3] Recognizing and dealing with past and present realities is, in part, what it means for TCU to acknowledge. At the same time, positive changes are occurring at the university, which should also be recognized as part of TCU's movement toward constructive acknowledgment.

Acknowledging TCU's Origin within Euro-American Christian Colonization

TCU's origin story typically begins with Addison and Randolph Clark opening a private school in Fort Worth (Tarrant County) in 1869 before moving to Thorp Spring (Hood County) in 1873, where they established Add-Ran Male and Female College, TCU's original name. Recent histories written as part of TCU's Race and Reconciliation Initiative, begun in 2020, have emphasized the brothers' prior service as Confederate soldiers and relationship to Black slavery and racism.[4] While these retellings are important, by themselves they obscure the school's origin as an institution of Euro-American Christian colonization, a broad and complex process whose ongoing goal is the taking of Indigenous lands and resources while destroying Indigenous peoples, cultures, and societies.

Euro-American Christianity inspired, authorized, led, and carried out this genocidal colonization in a variety of ways. Churches routinely worked in concert with governmental bodies to achieve these goals. Individual Christians throughout every level of Euro-American society chose biblical texts and church teachings to justify genocidal colonization and neglected others that would have potentially checked such actions. Euro-American Christianity helped normalize colonization, making it even seem natural and inevitable. The Clarks were ministers in the

Restoration (Stone-Campbell) movement, part of which became the Christian Church (Disciples of Christ) denomination, and they transferred ownership and control of the school to the Christian Churches of Texas in 1889. The school, therefore, is thoroughly rooted in US Christianity, although its relationship to the Disciples denomination is now more historical than governing.[5] Ignoring TCU's origin within Euro-American Christian colonization diminishes and disregards the violation of the sovereignty of the Native Nations in whose territory TCU resides. Failing to equally emphasize the role played by colonization throughout TCU's existence along with other influences such as discrimination based on race/ethnicity, gender, and sexuality is itself an act of colonization. It normalizes colonization's goals, values, and methods, thereby sustaining and allowing them to continue shaping, often unknowingly, TCU and the education it provides.

TCU is a newcomer to the lands we now call Texas. The earliest evidence for human habitation in Texas currently dates to more than fifteen thousand years. The homelands of the groups making up today's Kirikir?i:s, or the Wichita and Affiliated Tribes, stretch from what the colonizers renamed as Kansas to central Texas. The Kirikir?i:s, as we know them today, probably had formed by the early fifteenth and sixteenth centuries CE, although they developed from cultures that were much older. These Nations consisted of several Caddoan-speaking peoples, including the Kirikir?i:s (Wichita proper), Wí:ko? (Waco), Tawá:kharih (Tawakoni), Ki:che:ss (Keechi or Kichai), and others.[6] TCU has always resided on and benefited from lands that the Kirikir?i:s, or the Wichita and Affiliated Tribes, cared for and inhabited for centuries prior to the university's existence.

TCU (and its colonizing predecessors) never asked permission nor was granted the right to live in these lands by these Nations. Instead, it received this "right," as did other colleges and universities, through a violent invasion carried out by the Republic and State of Texas and the United States that began approximately forty years before TCU came into existence. While this invasion had European and Christian roots that were hundreds of years old, its most immediate manifestations grew from the Republic of Texas's efforts to eradicate and drive out the descendants of the lands' original human caretakers. The overwhelming majority of Texas's Anglo residents believed the Christian god had destined them to take these lands and spread what they thought was a superior culture built on a mix of Western notions of Christianity, democracy, capitalism, individualism, and rationalism. This meant destroying Indigenous peoples and the ancient cultures and relationships with the lands they had developed. These aims and ideals were cloaked and conveyed through terms such as civilization, savagery, freedom, destiny, salvation, reason, and more. TCU grew from, operated within, and was inspired by the goals, values, and actions advanced by such thinking.

When the Republic of Texas's second elected president, Mirabeau B. Lamar, declared in December 1838 an "exterminating war" against Indigenous peoples living in Texas, the processes making it possible for TCU to eventually obtain and benefit from Native American lands were put in motion. Failing to recognize that Native peoples were fighting to protect their families and Nations from invaders who wanted to destroy them and take their lands, Lamar admonished Texas's Senate and House members:

> If the wild cannibals of the woods will not desist from their massacres, if they will continue to war upon us with the ferocity of tigers and hienas *[sic]*, it is time we should retaliate their warfare. Not in the murder of their women and children, but in the prosecution of an exterminating war upon their warriors; which will admit of no compromise and have no termination except in their total extinction or total expulsion.[7]

It was in this context that Joseph Addison Clark, the father of Addison and Randolph, arrived in Texas from Kentucky in 1839. He first went to Austin, where he worked at the newspaper, the *Sentinel*, as a printer until January 1841. He then went to Nacogdoches County in east Texas, teaching school for about two years and, among other things, engaging in the land business, "untangling conflicting land titles, caused by recent locations overlapping old Spanish grants." He also made "surveying tours" in Nacogdoches, Shelby, and San Augustine counties.[8] His work in the land business made Clark a direct facilitator of Texas's colonization goals at exactly the time the republic was attempting to expel Native Americans and redistribute this land to Anglos as well as, to a lesser degree, Tejanos and even a few free Blacks.[9] Surveying and issuing titles to that land were essential to establishing non-Native control over it. The process of taking lands violently from Native Americans, then, would become integral to TCU's survival and success, just as it did for other colleges and universities in Texas.

The historical realities related to TCU's current location in Fort Worth illustrate the university's dependence on this process. The violent removal of Native Americans led to the establishment of the towns where TCU would eventually reside, Thorp Spring (1873–95), Waco (1895–1910), and Fort Worth (1910–present). Texans had for years been encroaching on these lands, as their European and American counterparts had been doing throughout the continent for centuries. These actions pushed many Native peoples living in other regions of the republic, as well as the United States, into northern Texas. In the area where the Trinity River's four major branches come together—known today as the Dallas–Fort Worth metroplex—a mixture of Native people from diverse Nations had gathered. Just weeks before Lamar's declaration, the *Telegraph and Texas Register* described the situation:

> The chief village of these Indians is situated near the Three (i.e., four) Forks of the Trinity, and contains about seven hundred warriors, who have congregated from the remnants of the tribes of Caddoes, Wacos, Keachies (i.e., Keechis), Towacanies (i.e., Tawakonis), Ironies (i.e., Ionies), Cherokees, and a few Seminoles. To the westward of this village, is another settlement containing about three hundred warriors. These savage refugees have been for some months concentrating their whole force at these two points, from which, as a common centre, all their plans of mischief are directed.[10]

The Republic of Texas frequently raised troops to send into north Texas while also seeking to dislodge Native people from the republic's eastern part. A significant battle, one among several, took place at Village Creek, also known as Caddo Creek, located near today's Arlington and Fort Worth city limits. On May 14, 1841, General Edward H. Tarrant, namesake for Tarrant County (where TCU resides today), led a group of Texas militia out of Red River County. They were searching for Native American settlements from which raids against Texans living along the Red River had been launched. Ten days later, Tarrant's men located three settlements on Village Creek. In addition to various Kirikir?i:s (Wichita) groups, members of other Native Nations lived in these settlements, including Tsa-la-gi (Cherokee), Mvskoke (Muscogee/Creek), Semvnolē (Seminole), Kiikaapoi (Kickapoo), Saawanooki (Shawnee), various Hasinai (Caddo) groups, and perhaps others.[11] The area seems to have been a gathering point for Native refugees from a variety of regions who were defending themselves from Anglo invaders.

The Texans surprised the diverse Native populations living there.[12] Decades later in 1887, Henry Stout, one of the participants, described how it began:

> We passed over a little knoll and around close to where there were a whole tribe of Indians, but they did not see us nor we them. We turned further on to the left, there saw two ponies and soon after two squaws. One of the squaws had a brass kettle preparing something. The other was an Anadargo [that is, Anadarko, part of the Caddo confederacy] squaw and had a baby in her arms. Tarrant, learning that Indians were in the brush, kept his men out of the way and let us go it alone. Bowlin and I concluded to charge the camp. When we got within seventy-five yards of it the squaws saw us. One running down the creek, and the one with the child ran directly towards me. I could have killed both of them and, thinking of the eight people killed in one [of] my neighbors' families, I wonder I did not.

Other accounts indicate that one of these women was killed, while the other and her baby were captured. Apparently, that woman later escaped, but General Tarrant kept the baby boy for two years before returning him on September 29, 1843, after Tarrant helped negotiate the Bird's Fort Treaty with ten tribes. The *Northern Standard*, a newspaper located in Clarksville, the county seat of Red River County where Tarrant lived, described the boy as "a little Anadahkah [i.e., Anadarko] boy," five years old, and "the nephew of Jose Maria, principal chief of the tribe."[13]

The people living in these settlements eventually collected themselves and repulsed Tarrant's attack. The militia's official report counted twelve American Indians dead but also noted that "a great many more must have been killed and wounded, from the quantity of blood we saw on their trails and in the thickets where they had ran." Captain John B. Denton, a Methodist minister and lawyer who a few years earlier had settled along the Red River and who would become the future city and county of Denton's namesake, was the only Texan casualty. The report made clear the Texans' intent: "It was not the wish of General Tarrant to take any prisoners. The women and children, except one, we suffered to escape, if they wished, and the men neither asked, gave, or received any quarter." The Texans, however, did take a few prisoners. They also destroyed homes and stole food and possessions. According to Stout, "The Indians had fled in consternation, and we picked up a great deal of plunder. Kettles, buffalo robes, eighty head of horses, and worlds of corn which they had made and hid out in the thicket. . . . We also found powder, lead, and more salt than a mule could pack. A Dutchman in our party got ten head of horses that were stolen from him previously and we were rich in plunder and spoils." Now that the Texans knew the location of their homes, Native people moved permanently from the area.[14]

Soon thereafter, White colonizers moved in and began creating what is now the Dallas–Fort Worth metroplex, complete with their churches, schools, businesses, governments, and systems for buying, selling, and distributing lands on which Native peoples had lived for centuries. A few months after the attack, the *Telegraph and Texas Register* observed, "Not an Indian village remains in this section. A vast region of fertile territory has thus been redeemed from the savage domination." This characterization, of course, failed to recognize the roles played by Native peoples in helping create the "fertile territory" itself, the very prairies and plains on which colonists settled. While debatable and complex, Omer C. Stewart's observation that "the extensive grasslands that we call prairies and plains owe their existence to fire set by Indians and continued by accident or design to the present" calls attention to Native peoples' contributions in shaping the environment. Rather than taking natural, uncultivated land, colonizers throughout the Great Plains benefited from centuries of work by Native people.

They also changed relationships to the lands. As Carolyn Merchant points out, "Indians developed sophisticated cultures in different environments throughout North America." Euro-Americans, however, "radically transformed" these environments and "altered native cultures and ecosystems." This transformation was well underway locally by fall 1841, with local colonists establishing Bird's Fort (later, Birdville), and in November, John Neely Bryan settling near what eventually became downtown Dallas. The Republic of Texas also entered into a contract with W. S. Peters and others for the introduction of six hundred families within three years. Eventually, twenty-six counties would be created out of Peters Colony. The *Telegraph and Texas Register* in spring 1842 expressed ideas that are still common today: "The hardy pioneer is pushing the lines of civilization beyond the Cross Timbers—so lately the secure retreat of the savage. A tract of land almost equal in extent to the whole settled portion of the Republic previous to the revolution, has been rescued from the domination of the savages, and will soon become the secure abode of peaceful settlers."[15]

More elements essential to the development of today's Dallas–Fort Worth metroplex appeared in the next few years: Texas joined the United States in 1845, Dallas and Denton counties were created in 1846, and both Fort Worth and Tarrant County were founded in 1849. By the next decade, Captain Denton was being hailed as "the Warrior Preacher of Texas." The United States established the Brazos River Reservation in Young County, near Graham, in 1854 and moved some Wichita (Waco and Tawakoni) and Caddo (Kadohadacho and Nadaco) groups onto it. A Penateka Comanche Indian Reservation was also established in Throckmorton County. The reservations lasted only a few years, as Texans continued their attacks and clamored for the complete removal of these Native groups from the state, which occurred in 1859 when Texas and the United States government removed them to what became Oklahoma. By the end of the 1850s, Texas effectively controlled all the places on which TCU would eventually reside.[16]

What does this have to do with TCU? The university's founders were part of the colonization of Native American lands. While there is no evidence indicating that Joseph Addison Clark participated in battles conducted by the Republic of Texas's military, he did carry out essential activities in redistributing these lands to non-Natives. He and his sons also acquired some of these lands and later used them to benefit TCU. Furthermore, TCU acquired the site of its current campus (as it did for its previous sites) through the colonized processes set up after the Village Creek battle.[17]

The history of TCU's current location illustrates how the colonizing process worked. In 1910, several cities sought to get TCU to move from Waco and offered various incentives for doing so. In Fort Worth, the Fairmount Land Company gave fifty acres of land, known as the Forest Park site, as part of the city's package that convinced TCU to relocate.

The ability to own and deed this land to TCU began with Tarrant and the Texas militia driving Native Americans out of the area in 1841. The republic, and later the state, quickly began giving and selling this land to non-Native colonizers. As Texas's General Land Office, established shortly after the Texas Revolution in 1836, explains:

> Because the new government was cash poor and land rich, land was used as currency to pay soldiers, public debt and build infrastructure, and was granted to veterans of the Texas Revolution as compensation for their services. Cheap public land was also used as a means to attract settlers to the new nation.

Texans believed "that an increase in the population of Texas would raise land values, provide tax revenue, and protect the frontier from Indian and Mexican raids." Therefore, the republic used head-rights and the empresario system to lure people to Texas.[18] The land became both a weapon by enticing military recruits necessary for expelling Native Americans and a means for personal and national/ state enrichment. For qualifying individuals, a land certificate was issued for a specific amount of acres, allowing the individual to locate and claim public land anywhere in Texas. Certificates could be bought and sold, even though they were not associated with specific parcels of land. Once an individual located and claimed a specific parcel, the land was surveyed. If there were no conflicting claims, Texas issued a patent to the claimant. At that point, the land passed out of the public domain and became private property.[19]

Most of TCU's original fifty acres are located within what is called the Wade H. Hudson 160-acre survey. Hudson, who lived in Grayson County, received a headright certificate on June 16, 1856, for 640 acres of land in Peters Colony. Two days later, Hudson and his wife, Lavina, sold the certificate for $350 to John Haning. Haning subsequently sold the certificate to John P. Smith, the so-called father of Fort Worth, for $370 on September 12, 1856. Three years later, the land itself had been surveyed and its boundaries established and superimposed on the prairie. A patent was issued to Smith on November 27, 1868.[20] Thus began the process that commodified the land on which TCU would eventually reside.

Once established on the land, the university altered the landscape. Such alterations are part of all human habitations, including those of Native Americans. TCU's use of the land, however, reflects a dominating relationship. Unlike its Native predecessors, who in varying degrees understood themselves as one of many beings intertwined with the land in interdependent, reciprocal relationships, the university made the land an asset, treating it as an object for achieving its goals. Rather than living with the land, TCU appropriated the land. Articles in the *Fort Worth Star-Telegram* described the site in 1910 as being located "three miles to the southwest of the city, topping a high knob of the rolling prairie which characterizes the land in that section" and being "just beyond Forest Park, which is hidden from view from the college by the deep swells of the land." The Trinity's Clear Fork approached Fort Worth, just three quarters of a mile from the campus, although it could not be seen due to the "heavy fringe of foliage" on the river's banks. Just to the south and southwest was "the rolling Western prairie." By October 1910, the newspaper reported that the site was being "rapidly cleared" and published a projected layout showing eleven buildings on a heavily treed campus. By the beginning of classes on September 19, 1911, three buildings had been completed. The *Star-Telegram* described these buildings as making "a pretty site" but noted that "the lack of trees and pretty grounds is at once apparent." Officials asserted, though, that this would be "partially remedied in the coming year" when its campus would be "plotted and adorned by a landscape artist." [21]

Creating "a pretty site" became an essential component to the university's image. It marketed the campus's physical setting almost immediately, touting the land's beauty as a way of uplifting the university. The 1910 university catalog described it as a "beautifully elevated place in one of the southern suburbs" of Fort Worth, having "all the healthfulness and freedom of the country." This was not the first time that officials boasted about the land's beauty when extolling the university's attributes. One account of TCU's founding indicated that one factor in locating the school at Thorp Spring was "the beauty of the wooded hills of the Brazos valley and Comanche creek." [22]

There is certainly nothing wrong with appreciating the beauty of a place, but appreciation soon contributed to its commodification. Throughout its history, TCU has considered "its" land largely as a financial asset, marketing tool, and aesthetic object, although in recent years it has admirably demonstrated a growing concern for environmental issues. In 2023, TCU touted its 302-acre campus as a "functioning ecosystem," with many sustainability practices implemented throughout a campus that is "nestled in a tree-lined neighborhood." Designated as a "Tree Campus USA" for several years by the Arbor Foundation, the "former 'prairie college' is now home to over 3,200 trees."[23] Ultimately, though, TCU's historical interactions largely reflect colonized power imposed over the lands and the Native peoples who were expelled from them. These kinds of relationships are not surprising, given the school's origin and existence within Euro-American Christian colonization, nor are they unusual in US society.

Acknowledging Systemic Colonization at TCU

Euro-American Christian colonization has shaped TCU's relationships with Native Americans, manifesting itself in what amounts to a systemic colonization that denigrates, appropriates, harms, and even makes invisible Native Americans and their experiences through the university's programs, curriculum, publications, and policies. Students, faculty, and administrators have engaged directly and indirectly in advancing colonization's goals and values, normalizing them to the extent that their presence in the university often goes unrecognized and unchallenged. While the violent removal and killing of Native Americans stands out for its heinous and shocking actions, systemic colonization plays an equal, though less recognized, role in the process. At its foundation lies the idea that TCU is the rightful heir and benefactor of Indigenous lands. These ideas have been encouraged and disseminated, often in subtle ways, in TCU's educational spaces. For instance, at a 1904 session of the Add-Ran Literary Society, a Mr. Williams (likely Robert Williams, a sophomore) gave an oration, "Passing of the Red Man." While the exact text is not known, the oration's title reflects a common notion that Native Americans had ceased to exist, a necessary corollary for residing on their lands. This idea, in turn, helps absolve the university of responsibilities to Native people and Nations, disconnects it from Tarrant's attack at Village Creek, and hides its participation in the colonization process. Native Americans are hardly given a thought, other than as objects of study of a romanticized past.[24]

TCU's fiftieth anniversary celebration in 1923 particularly demonstrates how systemic colonization works. The university put on a pageant written by the faculty and students of the English department, "These Fifty Years." Chronicling TCU's founding and progress, the pageant began with a prologue spoken by "an Indian." Informing the audience that TCU's location was once the "domain of the Tehas," the Indian tells of an old local chieftain whose dying wish was that the plains would remain "free and fruitful" and that a "lookout" would be posted on the hill to protect this freedom and fruitfulness. The Indian then asserts that a lookout was indeed standing on "the hill that crowns the river" and that the plains were "fruitful" and "free for freeborn men to till." The lookout, of course, was TCU, "Guardian of the Texas Youth." As the pageant recounts the 1910 move to Fort Worth, the city's fictional mayor proclaimed:

> To the south of our fast growing city
> Lies a hill that rolls down to the river.
> Long ages ago it belonged
> To a Red Skin of wisdom and vision.
> He decreed that this land
> With its broad view
> Should be used for the
> Youth of the Nation.

The mayor then gives the land—the fifty acres in the Wade H. Hudson survey—to TCU so "a stately structure of wisdom" may be constructed.[25]

While the pageant is certainly a product of its time, it is also quite revealing about TCU. It shows almost no accurate knowledge regarding Native Americans. The term, Tehas, is unclear, perhaps referring to *Tejas*, a Caddoan word used by the Spanish to refer to the Caddo peoples living east of the Trinity River but later applied to many tribes.[26] It is almost as if the diverse Native populations in Texas had been reduced to a single unnamed person. Furthermore, this cultureless "Indian" serves as a mouthpiece to transfer the land to TCU and cover over and legitimize the realities of how that happened. Additionally, the land's major geographical features—the prairie, the Clear Fork, and the hill where TCU is situated—now simply act as a backdrop to the university.

Colonization of Native peoples and the land appears natural, good, and is even rendered invisible by portraying TCU's history exclusively in terms of progress and freedom.

Fifty years later, little seemed to have changed when TCU celebrated its one hundredth anniversary. The chair of the centennial commission asserted that TCU's founding was a visible sign of the great interest in education on the frontier. He reportedly explained that TCU "has seen its own surrounding area progress from Indian infested territory to an urban center." At the Centennial Convocation held on January 25, 1973, a responsive reading, called a Centennial Affirmation, was conducted. At one point, the leader said, "In 1873 the great buffalo herds had not yet been run to ground just to the west. In 1873 Ishatai had not yet led the Comanches and their brothers in the last great Sun Dance, just to the north, and Chief Quanah was free."[27] These references seem to allude to some of the last events in what broader US society calls the "taming of the West." By the end of the 1870s, Americans had virtually exterminated the buffalo on the Great Plains. Ishatai and Quanah Parker were leaders in the 1874 fight against buffalo hunters at Adobe Walls in Hutchinson County, Texas. This battle helped spark the Red River War of 1874–75, which eventually led to the forced confinement of many Native American Nations on reservations in what is now called Oklahoma.[28]

Such vague, stereotypical references again reflect little understanding by the university. Characterizing Native Americans as an infestation suggests they have no rightful place in the supposed Anglo-Christian civilization of the Dallas–Fort Worth metroplex. Invoking the buffalo and Comanche seems to associate TCU's founding and its first century with a past that needs to be appreciated but moved on from, as the university embarks on a new century. The audience in the affirmation had previously said, "We have moved from Thorp Spring to a new world." Later, the leader said, "Remembering our past will not grant us a future, a new century filled with rich time." Alluding to the so-called demise of the buffalo and Native peoples portrays them as relics of the past that TCU had replaced. Native Americans were not involved or embraced in either of the university's anniversary celebrations other than as stereotypical figures used by the university to advance its own purposes. They certainly were not considered or engaged as modern people who can contribute to building a contemporary university.

TCU also openly embraced the pioneer/frontier narrative and a romanticized version of Texas history, while situating the university within it. These pioneers, of course, were invading Native American lands, but the narrative never mentioned that. In 1927, TCU's president Edward McShane Waits invoked this image in his annual report to the state convention of the Christian churches:

> If the University has a glint of romance in its history and development, let us not forget that Texas is a land of romance. Whether one is in search of alluring and romantic history or is attracted by great natural resources and bigness, Texas is an inviting field. The average Texan is a natural born dyed-in-the-wool, unblushing and indefatigable believer in his state. Texans have abundant cause for this pride . . . unsurpassed resources, great cities and the largest bloc of pure Anglo-Saxon blood on the continent with a romantic past and a future which lies toward the dawn . . . Texas Christian University has become a part of this romance. The worthy pioneers have left us a noble heritage.

Waits even called Mirabeau B. Lamar "that superb genius" for his support of education. Four years later, TCU's dean of the university, Colby D. Hall, greeted TCU students, telling them, "I believe in you, T.C.U. youth, because you are touched with the pioneer spirit of the West, ready for adventure, thrilling with enthusiasm, open-hearted and frank, looking to the future." Hall would go on to write *History of Texas Christian University*, in which he uses the pioneer/frontier framework to interpret TCU. The university also invoked this narrative in 1946 to raise money. A booklet developed by the university and its building committee, *The Meaning of Gifts*, began:

> One hundred years ago Texas was a sprawling, rowdy, unwieldy empire, known chiefly for its ability to divide its population into the quick—and the dead. It took men to change that. It was a man-sized job to develop Texas. The men who did that job—the pioneers from Virginia, Ohio, Tennessee, Kentucky, etc.—built more than a state. They created a way of living. They came to carve a livelihood out of a wilderness, and when they had done that, they found they had given America a great Gift: Texas . . . Nowhere is the spirit of Texas, or the Texas way of life, more vigorously broadcast than through Texas Christian University. T.C.U. is typically Texan.

The pioneer/frontier narrative appeared two years later at the university's convocation commemorating its seventy-fifth anniversary. TCU honored "its fellow pioneer organizations," saluting Texas business firms, "all of whom were founded during or before 1873" and "all of whom also helped transform the frontier into modern Texas." Of course, pioneers transforming the frontier into modern Texas was a seemingly more respectable way to describe a colonization process based on violently removing Native Americans, seizing their lands, and profiting from them. The narrative persisted, appearing in a 1999 article on the founding of Add-Ran College in 1873, explaining, "It was a time when buffalo herds abounded, when Indian raids were common, and when western and much of eastern Texas was still untrodden prairie land." The characterization of the prairies as "untrodden" was hardly accurate given that Indigenous peoples had been living on these prairies for thousands of years. The university continued to think of its relationship to Native Americans and the land in terms of raiding Indians, buffalo, and uninhabited land, all of which needed to be tamed or eliminated.[29]

In conjunction with embracing the pioneer/frontier narrative, TCU has used, perpetuated, and been shaped by Native American stereotypes and misinformation. This included romanticizing Native peoples, reflected in a 1903 poem, "The Legend of Lover's Leap," written by Ed. S. McKinney, TCU student and founder of the university's newspaper, the *Skiff*. While there have been many legends of Lover's Leap written in various places throughout the United States, McKinney expressed Waco's version. His poem begins:

I sing not of Caucasians,
Of their wooings and their passions,
Rather is my song of red men;
Of the children of the forest,
Of the prairies and the mountains.

He localizes the legend, "Where the city now called Waco stands . . . once where they lived . . . a tribe of red men called the *Wacos*," describing them as "brave and comely" and "free as were the fleetest mustangs." McKinney identifies a Waco chief named Black Bear whose bitter rival was the Comanche chief, White Eagle. Black Bear's son,

Rattlesnake, was taken captive by the Comanches and taken to White Eagle's "wigwam," where he met the Comanche chief's daughter, Chiwadassa. The chief declared that Rattlesnake would be killed the next day. The two young people, however, fell in love as they looked at each other and that night Chiwadassa freed the young Waco. They fled together, were pursued by the Comanches, and chose to leap into the Bosque River and die together, rather than be captured and separated.[30] McKinney's poem, which became popular at TCU during this era, transmits an image of Native Americans as simple people of Nature, while romanticizing their past presence on the lands that TCU and US society now inhabited. Rather than relating to the realities of colonization and how it brought the lands to TCU, such romanticized images allowed the university to overlook and forget them.

Many other destructive stereotypes and images can be found in TCU's history. Space limitations do not allow for an exhaustive exposition, but a few examples should suffice to demonstrate the point:

- **Redskin/Scalping:** On November 14, 1921, as TCU anticipated playing the Haskell Indians football team, a headline appeared on the front page of the *Skiff*, "Frogs Prepare to Get Scalps of Scalpers in Red-Skin Raid Friday." The article explained, "Creek and Cherokee, Comanche and Choctaw, in full war paint and carrying in their belts the scalps of many mighty warriors of the gridiron, will take their places side by side in the raid on the pale-faced Christians." Just over fifty years later, the *Daily Skiff* reported, "The Horned Frog cagers were scalped by the Oklahoma City Indians."[31]

- **Savage:** In May 1922, TCU began its forty-ninth annual commencement week with a "May Fete," in which Miss Rosa Driver was crowned May queen. The festivities included students posing as representatives from various countries coming to pay homage to the queen. Native Americans were described as "the savages from the far off colonies of America" who "are summoned to dance before her [Queen Rosa of the House of Driver]. They appear in all their characteristic paint and feathers, and in a solemn line await the pleasure of the queen. They portray to her the war dance and smoking of the peace pipe." Later that year, the Shirley-Walton Literary Societies

held a banquet in which the evolution of the American girl was
portrayed. Beginning with "the savage girl of the vast North
American forest, who stole out to meet her lover," the tableaux
continued with the "Colonial lady" and the "girl from Dixie,"
finally culminating in the "T.C.U. girl."[32]

- **Injun:** TCU student Hulbert Smith was touted in 1936 as
  a "real live Injun," or at least someone who looked like one,
  primarily because of his "Indian collection" consisting of items
  from forty reservations. The *Skiff* explained, "He could dress in
  his many multi-colored Indian shirts and vests, add turquoise
  jewelry, and top it off with a feathered war bonnet." The newspaper added, "Though considered primitive, the Indians have
  learned the art of making souvenir collectors pay for everything
  they want." In 1957, a *Skiff* "Editorial Comment" proclaimed, "A
  lot of folks say that Ranch Week is gettin' worn and faded just like
  the ole Levis stuck away in mothballs. It's down to a fine point
  now, they say, just like a [*sic*] Injun war dance. All ceremony and
  ritual an' not much action." Decades later, the epithet was still in
  use. Recounting a hockey game between the Fort Worth Texans
  and Dallas Black Hawks, the *Daily Skiff* explained, "This rivalry
  started way back when Dallasites thought Fort Worth was put 30
  miles to the west just to protect them from the injuns."[33]

- **Chief:** The 1925 yearbook described a picture of a man standing in front of a small wooden building: "Here, gentle reader,
  is a close up of Daddy Roberts [probably TCU student, Bill
  Kerr] and his Oklahoma school of which you have heard him
  speak so often. You would never suspect from the imperturbable
  expression on his face that he has just corralled Indian Chief
  Reademandweep and his band of renegades in this school-
  house and is getting ready to give them a lecture on the Literary
  Digest." The term was also applied to several athletes, Native
  and non-Native, nicknaming them "Chief." These included Lynn Brown (1932), Allie White (1938), and J. C. ONeal
  (1943).[34]

- **Squaw:** The 1960 *Skiff* column, "On Campus with Max
  Shulman," records "Little Stories with Big Morals." One story
  begins, "Once upon a time there was an Indian brave named

Walter T. Muskrat who had a squaw named Margaret Giggling
Water. Margaret was sort of a mess but she sure could make
beaded moccasins." The story continues and ends with the
moral, "Don't fight the hand that beads you."[35]

- **Drug users:** In 1966, the *Skiff* reported on research by a graduate chemistry student and sponsored by the TCU Research
Foundation. Perpetuating old and false associations of peyote
with drug abuse, the article began, "Long before LSD was ever
invented, certain Indians in the Southwest were taking psyche-
delic 'trips' by munching on pieces of peyote cactus."[36]

- **Threats:** In 1977, the *Skiff* used a common metaphor associat-
ing "Indians" with violent behavior and criminal activity when
it urged TCU's security to establish foot patrols on campus,
rather than only relying on patrol cars. "It does little good for
the cavalry to drive up after the Indians have left."[37]

- **Evil:** In 1983, TCU history professor Dave Edmunds's book,
The Shawnee Prophet, was nominated for the Pulitzer Prize. The
Daily Skiff compared the book's subject, Tenskwatawa, a highly
revered Shawnee leader, to the leader of Iran, who at the time
was reviled by Americans: "*The Shawnee Prophet* deals with an
Indian politico-religious leader whose beliefs were somewhat
akin to those of the Ayatollah Khomeini." Two years later, a
comic strip published in a TCU newspaper, *Au Courant*, showed
a young writer going to his editor in chief for advice on a story
he is writing: "I'm doing it [the story] on TCU being cursed
because it's built on an ancient Indian burial ground, but it
lacks pizazz." The editor resolves the problem by suggesting he
change the story to say that research indicates the administration building was "built over the tomb of a bizarre cult of Gay
Venezuelan belly dancers."[38]

While these few examples certainly reflect the norms of their
respective times, they cannot be simply dismissed for this reason. Each
term and characterization had long been used by Americans to communicate derogatory ideas. They collectively indicate a general attitude
held for decades at TCU about Native Americans, creating a framework

and environment for how the university related to Native people. TCU accepted and participated in the broader US society's disdain and mockery of Native Americans. It joined the country's efforts to construct and enforce images of Native people that amounted to a sort of psychological warfare, even when done lightheartedly. Belittling Native Americans helped destroy their traditional identities, cultures, and even self-images, thus fulfilling one of colonization's goals—their physical and cultural eradication. Survivors of physical eradication had to confront attempts to eradicate their cultures and, in turn, their identities. Enforcing these colonized identities helped maintain and justify the seizure of Native lands and resources. By accepting and allowing such characterizations to be used, the university participated in a systemic colonization that was normalized and never questioned. These characterizations freely did their work in service of colonization.

Such characterizations worked in concert with appropriation of Native American cultures, frequently expressed in teaching about Native Americans as objects of study, rather than learning from and working with Native peoples and communities as equal partners. Nowhere is this more apparent than in the "Indian Spring Festival" staged by the girls' physical training classes in 1928 as part of Music Week and in honor of Mother's Day. Mrs. Helen Walker Murphy, director of physical education for women, wrote and directed the festival that over three hundred female students participated in, and TCU's band provided music. The pageant presented "the folklore of the Indian spring, representing the planting, growing, and harvesting [of] Indian corn." Held in TCU's Clark Field football stadium, which was located east of the Mary Couts Burnett Library, approximately four thousand people attended the presentation.

The football stadium "was transformed into a Zuni Indian village and the surrounding Indian reservation. Indian tepees, totem poles, softly colored lights, Indian costumes and music formed the background for the enacting of the story of an American girl who was captured by Indian braves to take the place of 'Silver Heels,' the 'Old Chief's' daughter." TCU's students told this story largely through dance, "corn dances, including the Spirit of Sun, Corn Planters, Rain Dance, Spirit of Green Corn, Green Corn Dance and the Hopi Corn Dance; the Bow and Arrow drill and the two concluding solo dances, the Spirit of

TEXAS CHRISTIAN UNIVERSITY

PRESENTS THE PAGEANT

"INDIAN SPRING"

SATURDAY, MAY 12, 1928, 7:30 P. M.

ATHLETIC STADIUM

Directed by HELEN WALKER MURPHY

EPISODE 1

Ho-o! Ho-o!
Dance we singing,
Promise bringing
Of the prize of maiden fair;
Hearts beat lightly,
Skies shine brightly,
Youth and Hope are ev'rywhere.
Ho-o! Ho-o! Ho! Ho! Ho!

INTERPRETER	Rosalyne Tiger
YOUNG CHIEF	John Simmons
CHIEF	E. M. Waits

HIGH CHIEF

EDWARD McSHANE .... *of the House of Waits*

INDIAN PRINCESS

PAULINE	*of the House of Richardson*
LITTLE BROTHER	Jack Murphy

INDIAN MAIDS

TEXORA	*of the House of Pierce*
DOROTHY NELL	*of the House of Broad*
DORIS	*of the House of Shaw*
JENNIE LOUISE	*of the House of Copeland*
FRANCES	*of the House of Fry*
MAE	*of the House of Morgan*

BRAVES
Alvalene Lawrence, Dorothy Louise West, Ruth Ragon, Margaret Roberts, Doris Newberry, Osie Blackwell, Mildred Meggs, Anna Lee Payne, Ora Claire Humphries, Adalene Bounds, Mary Elizabeth Cunningham, Margaret Carpenter, Catherine Wills, Elizabeth Carter.

TORCH BEARERS
Jeanette McLean, Anna Harriet Heyer, Nettie Lee Barton, Elizabeth Fulford, Margaret Cook, Margaret Monnig, Edna Estes, Lorena Houtchens, Virginia Bond, Winona Brock, Estelle Klingsted, Helen Smith, Grace Bucher.

OLD WOMAN .... Edith Armstrong

FIRE TENDERS
Virginia Douglas, Elizabeth Bacon, Elnora Rice, Mary Hamilton. Opal Tedford, Grace Leath, Odie Atkinson, Janie Miles Monroe.

Program of "Indian Spring Pageant," Episode 1, presented by TCU students and faculty on May 12, 1928. *Special Collections, Mary Couts Burnett Library, Texas Christian University.*

the Hunt and the Dance of the Medicine Man." TCU President Waits, playing the part of the Old Chief, sat on a throne with the Princess and "wore the feathers and the blanket that made him chief of the tribe."[39]

Once again, the people of TCU and Fort Worth were entertained by constructed images of Native Americans, described as "weird Indian characters," "weird Indian reservation," and "haunting Indian melodies." Presenting inaccurate but exotic images seemed to reflect an academic voyeurism that entertained while simultaneously perpetuating stereotypes and misinformation designed to exert control over Native people. The pageant revealed more about its Anglo audience and participants than it did about Native Americans. It disregarded accurate depictions of Native Americans and their cultures, instead choosing to present a mixed-up conglomeration of separate cultures. The fictional capture of an American girl emphasized Anglos as victims of Native American barbarity. At the same time, TCU's president assuming the role of the tribe's chief and disrespectfully donning a headdress reflected the university's assumed power over Native Americans. Native people were not at all present in the production, nor were their voices heard. Instead, TCU controlled and perpetuated images of Native peoples that asserted Native Americans could only exist in US society under terms dictated to them.

The 1928 pageant was hardly exceptional at TCU. Both before and after, the university expressed its institutional appropriation through a variety of Indian-themed presentations, including:

- "A Pleasant Evening with the Indians," staged in 1913 by the Clark Literary Society and including "an Indian Dance, and Indian Pipe Dream, a Eulogy to an Indian Girl, and other things that were strictly Indian."[40]
- The TCU Glee Club performed "Indian War Dance" during its 1915–16 season.[41]
- TCU's first annual May Fete of 1927, "The Ode to Spring," included "The Indian Spring of 1620, which was led by Pocahontas and consisted of songs by the Indian Maid."[42]
- In 1930, the Women's Athletic Association (WAA), directed by Miss Helen Walker Murphy, presented a pageant depicting "the life and religious ceremony of Texas Indians." The following year, the association invited one hundred "camp-fire girls" and

250 "girl reserves of Fort Worth" to be their guests on "play day." Using "the Indian motif," "games to be played will be given Indian names, and different kinds of feathers will be given to the tribes." Two years later, the association staged an Indian Water Pageant in the TCU swimming pool to aid a poor family they had adopted: "The story is concerned with the efforts of a tribe to find a new princess who will please their gods," and "dancers, braves, and squaws were participants in the show." In 1936, the WAA's annual pageant focused on the Texas centennial, emphasizing the numerous flags that have flown over Texas. At the beginning of the play, "Indians come on the stage in old Chevrolets filled with little papooses. They get out to smoke peace pipes in the form of cigarettes passed around by little Phillip Morris boys. They hear the rumble of guns and jump in their wheezing cars and rattle off."[43]

- Charles Wakefield Cadman's operatic cantata, "The Sunset Trail," was performed in 1931 in TCU's football stadium. Sixteen thousand people witnessed the combined efforts of the Fort Worth Civic Chorus, the Fort Worth Symphony Orchestra, and three hundred students from TCU's physical training department, directed by Mrs. Helen Walker Murphy. The cantata depicting "the struggle of the Indians against the untiring advance of the white people" was set in a "realistic" Indian village with six tepees "decorated with weird Indian symbols" and arranged around a campfire and totem pole. Standout TCU basketball player, Adolph Dietzel, played the role of the tribe's chief, which seems to have led to his receiving the nickname, "Chief."[44]

- In 1935, the Music Club presented a comedy, *The Daze of '29.* The song titles, it was said, reflected "the Indian setting of the play": "The Indian Death Dance," "You're a Chiseler," "Prayer of an Indian Maiden," "The Cats of Rangoon," "Let's Get a Little Wigwam," "A Course in Campustry," "Under the Blue Eagle," and "I'm a Red-Headed Indian Gal." Characters in the musical included a young Indian princess named Tonawanda and her maid, Whatamamma, White Feather, Blue Eagle, Falling Hair, Drooping Spirits, Horsefeathers, Fallen Arches, and Sally Wigwam.[45]

- Four thousand people watched the university's annual pageant in 1936, which addressed *The History of Tarrant County* and was held in the football stadium. The play divided Tarrant County's history into five episodes: the Indians leaving; the melting pot of French, Spanish, and Mexicans; the later pioneers; Tarrant County giving her sons to the Confederacy; the cowboys and the march of progress of Tarrant County. Two of the play's leading roles were Young Chief and Medicine Man.[46]

- At the university's 1939 pageant, which began with a medley of "old-time tunes," Indian clubs were swung to "The Stars and Stripes."[47]

- The 1940 pageant's theme was "Dance of the Nations." It included the song "Indian Love Call," played to the "haunting strains of the Cherokee," and featuring "six prairie dancers, wearing pastel shades of China silk, [who] will do a classic dance to 'Indian Love Call.'" Then "Indians" performed an "Eagle Dance," copied from "a characteristic ceremony of a tribe of American Indians."[48]

- In 1942, TCU staged a play for the Federated Women's Club, *A Romance of Texas*. The play depicted four periods of Texas history through Indian, French, Mexican, and pioneer scenes. The Indian scene included the song, "Indian Love Call," with an adagio dance performance.[49]

Teaching and researching about Native Americans also participated in the university's appropriation. The documentary record suggests that these kinds of activities seemed to have become more prominent at TCU beginning in the late 1920s and 1930s, and have continued ever since. It is unclear how or if these topics were addressed previously. Professor and Mrs. W. M. Winton of the Science Department were especially active during this period. They spent several summers in the US Southwest filming and photographing Native Americans and brought this information back to TCU. Mrs. Winton spoke to an English class on "Indian folkways," along with Mrs. Helen Walker Murphy, who spoke on "Indian Folk-Music and Folk-Dances." Mrs. Winton also showed some of her films, which included "Indian cere-

monial dances, a sand painting in the making," and "the dance accompanying the 'Navajo Night Chant'" to the Natural Science Society. She
also spoke to a Southwestern Literature class on "Experiences among
the Indians," illustrating her talk with records of Native music that she
and her husband had recorded. Mrs. Helen Fouts Cahoon, head of the
Voice Department, gave a lecture to the Mission Society of TCU on
"Indian music," performing several numbers based on "tribal melodies."
The English Department's Rebecca Smith and Mabel Major gave an
interpretation of a Southwestern Indian dance at a meeting of Sigma
Tau Delta, as well as lectured on "Indian souvenirs" collected from
the Southwest. They also published a book, *Southwest Heritage: A Literary
History with Bibliography*, which included "the mystical beauty of Indian
superstitions." Engaging in questionable practices, such as filming and
recording sacred ceremonies, did not seem to be a concern in the quest
for harvesting information for teaching and publishing.[50]

Native American topics continued to be addressed in courses,
research, and presentations during the following decades, although the
disciplines and programs engaging them seem quite limited despite
the *Daily Skiff*'s proclamation in 1977 that "the American Indian and
their traditions are alive at TCU." It cited as evidence teaching about
the life, history, and art of certain tribes, as well as books produced by
faculty members on the Apache, Navajo, Otoe-Missouria, Shoshone,
and Kiowa. Five years earlier, members of TCU's Theatre Department
had staged a play by Arthur Kopit at Scott Theatre, *Indians*. Set in the
arena of Buffalo Bill's Wild West Show, the play depicted "the American
Dream myth in its last acts of destruction against the red man." The
play's author believed that "the Indian crisis in this country was our first
Vietnam." During the early 1980s, history professor Maurice Boyd published a two-volume work, *Kiowa Voices*, for which he consulted with some
Kiowas and even brought them to campus. In 2000, TCU's Department
of Ballet and Modern Dance presented "The Union of the Spirit and
Native American Dance," led by a Kiowa dancer.[51]

It is difficult to know precisely what was taught and what roles
Native Americans played in developing courses, research, and performances. Were Native Americans consulted and, if so, was it a sufficient
number to reflect their diverse opinions and practices regarding particular topics? Did Native communities give permission to use the cultural

knowledge that faculty were conveying to students and others? Did faculty learn from Native people and communities how this knowledge should be understood, or did they present such knowledge in light of Western academic theories? Did faculty allow Native American knowledge and experiences to critique and stand as equal to Western theories and presentations? Were Native knowledge keepers compensated and accorded the same respect and status as Western academics? We can make assumptions about the answers to these questions, but ultimately, we do not know. If the answers to these questions are "yes," then TCU would be exceptional in academia.

Acknowledging Minimal Native American Presence at TCU

Native American presence at TCU has been sparse. While benefiting from the invasion and the expulsion of Native Nations, TCU did little to create mutually respectful and reciprocal relationships with Native people and communities. This is reflected in the exceedingly small, visible Native representation throughout the university's history. At the time of this writing, the first Native student that can be clearly identified at TCU was Bert Peters, a Pawnee citizen, who attended TCU for one year in 1929. In the previous fifty-six years, there may have been others, but they remain hidden. The *Skiff* announced Peters's arrival on February 27, 1929, in the story, "Oklahoma Indian, Son of Pawnee Chief, at T.C.U.," explaining:

> Among our students there is a psalm-singing, football-playing, full-blood Pawnee Indian. Bert Peters, son of a chief, is studying evangelical singing over at the Baptist Seminary (i.e., Southwestern Baptist Theological Seminary in Fort Worth) and also attending T.C.U. He has completed three years on his A.B. Peters attended Ottawa University and Ouachita College and has played two years of college football. When asked what position he played, he answered, "Tackle and full-back, but mostly sat on the bench." His Indian name when translated into English means, "Little Sun." Pawnee, Oklahoma, is his hometown.

That summer, the *Pawnee Courier-Dispatch* indicated that Peters "sings to help earn his way through Texas Christian University." It also identified his grandfather as "White Eagle, who fought in the Civil War under

General Miles." His father was Robert Peters. We do not know why he only stayed one year at TCU, but he apparently graduated in 1932 from Oklahoma Baptist University.[52]

Between 1929 and 1990, these individuals were identified in TCU's publications as Native American:

- Standout TCU football player and later assistant football coach, Thomas Allison "Allie" White, was nicknamed "Chief" and purportedly had "a lot of Indian blood." Part of TCU's 1938 National Championship team, he was eventually elected to the Texas Sports Hall of Fame. An orphan, he grew up in Fort Worth's Masonic Home.[53] His specific Native American identity, however, has not been confirmed.

- Jack Jordan in 1939 was identified as "a registered Cherokee Indian," who was raised in and around "Keeneton," Oklahoma.[54]

- J. C. ONeal, a sophomore from Anna, Texas, played guard on TCU's 1943 football team. He was nicknamed "Chief" and said to be "from the Indian country."[55] His specific Native American identity has not been confirmed.

- Otis Albert Penn, an Osage from Pawhuska, Oklahoma, attended summer school in 1948.[56]

- In 1952, an article appeared in the *Skiff*, "Calm Down, Men, It Ain't Injuns: That's Ole 'Gaterfoot' Harris." It began, "If by any chance you happen to be startled one of these beautiful fall days by a blood-curdling Indian war cry, calm yourself, the Apaches aren't on the warpath. It's only Marshall 'Gatorfoot' Harris letting off steam." Harris, who was from Deland, Florida, was also a cadet colonel in the Air Force ROTC and a starting offensive tackle. He had been nicknamed "Great White Feather," by dormitory students "who often try to imitate his Seminole war-cry."[57]

- In 1952, three first-year nursing students who went to high school in Globe, Arizona, Claire Taylor, Maxine Linn, and Donna Gay Knox, may have been Native American. Linn, who was from San Carlos, Arizona, said, "We have a hospital on the Indian reservation where I live, but they don't have a nursing school." Knox, who was from Globe, enrolled in the four-year nursing plan, while Linn and Taylor, who was from Mesa, Arizona, pursued the five-year plan.[58]

- The *Skiff* ran a story and an accompanying photograph in 1953 titled "Cherokee Lassie Ah-Neu-Et Finds Happy Stomping Ground at TCU." It told of Joyce Hammett, who was KTCU's radio station manager and a twenty-one-year-old transfer student from Oklahoma A&M. Described as an "Indian maiden" and "the seductive voiced lassie," she was a great granddaughter of survivors of the Cherokee Trail of Tears and her brother, James, was said to be "chief of the Cherokee tribe in Oklahoma and is a member of the Indian Legislature at Tahlequah, Oklahoma."[59]

- During the mid-1980s, Choctaw graduate student Devon Abbott [Mihesuah] was active in a variety of causes, including protecting Native American burial grounds and working to repatriate stolen items. Mihesuah has gone on to have a distinguished academic career and is currently the Cora Lee Beers Price Teaching Professor in International Cultural Understanding at the University of Kansas.[60]

The preceding list is certainly not exhaustive, but clearly there never have been many Native American students at TCU. There was an effort to engage "native American" students with a campus organization in 1965. The International Friendship Club, designed to "create opportunities for our foreign student body and our native American student body to come together," held an international festival. It is unclear if "native American" refers to Indigenous people or all who were born in the United States. There is no indication that any Indigenous students participated. Between 1989 and 2004, Native Americans made up between 0.2 percent and 0.5 percent of the student body. When TCU assistant professor of history Nancy Shoemaker decided to leave the university in 1993, she cited the small number of Native students and the lack of course offerings in race and ethnicity among the main reasons motivating her departure. She stated, "This is the only place where I've taught where I've never had an Indian student in my class. I really feel isolated from people who do Indian studies or from people who are Indian." Available data suggests that the number of students self-identifying as American Indian/Alaska Native peaked in Fall 2013 at ninety-two (0.9 percent of the student population). That number, though, had fallen to twenty-seven students in Fall 2022 (0.2 percent of the student population).[61]

The 1990s, however, did see the rise of TCU's first Native American Student Association. In 1991, Native students began organizing the association, hoping to educate the campus about "Native American culture, heritage and traditions while increasing the existing bonds between the 14 Native American students currently enrolled." Cherokee, Kiowa, Navajo, and Sioux students were identified as part of the Native population at TCU. As Navajo freshman Julius Charlie explained, students often mistook him for being Hispanic and also asked "real strange questions" about scalping, rain dances, and other issues. Associate Vice Chancellor for Academic Affairs Larry Adams, a member of the Shawnee Tribe, and Student Activities Minority and Program Adviser Monica Mendez co-advised the group. By Spring 1992, the group had formed with Charlie being joined by fellow Navajo student Michael Charlie (unrelated), both from Shiprock, New Mexico. Three years later, another Navajo student from Shiprock, Robyn Mitchell, a junior Geology major, served as president of the association, which had about ten active students (thirty-seven Native students were enrolled at TCU). Tabitha Tan, also from Shiprock, participated in the association and as her interview in this volume indicates, Native students faced many challenges. Under Adams's influence, TCU had recruited Native students in Shiprock, as well as elsewhere. Adams explained in a 2012 interview, "I worked specifically with a great financial aid director Mike Scott who said, 'We will match every tribal scholarship at TCU to bring those students.'" Unfortunately, the student association ceased to exist soon after this core group of students left TCU.[62]

Among TCU's faculty, Native representation has perhaps been even worse than student representation. No Native American faculty member has been identified before 1974, although that does not necessarily mean there were none during the university's first century. In that year, the university chapter of the NAACP filed a discrimination charge against TCU for its lack of minority hiring, citing the university's 1973 Affirmative Action report revealing, among other things, that there were no American Indians out of 322 faculty. Also in 1974, Mrs. Gail Pate, "part-Choctaw, part-Cherokee Indian" joined the Art Department, specializing in what was then called "Indian Art." Originally from McAlester, Oklahoma, she believed a course should be offered in Indian art "because it involves an aspect of America's heritage that is much neglected." Little changed as the years went by. In 1988, the *Daily Skiff* reported, "Of the twelve minority faculty who are at TCU, half are Hispanic, three Asian, one American Indian, one black, and one native of India." The number of full-time faculty self-identifying as American Indian/Alaska Native peaked at nine in Fall 2020 and remained there through Fall 2022 when nine out of 709 faculty were counted. Among staff, nine self-identified as American Indian/Alaska Native in Fall 2022 (0.5 percent of total staff). It is not known if TCU has ever had any Native American upper-level administrators, other than Adams, or trustees.[63]

Occasionally, TCU's faculty, staff, and students created interactions with Native Americans, usually in the form of on-campus presentations. Some Native speakers were quite prominent, such as two members of the renowned Kiowa Five, Tsa-To-Ke (Tsatoke) and Auchiah, who in 1933 spoke with the Art department and the Southwestern Literature class. The following year, Rebecca Smith and Mable Major loaned to the Mary Couts Burnett Library two works by Tsa-To-Ke, "The Kiowa Sun Worshipper" and "The Kiowa War Dancer." In 1972, the White Roots of Peace, described as "ambassadors for the Mohawk Nation," came to TCU as part of their national tour of universities designed to "bring an understanding and mutual respect between the white and red races." Seventy-five students met in the Student Center ballroom and listened to speakers, as well as participated in a few Mohawk dances. Two years later, one of the group's speakers, Sakokwenonkwas (Thomas R. Porter), returned and spoke on a variety of topics, including, as the *Daily Skiff* reported, a speech in which he noted that "it is time to reconcile differences between Native Americans and whites (or foreign imports)." Kiowa author N. Scott Momaday, who won the 1969 Pulitzer Prize for Fiction for his novel *House Made of Dawn*, spoke at TCU's 1973 Honors Day Convocation, saying among other things, "No segment of humanity was more closely brought to extinction by religion than the American Indians." In 1976, a TCU Muscogee/Creek staff member, Ken McIntosh, who was the Brachman Residence Hall director, took thirty students to Holdenville, Oklahoma, to experience a Stomp

Dance. The *Daily Skiff*, though, disrespectfully titled the story, "Come to Church—but Bring your Loincloth." Momaday returned in 1983 as part of Creative Writing Week. It was about this same time that a Brite Divinity School student, Larry Crocker, who had been working with the Kickapoo Tribe and its efforts to obtain land and citizenship in the United States, brought their cause to TCU. While Brite Divinity School is an independent institution with its own board, assets, and employees, it is located on TCU's campus and the two institutions often work together, as they did in this instance. At the time, nearly seven hundred tribal members were living in deplorable and hostile conditions on one acre of land in Eagle Pass, Texas. The next year, TCU's House of Student Representatives organized a collection drive for the Tribe and gathered clothing, food, and money. The drive was also held the following two years. The TCU Forums Committee invited Cherokee Nation Principal Chief Wilma Mankiller to speak at TCU in 1987. Addressing "The Future of the Cherokee Nation," she discussed a variety of topics, observing, "It's amazing how little American people know about American Indians."[64]

While this is an admirable list of speakers and activities, it represents an overall meagre engagement with Native Americans on the part of the university, especially in comparison to how it has engaged other groups and issues. The environment and relationships created by TCU ensured that any significant Native American presence would be limited. Technically, Native Americans could enroll or work at TCU, but why would they want to come or remain in a place where it was acceptable to deride or exploit them, ignorance about them was rampant, and false information and stereotypes continued to be transmitted? Only the heartiest could survive such an environment. Furthermore, these engagement efforts were neither sustained nor institutionalized, thereby severely limiting their impact. They were the efforts of individuals or small groups that did not survive beyond the time and interest of those people. While the university allowed some of its spaces to be used for these expressions, it did not value or prioritize them enough to embrace and invest resources necessary for ensuring their long-term sustainability.

There have not been many bright spots in TCU's past relationships with Native Americans and the land. Thoroughly enveloped in Euro-American Christian colonization, TCU has participated in the intentional destruction of Native American and Indigenous peoples and the seizure of their lands by benefiting and profiting from their devastation, perpetuating harmful stereotypes and misinformation, appropriating their cultures, and creating an environment where they may not have been formally excluded but were largely inhibited and discouraged from attending and working or rendered invisible. TCU's Land Acknowledgment calls our attention to relationships and the essential role played by acknowledgment as a necessary ongoing step in healing and creating healthy relationships. Acknowledging that TCU's historical relationships have largely been destructive and self-serving may be painful and uncomfortable, but it is crucial. More than retribution or "White guilt," constructive acknowledgment shines a light on serious issues that must be addressed. It recognizes that there is an ongoing problem, not just a historical one. It also is a gateway to exciting opportunities rooted in interconnected, interdependent, respectful, and balanced relationships. As the university's Land Acknowledgment reflects, TCU is interconnected and interdependent with the land, all living beings, all Native Americans, and the Wichita and Affiliated Tribes. What, then, do respectful and balanced relationships between all involved look like? Acknowledgment opens the door to meaningful actions seeking to create such relationships, a process, as outlined in this volume's introduction, the university has increasingly embraced since 2015.

PART II:
BEING IN RELATION AS A NATIVE PERSON WITHIN THE TCU COMMUNITY

RESILIENCE KICKS IN:
An Interview with Tabitha Tan (Diné)

Tabitha Tan attended TCU as an undergraduate from 1994–1999, graduating with a degree in environmental science. She was part of a small but significant cohort of Diné students recruited to TCU in the 1990s and cofounded TCU's first iteration of a Native American student organization, which was active during the 1990s. A scientist with a successful career in the personal care industry as associate principal engineer in the Corporate Quality department for Mary Kay Inc., Tabitha continues to live in the Dallas–Fort Worth metroplex. She is an active TCU alumna and a guiding force behind TCU's Native American and Indigenous Peoples Initiative. Her interview details the importance of the support given by generations of strong Diné women in her family and by faculty/staff mentors at TCU in helping her adjust to university life far away from the Navajo reservation where she grew up.

Yá'át'ééh.

Shí éí **Tabitha Tan** yinishyé.

Naasht'ézhí Tódik'ǫzhi nishłį.

Tó'aheedlíinii bashishchiin.

Bit'ąą'nii dashicheii, áádóó

Tábąąhí dashinalí.

Ákót'éego Diné Asdzáán nishłį.

Above: Tabitha Tan speaking at the dedication of TCU's Native American monument, October 15, 2018. *Photo by Cristian ArguetaSoto.*

Hello.

My name is **Tabitha Tan**.

I am from The Zuni Bitter Water People.

Born for The Water Flows Together People.

My maternal grandfather is from The Leaf People, and

My paternal grandfather is from The Water's Edge People.

In this way, I am a Navajo woman.

Life prior to TCU

I am originally from Shiprock, New Mexico, which is on the Navajo Reservation. I was born and raised on the reservation. I left my hometown for a few years because my mom thought I needed to get a better education off the Rez. We moved to Albuquerque, and I ended up going to school at Albuquerque Academy up to my tenth-grade year. Then I was a rebel and decided I wanted to go back to my hometown to live with my dad. I ended up going to Shiprock High School for my junior and senior year and graduated from there with the class of 1994.

During your senior year, you have a lot of different colleges coming to visit your high school, and TCU happened to be one of them that came to visit my high school. There were two other students previously who had gone to TCU, Robyn Mitchell and Michael Charlie. TCU at the time was aware of a Navajo Nation scholarship for Navajo Scholars called the Manuelito Scholarship. I still have my plaque. The Manuelito Scholarship is given to Navajo students who meet a certain GPA, a certain SAT/ACT score. At the time, I think it was a $25,000 scholarship over four years. One of the initiatives that TCU had is that they were willing to match that scholarship. So that was an incentive, apparently. A representative from TCU came to Shiprock and spoke to the students, passed out the purple pens, my favorite color, and we just kind of had a conversation. I was there with three of my best friends from high school, and we're still best friends today.

We were very interested in going to TCU, obviously, from a financial perspective, knowing that TCU was going to match our scholarship. TCU invited the four of us to come out to Fort Worth to visit and paid for our airfare. We stayed in the actual dorm, in Shelby Hall, and just had the TCU experience. We met up with Robyn Mitchell, our Navajo friend who was already at TCU. She took us on a school tour. We went around Berry Street and went to get Slurpees at the corner 7-Eleven and so forth. Then, we went to lunch, we went to dinner. We had dinner at a Mexican restaurant called Dos Gringos. It was the four of us, Robyn, and some other minority students, and then some of the administration from TCU. There were about twenty of us at this dinner. So we got to visit TCU and again for me, I was very attracted to the university because it wasn't in New Mexico or Arizona. From there, we applied to TCU. I got accepted. Did a submission, wrote a letter, an essay, and I got this nice big packet from TCU saying that I got accepted. And I was like, "Okay, great. This is my school of choice."

At the time, I had gotten another scholarship, which was the Indian Health Service Scholarship. That was also a full scholarship, and I put TCU on the application. In the midst of all that, I decided to go to a whole other school, which was Dartmouth College in New Hampshire. One of the reasons why I chose Dartmouth was because they definitely had a very strong Native American student program, meaning a circle of students and a center where I knew I could go if I needed something, whether that was somebody who looked like me or a guidance counselor who looked like me to help me work through things. That was one of the reasons why I chose that school.

Probably in the end of August, I got a letter from this Indian Health Service Scholarship saying, "We've awarded you the scholarship." I said, "Well, I'm going to Dartmouth now. I'm not going to TCU," but they said, "Well, we only can give you the money for what we allocated for TCU." At that point I figured, I'll just go to TCU. It's close by. When I had decided to go to Dartmouth, I bought my plane ticket for the fall semester and to get there, it was probably two planes, three planes maybe just to get to Hanover. I remember asking my mom and dad, "Hey, so are you going to buy my ticket for Thanksgiving and Christmas?" And they're like, "No, you're not coming home for those days. Do you know how much it is to fly out there?" So I think that kind of helped me decide, "Hey, TCU is a little closer," and I'll have more money because I have three scholarships now.

So that's how I came to TCU in fall of 1994. I called Dr. Larry Adams. I said, "Hi Larry, I decided to come to TCU." He called somebody since school had already started at TCU, and I was able to enroll into most of the classes I needed as a premed major. My mom and I booked a flight, and we were off to TCU with the big black trunk full of stuff. I remember my mom and I pulling up in a taxi, getting off, unloading my things in front of Shelby Hall. Larry Adams had somebody pick us up and drove us around to the stores to get things like a TV, phone, refrigerator, and microwave. I didn't come from an affluent family, but what I do know is my grandfather had sheep, cows, horses, and so did my dad. They raised them, they sold them, and made a living off of being ranchers. I even got to go on the exchange program to Paris, France when I was in tenth grade because my dad and my grandpa sold their cattle and gave me a $2,000 check. So somehow they made a living off being ranchers and my dad worked a full-time job too. My grandpa even bought me a red Honda Prelude with a sunroof while I was in college and I cherished that car. I have no idea how they made that money off of a ranch, but it was what helped support my family and my ability to go to college.

Tabitha Tan's graduation day from TCU, May 13, 1999. Left to right: Ray Tan (father), Tabitha, Maggie Slowman-Brown (mother), and Troy Brown (brother).

One of the things I always think about and am grateful for is that I'm a first-generation college student. I know my mother's story. I know both my grandmothers' stories, and I know both my great-grandmothers' stories of how they got to where we're at. So I think about all that, and I reflect on the progression over time, because those women were definitely very strong-willed, determined, and resilient.

So my maternal great-grandmother, she was given an English name, Mary Slowman from Teecnospos, Arizona. Her Navajo name, Dezbah, means "prepare for war," I guess, in a sense, like she's fire. She lived to be over one hundred years old. She was a sheepherder, and she was also a Navajo weaver. A lot of her rugs are out there somewhere being sold, but I do have three or four of them that I cherish.

Then, there's my paternal great-grandmother, who I also met, her name is Yit'sidíí Bidá'í Bitsí', and that means the silversmith's daughter. She was really the inspiration for me to go into environmental science. She was a medicine woman, too, who used herbs to heal people. You would go in her house, and she'd have tons of herbs lined up in clear glass mason jars on her windowsill and shelves. If you said your ear hurts, she knew something to mix up to make sure that went away. She had the cure for acne. She had the cure for pain in your back. She definitely influenced me in that sense, and maybe that's the scientist side of me. And then she was six feet tall, go figure. She was married to my great-grandfather, Joe Tan, who was a medicine man, in Oaksprings, Arizona. He was half San Juan Paiute and half Navajo. His Navajo name was Báyóodzin Begaye, which means the Paiute Indian man. My dad also told me my great-great-grandfather was full San Juan Paiute, a true warrior.

Then, there's my maternal grandmother, her name is Etta Slowman from Teecnospos, Arizona. She was very well-educated. She spoke English, she knew how to drive, and she worked full-time at a hotel close to Mesa Verde, which was a popular tourist location in Cortez, Colorado.

Then, my paternal grandmother, who I was closest to of all my grandmothers: her name was Elsie Tan from Red Valley, Arizona. She was a weaver, a sheepherder, and a homemaker. She's the one who pretty much raised me alongside my grandfather and my aunties. My parents were young when they had me and she wanted to make sure not only I but my other cousins were taken care of. She actually let my parents go off to college and go work out of town while I was growing up, and I always loved it when we would go see my parents. She didn't speak English or drive, but she knew that I always had to do my homework, read my books, and sign my permission slips. I actually translated for her and my grandpa or even counted money for them when we would go shopping, and there's one time I took them all the way to the "big city," Albuquerque, using my English/Navajo skills so they could go shopping for a truck.

All these women definitely were the matriarchs of our family; the Naabeehó sáanii (Navajo women) are the center of the family, the family decision-makers, family protectors, outspoken, full of wisdom, determined, and motivated. Both of my grandmothers had nine kids and one of them, the one that helped raise me, Elsie, she had an arranged marriage to my grandfather, Sam Joe Tan from Sheepsprings, Arizona. My paternal great-grandfather was a medicine man, so it was kind of like, "Hey, the medicine man wants you to marry his son." So, from their stories, she just rose to the occasion and married a man she didn't know and probably didn't care for and learned to love him while raising nine kids. She always had this smile on her face when she would tell me the story of how she met my grandfather.

Definitely, they were matriarchs, meaning that they really were the leaders of the family—had kids, raised kids, raised grandkids. I think that's where I kind of get my leadership from, my outspokenness, my determination, which my brothers say all the time. In the Navajo culture, from a clan perspective, the woman is the lead. When you say your clan—my clan is Naasht'ézhi Tódik'ǫzhi Dine'é —I'm saying my mother's clan first because she's the lead. That's who I am. That's my root. So when you go to my mom, my mom's mom, and her mom, we all have the same clan. We're all from the same lineage, and that's number one. Then, your father's clan comes second. I think that's indicative of the matriarchal society within the Navajo culture.

My mom, Maggie Slowman-Brown, was raised by a strong woman. She lost her dad when she was six. My grandmother, her mom, was left with nine kids and no husband to help her raise these kids. So she educated herself. She got herself a job. She raised all these nine kids. She really was hardcore. She was no holds barred. I was scared of that grandma. She wasn't going to sneak you candy like my other grandma did—again, going back to the resilience thing, right? She definitely was. She definitely did not show emotion. She was tough toward me, but she loved my brothers.

I think because of that and how my mom was raised, this made my mom a very strong woman, and she did educate herself too. She did go to college, didn't quite get her degree, but exposed herself to education, the city life, and was very well-spoken. We were having a Peyote meeting one time at my grandma's house. The medicine man said, "Hey, who's that White lady in the teepee?" And it was my mom. My mom definitely didn't look Navajo. She was very fair-skinned, light, kind of reddish hair, beautiful, spoke English and Navajo very well, and carried herself very well. Not that Navajo women don't, it's just that she just stood out like that, and I think part of that, too, was just that she could function in the other world and in the Navajo world. But she definitely was a matriarch of her family. After my grandmother and my great-grandmother got older, my mother stepped in and became literally the leader of that side of the family. I think that is indicative of my mom.

My great-grandmother on my mom's side, this is Mary Slowman, or Dezbah, she wove these two beautiful red rugs with black patterns made from 100 percent wool, and then she sewed them together to make a traditional Navajo rug dress known as the Bíil. They are worn in celebration when a woman has accomplished a great milestone in life or may be worn for special occasions and were worn historically during the winter and prior to the Long Walk. That's probably almost a seventy-year-old rug dress. My mom's sister keeps it, and she loans it out to family members who want to use it, but you have to give it back since it's a very valuable family heirloom. Yeah, that's a true Navajo rug dress. I mean, it's heavy. It's hot. I have no idea how women wore that a long time ago, but it keeps you warm in the wintertime for sure.

I think if I get my strength and my resilience from anywhere, it's really from this line of women, because I know my grandmothers don't play. So that just kind of stuck in the back of my head. My grandma prayed for me, did a prayer over me before I left, and both grandmas covered me with cedar, covered me with corn pollen, and feathered me down. And I thought, "Okay, this is something I have to do. This is not an option for me." All the sacrifices they made for me, I got to finish this. I'm just a competitive person anyway. And growing up—obviously, I grew up on the reservation—sometimes you don't have water, sometimes you don't have electricity. But somehow, we made it, and somehow we survived it, and we never went hungry. I knew, "I have the survival skills because of them. If they can survive that life and still get here, I can survive this college life on a scholarship and have TCU fully paid, then I think I'm going to be okay. Obviously, there's a reason why I got here, and there's a reason why I need to stay, and I need to finish this." So, literally, that went through my whole mind, probably that whole first week at TCU.

Experiences at TCU

Being at TCU, I didn't feel like I struggled, because I was able to talk to my family since they paid for my phone. I had a cell phone and a pager, and somehow they made it happen. Maybe for them, it was like, "Okay, she's out in the White man's world and she's going to survive it, so we're going to help her do it." It literally was a family effort for me to be at TCU. It was just not me. It was just not my parents. It literally was my whole tribe that did everything to make sure that I was at TCU and that I stayed there. So if it meant they all chipped in to get me a cell phone so I can call home, that's what it meant. That's why my family is so important to me, and I am very close to my family. I'm talking down to my cousin's kids who are in elementary school, that's three generations apart and I'm close to those kids. I think it's really this lineage of women, or just my family in general, that means the world to me. One way or another they made it happen for me.

When I got there, I think I was in culture shock. I had gone to Albuquerque Academy for my freshman and sophomore years, so I was familiar with other cultures, but when I was at TCU, I didn't see other people who looked like me. I think it kind of started to sink in. At the same time, I had two other Navajo friends. We had all visited TCU together our senior year and they decided to go to TCU, so they were already on campus. And it wasn't the same for my two other friends who came. It wasn't the same for them. They struggled a lot with just the environment, meaning the non-Native people, because obviously 99.9 percent of our high school was Navajo, and if you were White or if you were Black, you knew who that family was.

I think when I knew that I was different—when I say I was different, meaning I look different, I probably sounded different at the time—is when we had bought all the stuff for my dorm room, and I was in Shelby Hall. When I first met my roommate from Ada, Oklahoma. She was very surprised at what my mom had bought, which was all set up in the room, like the microwave, the phone, because she didn't bring any of that with her. I just happened to watch movies and knew that "Hey, if I want to be cool, I want a cool dorm room. I know this is what I need to have." I think I've told the story before. She said, "Oh, you speak English?" And I thought to myself, "Yeah, we all speak English. I wouldn't be here if I didn't speak English." She told me that the RA had told her there's this Native American—at the time, "Indian" girl—that was coming to TCU off the reservation. They didn't know if I spoke English or still lived in tepees. My mom was with me. My mom was very vocal, very well-educated, and very in tune with the world off the reservation. So she was not very happy about that, at all. She was quite offended, and I think I didn't know any different, I guess. I didn't know what it meant at the time to me. If my mom was upset, obviously I was upset, too. So she ended up going to talk to Dr. Adams and the administration. We got an apology. I don't know if they ever spoke to the RA or not, but during that time I just realized, "Okay, this is going to be different."

I didn't quite express it to my mom because I knew she would worry, but I just remember after all was said and done, I clearly remember when she was leaving. I remember this because I lost my mother when I was twenty-two and I will never forget this moment. So she looked at me and said, "Honey, I know you can do it. It's okay. It's scary, but it's okay. If there's anybody that I know that can do it, it's you." And I remember she gave me a kiss on the cheek and a huge hug, she jumped into the taxi, and went on her way to the airport. I think at the time, it's resilience that kicks in, right?

During my freshman year, TCU had this organizational fair in the main area of the student center, where they have all the tents outside and you can walk around and see what clubs or organizations you can join. One thing I knew that we did well back home was we played basketball. Our girls' high school were back-to-back state basketball champions in New Mexico. So I'm like, "Hey, maybe we do intramural sports." At this point, I think for me, it's really, like I mentioned, just survival, and figuring out, how do I survive this? And how do I make this better for myself, but also, for my friends, because I knew that they were struggling. They wanted to just stay in their rooms. I wanted to go out, eat in the Commons area, and meet new people.

So you just can hang out in front of Frog Fountain, and everybody is hanging out there. So I'm like, "Okay guys, maybe let's join intramural sports." For me, I did recognize people who looked like me. They weren't Navajo, but they were Brown with brown hair. So I'm like, "Okay, let me see what this is about." There's another freshman person we met named Carlos Alvarado, who's actually still my best friend to this day from TCU. He saw us and started asking us questions. And there was an organization that he was a part of called Organization of Latin American Studies, OLAS. Although we told him we were not Hispanic or did not speak Spanish, he still wanted us to come join the meeting to get to know other people like us. He was also a part of Frog Camp, so he met a lot of people. He was just a social person, so I kind of just gravitated toward him.

Then he introduced me to all the other Hispanic people, and that's how the three of us—the other two Navajo friends, Melissa and Roxanne—we all got introduced to the Hispanic sorority, Sigma Lambda Alpha. So I thought, "Okay, they all look like me," and they

Robyn Mitchell (Diné and president of TCU's first Native American Student Association during the 1990s) and Carlos Alvarado, Tabitha Tan's best friend from TCU.

were so loving and caring. They knew that we were, I guess, "Indian" at the time, and they thought that was so cool. The chapter at TCU was the Beta Chapter, so they had just started. They were wanting to get as many girls as they can, obviously—not to meet numbers but just to learn about other cultures, too. They were very loving and very caring, and I thought, "Okay, so why not. They look like me, so let me just join them." And I pledged.

And then, my other two friends, they just stopped, and they ended up leaving TCU after their first semester. I lost my two best friends from high school, the women who I grew up with in Shiprock and even stayed friends with even when my family moved to Albuquerque. It was an adjustment, but it just meant I had to be more resilient and maybe their experience at TCU wasn't the same as mine. I was sad when they left. I wasn't mad or upset because I knew how they felt. I say that because I had those same feelings when I went to Albuquerque Academy. When I went to Albuquerque Academy, the majority of the students were Caucasian students with sprinkles of Native American students. So I already knew that. For sure, the experience that I had at Albuquerque Academy, I think, was far worse for me than at TCU, and maybe that's why I knew what to do. When I got to TCU, it was uncomfortable, but I'm like, "Hey, I'm not going to go through what I went through again at Albuquerque Academy, so I'm going to make sure that I make it happen here at TCU."

They're still my best friends to this day. I think when you're not exposed to cultures outside, especially if you grew up on the reservation, it can be painful in the sense that you feel like sometimes you lose your identity. Because at home, you're speaking your language, you're eating your foods, your native foods, and you're surrounded by family. We grew up with our whole family. My grandma's house, everyone went there every evening. Then you go from having that to not having anything. That's really hard. So I think my friends were that for me, but when they left, I knew I had nothing. That feeling was definitely difficult.

When you get on campus, I guess you don't feel safe anymore. In the sense of not physical safety, but emotional safety, because you can't express yourself to somebody or somebody doesn't understand what you're having to deal with or what you're having to feel. That was very short. Again, resilience kicks in, you put on your big girl pants and you keep it going. And my mother was very good at helping me through a lot of that. And there's times she would just jump on the plane or in the car and come visit me. She just knew by the sound of my voice, if I called her and she heard something in my voice.

There's a time where I remember we were walking back from a class and my friends were like, "Is that your mom?" She was sitting right by the student center on the bench next to Frog Fountain with my grandma. I'm like, "Oh my God, how embarrassing," but I was so happy to see her. She just grabbed me and hugged me. My grandma was like, "I don't know, your mom said we're going for a drive, and next thing you know we're here." They stayed with me for a week because I had my own apartment. They cooked, they cleaned, we went shopping. My grandma did a blessing for me again, and this time she blessed my apartment. So it's things like that, made me feel like I was covered by blessings. You have people like my mom come and rescue me, just because of whatever she heard in my voice. Like I said, I don't have to say anything. She just hears my voice, and she knows. I guess that's just a mother's trait, but she was always in your business, too. I always joke around and say that I chose TCU because it was just far enough away to where my parents can't just show up, but it didn't matter to her. She still jumped in that car and drove twelve hours, and she wasn't stopping. Also, all of my life growing up, I've always been told, "Tabitha, you live in two worlds, the Navajo world and the White man's world," all the time. Whether it was my grandparents or my parents, especially my dad. I felt like they knew how it was because of things that they've experienced, and they were trying to tell me, "Hey, we're preparing you because we don't want you to have those same feelings that we had." So I think I was prepared, but when you're by yourself and you're alone, kind of like a lone soldier, that definitely is a lot harder than if you had your friends or family who are from your hometown next to you.

At that time after my friends from Shiprock left, after the first semester, I kind of just gravitated toward my sorority and the OLAS organization. Most of my friends were Hispanic and I didn't grow up with Hispanics, but they embraced me and invited me to their homes. I had one friend, she lived in Laredo, Texas, and she had this ginormous home and invited fifteen of us during fall break. We all drove down there, ate some good Mexican food, went shopping in Nuevo Laredo, and danced to Tejano and Spanish rock music. So that's really how I survived in the beginning and just expanded on that. So with my sorority sisters and Carlos, they were sensitive to my experiences and were even more loving because of them, which I definitely am grateful for, because I don't think my experience would have been the same without them.

There was another organization called International Student Association, and they had an annual cultural event. They invited us to dress in our Native regalia and do a presentation or be a part of the fashion show at the time. I think people started to notice us, as Native Americans. Well, actually, we were known as the Shiprock girls, our hometown, because we played basketball and we did really well on the intramural basketball teams. So everyone would come and watch us play down in the Rickle. Everybody knew we were the Navajo girls. It just kind of grew on other people.

People knew to come to us, to ask us questions about our culture or ask us to be a part of the fashion show, which kind of led to starting that Native American student organization. The first time we did an event for Native American Heritage Month, we found local artists to come to TCU and I remember Harold Rogers as a Men's Fancy Dancer. I don't know if he remembers that—I remember his regalia. There were also another couple of females and kids that came, and there was a drum that came. These were events that were held in the Student Center as the students were walking by and you can share information with them or pass out a flyer. That's really kind of how the events were done. I mean, whether that was the Native American event we had, or whether it was during Hispanic Heritage Month, Black History Month. I mean, that's really where a lot of us—I say us, minorities—had our events, but it's something you had to advertise for yourself.

Opposite page top: The "Shiprock Girls" (Diné) with members of the Organization of Latin American Students at the TCU-Baylor football game, October 1, 1994. Left to right: Melissa Caddell (second), Tabitha Tan (third), and Robyn Mitchell (fourth).

Opposite page bottom: Students from TCU's first Native American Student Association participating in the International Students Association's Annual Spring Banquet Fashion Show during the 1990s. Kathy Whitekiller (Cherokee, second from left), Robyn Mitchell (Diné, fourth from left), and Tabitha Tan (Diné, fifth from left).

That's kind of how the Native American student organization start-ed, but it was really probably four of us—myself, Robyn Mitchell who is also from my hometown, Shiprock, and was a sophomore at TCU during that time, and there was another Navajo guy, Mike Charlie, also from my hometown who was a junior at the time. He was kind of like our big brother when we came to TCU, and Robyn was kind of our big sister. I guess they kind of led the path for us. There was another lady, her name was Kathy [Kathleen Whitekiller]. She was Cherokee from Oklahoma and attended TCU for a year or two as a nursing student. Her experience may have been different, but we were able to connect on campus. We were all able to be in touch with our culture on campus, no matter what tribe we were from.

We started the student group for awareness. I just believe in edu-cating others. I think what sparked that, too, is being asked about being Indian and if I knew how to speak English or if I still lived in tepees. Having a lot of different questions being asked of me that you think would be basic. I thought, let's see what we can do to educate the com-munity, in this case TCU. I think the other thing is I felt at the time, you kind of feel exotic. People are like, "Oh, you're Indian." Then, the fact that we grew up on the reservation, people think that you're 100 percent, that you're "real." We've never really met somebody whose both parents are 100 percent based on our CDIB [Certificate of Degree of Indian or Alaska Native Blood]. For me or for us, it was really, "Let's just educate them and teach." That was really our goal. I think when people think Indian or Native American, the first thing they think about is powwow, the drum, flute music, and what you see on TV like *Dances with Wolves* or I don't know, all these other movies that you see. So it's kind of like, "Okay, let's start them with this."

And then, we go and do other things, too, which in this case was really working with some of the younger kids at one of the schools there at TCU. I think after a while it was only maybe two of us that were left because Robyn graduated, Mike graduated, and it was just me and maybe Kathy. That's when it just dissipated after that [after 1996]. We weren't able to sustain it because of the numbers of Native American students were not present or at least we didn't know if they were being accounted for. There was really nobody else. Again, I mean, it was a good start, and we really enjoyed what we did at the time.

Robyn Mitchell (Diné) and Tabitha Tan (Diné) at the International Students Association's Annual Spring Banquet during the 1990s.

I think the knowledge at TCU about Native Americans was, I would say from a scale of one to five, probably one, and we maybe moved it to a two or three. Again, it's really what you see on TV, right? And this is also for me, I didn't realize there were reservations in Texas. I knew there were reservations in Oklahoma. You have Native Americans in Oklahoma who are Cherokee or those other tribes in Oklahoma, but they don't exactly look like me. There were probably Native students who were Native or part Native, but they weren't going to be open like, "Hey, I'm Native American," because they had blonde hair and blue eyes. When people started to feel comfortable, then they would come out and say, "Hey, I'm Native too." They would start talking about their grandparents or even sometimes knew the language. I don't feel like it was an environment where if you had blonde hair and blue eyes, you were open to saying, "Hey, I'm Native," because obviously, that may be looked at a little differently. To everybody, I was Hispanic, I was the Mexican girl from New Mexico.

Growing up, Navajo was my first language. The way it's been explained to me from my family is you have the Navajo culture and then you have the Native American Church and then you have Christianity. My family was very different. My mom's family was Native American Church. That means they're having Native American church ceremonies, eating peyote, drinking peyote, praying to, I mean, both my grandmothers would debate this all the time, whoever is up there. My great-grandfather was a medicine man on my paternal side, so my dad's family was very respectful of him in that, seeing that that's the Navajo culture. He practiced the Navajo culture and then you bring in Christianity into that. So they kind of functioned with that. So I think growing up—I explained that story because growing up, I just went whichever way my parents went. If I was with my mom, I did Native American Church. When I was with my dad and his family, it was church with the medicine man. So one of the things I personally chose is to respect both sides of my family.

Coming to TCU, I got blessed with the corn pollen, the cedar, and the feathering down, and would even have a ceremony before I would leave for college. Then, on the Christian and the Navajo side, I have my great-grandfather, Joe Tan (Báyóodzin Begaye), the medicine man, doing a ceremony for me in Hózhójí, meaning the Blessingway, to Walk in

Beauty Ceremony. And then my grandma Elsie, praying for me while putting olive oil on my forehead. Everybody in my family was blessing me all sorts of ways before I left for college, but when I got to college, I didn't do any of it because I think for me, I was always afraid—I don't know why, now that I think about it—of what people would think of me feathering myself down or taking corn pollen or even sitting in prayer with the Bible. It was a Christian college, and I've seen other people do it. During my freshman year, my roommate's father was a pastor of a Lutheran church. So, she always had her Bible out, did Bible study, and I just never did. I just didn't know which way to go at the time. And I just didn't want to be looked at as, "Oh, she's eating some corn pollen" and has these feathers with her. Is it witchcraft or is it juju, because anybody can interpret some of those things differently. So I just chose not to do it. If I did it, I did it in silence. It was more that I just would rather not do it than have somebody see me do that and say, "Oh, well, she's doing something in the room with her feathers." So I just didn't do it out in the open.

Larry Adams was very vocal about him being Native American and obviously, in his position [associate vice chancellor for academic affairs] at the time, it's very well-respected where he was. And the fact that he supported us, whether or not that was, "Hey, if we needed help with something." I think from that perspective, maybe there was more sensitivity because if you're affiliated with him as somebody at that level in the administration, I feel like that was more helpful. I think for us, I was happy we had that access. I think the relationships that we also built with our professors and our advisors were also very helpful. My advisor was Dr. [Leo] Newland, and he respected my culture and where I came from and was very sensitive to the differences of how I grew up. The other person was in the Geology Department, [Nowell] Donovan. He loved Robyn Mitchell. He was her advisor because she was a geology major. He was very caring to her and her family and then, that was extended to us, too. Holidays, if we weren't going home, we would get invites to some of the professors' homes and introduced to their families. So I think the sensitivity from that perspective was tremendous and was very helpful to us. If it wasn't a student, at least we have a professor or advisors on our side to understand our background and our struggles when it comes to being on campus. I think the other thing is the geology professors knew the history of the geological aspects of my hometown,

Shiprock. Shiprock, also known as Tse' Bit' A'i, meaning "rock with wings," is a volcanic rock in my hometown. Being in geology and environmental science classes, this was an area that they had interest in already, and they've already studied it and researched it, which we thought was cool at the time as we, being from Shiprock, did not know the geological aspects of the area. So them knowing we were from there, it just kind of worked out for us.

Classes addressing Native American issues or perspectives were almost nonexistent. TCU is in its own little bubble, right? I don't think even that was on anyone's agenda or anyone's thoughts. I don't even remember a book in English class, even in a religion class. For example, you had to take World Religions or you had to take the Bible class. I didn't take those two classes, so I had to take another 300-level class. The only class I was able to take at that time was an Islam religion class. Even that class was an option to take, but nowhere was there any Native American, American Indian, or anything like that as a part of any discussion in any class that I am aware of.

As far as staying connected with family or just missing home, with the scholarships I had, I had extra money that allowed me to buy a plane ticket home if I got homesick. That extra money that I had really was a lifesaver. I know that my family probably couldn't have done that financially every single time I wanted to buy a plane ticket. I may have gone home a lot since my family would ask, "Do you even still go to college?" I went home quite a bit and eventually my parents would say, "You have to stay there sometimes. You have to." There were other students, such as Kathy who was Cherokee, who drove back to Oklahoma every weekend. She never stayed on campus—only for classes. And she was out the door the minute her last class was done on Friday and was back to Oklahoma. She drove in Monday mornings and went to class. I didn't have the luxury, but I knew that, hey, if I had some money, I was going to jump on that plane on Friday afternoon, and I was back at DFW or Love Field on Sunday evening. And I think that happened more often than not, to help with that homesickness.

I think loneliness was a feeling I had at times because no one can relate to you, or I felt like I was missing out on things like birthday parties or celebrations with family. And I wanted to be there because I was very close to my family. Even now, I went home for a graduation and then, I went home for a baby shower two weeks later. So even at this age, I still am the same way, but I think that keeps me grounded and it keeps me in tune with where I come from. I feel like that was really, really my saving grace, I guess. Now, this is what, almost thirty years later since I came to the DFW area in 1994, I still go home just as much as I did when I was in college.

Going home, I was happy to be with my family, but also to see my friends. Even though my two friends left TCU, we still spent time together. We would drive from Fort Worth back to our hometown together during the holidays. Going home to see family or friends, I know I was 100 percent sad, but I never cried. Because at the time, I kept telling myself, "You're not allowed to cry, Tabitha." Because when you leave, everyone is praying for you. I have a whole line of family members in front of me ready to bless me, pray for me, feather me down.

And it's like, "Okay, you can't cry," and I say that because it was hard not to. But when you're told not to cry, it's just unspoken, you just don't cry, you don't show fear, and you stand in pride. I think that goes back to a cultural perspective for Navajo women in general. You're the matriarch, you're the leader, you don't falter, you stand your ground or you resist or you—what is that word I used earlier? Resilience kicks in. But believe me, there were a lot of times when my dad dropped me off at the airport and I wanted to cry. That definitely was very hard to not be able to express your emotions. I think in the Navajo culture, you just don't. Now, it's a little different because back then, you had to be strong, you can't show your weakness. I will say there's not a time I've ever seen people cry, like leaving at the airport, unless there was a death in the family. It's almost one of those things, an emotion you don't show, I guess. That's probably not good, especially at that age. Even now, I teach my niece, it's okay. It's okay to express emotion. I even have a feeling wheel that helps label my emotions or whatever I'm experiencing at a specific time. It's not easy for me to express my feelings at times. It's just one of those things where maybe if I did it in the past, I wouldn't have to have that feeling wheel in front of me now. Not to say anybody ever told me, don't cry. It's just one of those things you just don't see anybody doing, so you just didn't do it.

What stood out to me the most in how I changed at TCU is knowing how to function off the reservation. I think I mastered that. So I think that also prepared me in a sense for the real world, after TCU. It also helped me know how to help others who come after me, meaning my cousins' kids, my cousins' friends, and anyone who may want to go to college. Because it's not the same, meaning that I feel like kids today aren't as resilient and for those who are, I try to share my story with them so they know it will be okay. Let's use my niece Moné as an example. By showing her the way, the challenges that I faced, she can use that to her advantage and she can also help the next generation that's coming after her.

So there's less stories of having the hurt or the pain or the missing home and more of the success—of how do I pivot and how do I adjust to this environment? Because I'll be honest, I don't feel like the reservation has changed since I was there. It's still the same. The only difference I think is you have a McDonald's now, you have a Sonic, you have streetlights, but other than that, it's the same. Maybe the school system has advanced just a little more, but I will say that I feel like my time at TCU has helped me be better prepared for life as an adult and even for my first "real job." Recently, my cousin told her daughter, "I don't think you should go to college because it's in Seattle. It's far. I'm not going to be able to see you, and how am I going to get to you?" Obviously, her daughter had to listen to her mom. I inserted myself and had a conversation with my cousin. She's my older cousin, Jeri. My first question to her was, "Why are you holding her back?" She has potential to get a full wrestling scholarship, so I said, "Let me tell you what, why don't I take her up there? Let me talk to her coach. I'll fly up there with her. Let's just see what happens. She may like this. She may not. She may get homesick. I don't know. Let's just see." So, we went up there. My cousin ended up coming with me, and my goddaughter ended up loving it. They offered her a wrestling scholarship. I negotiated with the coach for room and board, and she ended up going to college in Seattle and wrestling for a Division II women's wrestling team. In March, my goddaughter went to the national championship in Puerto Rico and took second place as a freshman female wrestler in her weight division. My cousin also took her other kids, and they all flew out to Puerto Rico for the championship. I couldn't go, and I really wanted to go, but I said, "Hey, this is your time. You got to do this. This is your daughter." So that's just kind of an example of knowing what the struggles were during my years at TCU and adjusting. I was able to share that with my cousin and her daughter. Her daughter loves it. She can't wait to go back. I just saw her last weekend when I was at home and she's like, "I can't wait to go back. I need to get out of here." I feel like that's the benefit. If I can have endured all this through my college years and those who come after me, do not, then I'm okay with that.

It's difficult to go back to the reservation. I used to go all the time to visit my grandmother Elsie, but since she's passed on about two years ago, the only reason why I go there to Shiprock or the Rez is to get a roast mutton sandwich or a Navajo taco and to see my aunts and my cousins who still live there. Outside of that, I make sure I get there first thing in the morning, and I leave before it gets dark. I think it's hard to see that. It's hard to see that the progress is very minimal. And I have these discussions with my dad all the time. I'm like, "Why? Why?" I think part of it is—I'm only speaking for myself, and what I've seen my family—you get content, and sometimes you don't know what else is off the reservation, or you only know what's in a border town. Meaning, for us, Shiprock is my hometown. The border town is Farmington. Sometimes, people don't see outside of that. So when I'm talking about my cousin, Jeri, she's forty-nine years old and just recently flew on a plane in 2022 to Seattle. She's never been anywhere, outside of the United States, and now I told her, "You're in Puerto Rico!" So that's really hard for me to see, and I guess sometimes I feel like, this Navajo scholarship helped me get to where I'm at. Can I go back and help my people? Yes, but I feel you have to change the mindset. You have to change, and I say this with my own family, too, because I feel like we've always been given things. Maybe we've just gotten used to it and we become complacent with it.

Advice to TCU

As an alum, I am a Horned Frog [TCU's mascot] for life. I bleed purple [a phrase conveying loyalty to TCU's school color]. My experience at TCU was a little different, and I learned a lot. I'm definitely very grateful for Dr. Newland and the advising there. Also, as an alum, just the transition that TCU has made from 1994 to 2023, which is almost thirty years later, in my mind, it's great—it's phenomenal. Although it took a long time, I think having the Land Acknowledgement, and even the scholarships, is definitely showing respect, as it states, to acknowledge all Native American peoples who have lived on this land, where TCU now stands. I definitely am grateful for that because I think not all colleges have done that. Not all businesses have done that. I think the fact that they're open to conversation and have recognized their role in the process, meaning TCU recognized that, "Hey, we are on Native land." Did anybody ever bring that to their attention? Did they even know? I didn't know. I think as an alum, I'm definitely appreciative that they have recognized that we are here, that we exist, and that the land that the beautiful campus is on was once land of Native Americans. And that is great, and no wonder I felt at home surrounded by my ancestors. Can they do a little more? Absolutely.

The scholarship aspect is where I would say that, because TCU is very expensive. And there's no comparison to someone coming off of the reservation and being able to afford TCU and for TCU to think, "Oh, well we want more Native Americans." When you're wanting to recruit Native Americans, say from the reservation or near the reservation, there's no way they can afford TCU. And not even the tribes that provide the scholarships would be able to pay for TCU. So, for example, the Manuelito Scholarship is an academic scholarship I was awarded by the Navajo Nation, however, it would not cover TCU's tuition today. I hear it's still the same amount as when I first got it. We're in 2023, and that's going to cover nothing if the prices of the university tuition have increased by ten since then, right? Well, I say that because my niece has been researching the current amount of the Manuelito Scholarship and it's still the same amount. So I think in that sense, I think a little more work could be done in that area.

In the future, I would still like to see the Land Acknowledgement at sporting events, and at each of TCU's colleges, and for TCU to continue student recruitment on/off the reservation. And again, I think for me, it's the scholarships and the availability of financial aid to Native students I would like to see. I think that would be key for me. I would like to see more of that, but also, understanding the culture. I know we've kind of started with the Native studies program, but I think also introducing a little more of that for awareness and education for me would be key, because I still feel like TCU is still in its bubble. When I say TCU, I mean also the students. Something else that would also be very helpful in the sense of just relationships when a Native student comes to TCU would be being able to have somewhere to go or someone to turn to who looked like me to help me work through things. I think when I was there, the person that was that for us as minority students was Darron Turner. He was that person for us. He didn't just accommodate the Black students. He accommodated all of us people, the students of color, who were at TCU at that time.

Luci Tapahonso (right), inaugural poet laureate of the Navajo Nation and keynote speaker at TCU's third annual Native American and Indigenous Peoples Day Symposium, with Tabitha Tan (left) at the Horned Frog statue, October 1, 2018.

BLEEDING PURPLE AND NOT DEAD YET!

by Albert Nungaray (Tewa)

Albert Nungaray (Tewa) graduated from TCU with majors in history and anthropology in 2017. As a student, he participated in the first Native American and Indigenous Peoples Day Symposium and worked to revive the Native American Student Association in 2017, serving as its vice president. In this autobiographical essay, Nungaray writes candidly about his path to TCU, the alienation and discrimination he experienced after enrolling at the university, his gradual discovery of community, and how he came to play a leadership role on campus. At the time of the writing of the essay, he was pursuing doctoral studies in history at the University of Texas at Arlington and working as a history and culture educational consultant with various organizations in Fort Worth, including Log Cabin Village, the Fort Worth Art Commission, and the Fort Worth Independent School District. He remains a guiding participant as an alum in TCU's Native American and Indigenous Peoples Initiative. "Bleeding purple," a phrase appearing in the title of this essay, is a common sentiment that members of TCU's community express to indicate identification with and loyalty to the university, which has purple as its school color.

Above: Albert Nungaray speaking at the dedication of TCU's Native American monument, October 15, 2018. *Photo by Cristian ArguetaSoto.*

Can I tell you a story? In a world of formality and stylistic standards, with your permission, I wish to simply tell you a story. Since time immemorial, storytellers have been telling our histories and preserving our lore. They pass on lessons and ideas generation after generation to ensure that who we are and who we want to be is not lost to time. As a historian, I do my best to balance academic and cultural storytelling. The stories I tell are of creation, legends, and ancestral lessons, tales of historical figures and events, the contexts of grand design and individual alike. However, today I find myself in a strange role. I have been selected to contribute to the history of my alma mater in a book that will document my microscopic part in its 150-year story. My contribution will not be of facts and citations or historiography, that which I have been trained for at university. I will be tossing formality aside for a moment and simply be. Because somehow, of the tens of thousands of students who have walked the grounds of TCU, my voice, my story will be on these pages in perpetuity. I struggle to figure out why and how that came to be. I struggle to process what makes my time in our Horned Frog community special enough to put into print. I graduated in 2017 with mediocre grades, and I have no grand narrative of success. Surely there is someone more deserving! It is simultaneously humbling and a boost to the ego. Yet, in that struggle, memories have forced their way to the forefront of my mind. What sits on the pages before you are the memories sweet, comrades true, the good and the bad, the bruises and victories, the absurd life of a Horned Frog on a mission to break the cycles of generational trauma that led him on a winding path of endless disappointment and rare but treasured life-altering victory.

See, I grew up in El Paso, Texas. I was a mixed-race child of poverty and am still known for my notoriously bad luck. Most of my core memories from childhood are trauma based. I was raised in a home that saw an extremely violent divorce, with my father replacing me the first chance he got to start a new family. I grew up feeling expendable, disposable, and forgettable. By the time I was a teenager, I had learned my purpose was to be a commodity to be used for the good of those around me, nothing more. I was to put all I am into all I do and keep the needs of others—especially my siblings—ahead of my own. People like me are here to work themselves to death as tools to be tossed aside when worn out so that those around them could have slightly better lives. While I wouldn't say I was comfortable with that mentality, I got used to it and accepted it as simply how life was. As much as my parents hated to admit it, we were poor, and I always knew it. We had improvised involuntary skylights—my loving term for holes in the roof that came from leaks and collapses—and only intermittent running water for the last few years I lived there. The pipes leaked so badly that if we left the water on it would flood the walls and floor, so we would turn it off at the street and only turn it on for an hour a day if we absolutely needed it. We would go for weeks eating nothing but beans and my stepfather's "famous" chili. At one point, my bedroom was rented out to a "family friend" while I was still in it so that we could afford food and utilities. While most people I grew up with look back at their first paycheck with fondness, I look back and remember I didn't see a dime of it as my mother used it as soon as it was in my account. While that feeling of disposability has often followed me into adulthood, over the years I have learned the details of the full story and have largely forgiven all involved in most of these past traumas. I still acknowledge it was traumatic, I still often feel expendable, but I also realize the feelings of a child did not quite reflect the reality of the larger overall context.

Still, I know my parents tried their best with what they had. My stepfather thanklessly worked hard to give what he could to children who were not his blood. I admire him greatly. My biological father didn't replace me or forget me, he simply needed to save himself and didn't know how in a complex and chaotic situation. My mother didn't see me as a commodity, she was just desperate to make ends meet for our family. They are all human and far from immune to humanity's wealth of flaws. I don't think for a moment these struggles were malicious. As an adult, I understand this, as now I try my best with what I have and look back on the moments when I wondered how hard it could possibly be to do things right. The schools I went to did not help my case. In fact, my high school guidance counselor once told me I needed to "focus on jobs which were more up [my] alley." I remember his words piercing my heart when I asked about college: "We both know you're not academic. Have you thought of metal working or truck driving? Things that are more realistic for you?" As you can imagine, the psyche of a high school kid growing up with nothing did not take that well. Yet, it didn't matter, and I didn't let it deter me. I wasn't smart enough for college, and I knew that. In my mind I was joining the military anyways, so I would learn a trade there regardless. I almost dropped out that week. My mom refused to let me, blocked calls from military recruiters, and made promises she couldn't keep. Having recently been diagnosed with multiple sclerosis, she did all she could to make sure I didn't give up. So I kept pushing and graduated.

I'm sure at this point, you get the idea of what kind of life I had as a child—so that covers the poverty. I don't have to get into much detail there because no one wants to read pages upon pages of trauma and heartache. My bad luck is another story entirely, however. As I mentioned, while in high school, my dream was to enlist in the military like my father, stepfather, uncle, cousin, and grandfather. After all, Native Americans and Mexicans are vastly overrepresented in the military. Who am I to buck the trend, right? I could be a warrior and somehow make my family proud. My tribe, the Tewa, are traditionally farmers and aren't known historically as warriors, but in my mind it was my duty to serve. Much to my shame, however, that was not my path. I eventually found out the military would not take me because of health issues. With that, I attempted to get my certification to be a paramedic. If I couldn't serve the nation, I could serve my community. However, that was not to be as well because I fractured several vertebrae in a work accident. In pain, depressed, and with a complete lack of priorities, I dropped out of community college with a 1.4 GPA. For several years, I floated around odd jobs. From digging ditches and cleaning up the leftovers at crime scenes to working at dollar stores and teaching survival classes, I did my best to help my family get by and failed every step of the way. In no particular order of events: I have been hit by a car, have survived severe sepsis, have had a tree fall on me, have been stabbed, have been knocked unconscious by lightning, and have had more injuries than I care to count. Still, I worked as much as I could and made sure my brother and sister had what they needed to succeed. I drove them to and from school so often that people thought I was my brother's dad. I wanted them to succeed and did everything my young mind could think of to make it happen. I wasn't the smart one; they had a much stronger chance to succeed than I did. So, after so many setbacks, once again it felt like to give like this was my only way to contribute and my purpose in this life. Needless to say, Lady Luck and I have never been on good terms. My notorious luck is not a thing of the past. It has followed me every step of the way. I'll always remember the response my TCU friends and professors had when a squirrel refused to leave my truck and I missed a meeting, only to have that truck catch fire the next week. I can get a good laugh out of most of this now, only because of how ridiculous it all is. But at this moment, I find myself laughing at how ridiculous it is that the poor and unlucky kid from El Paso is now writing some of his story down for a university he never thought he would get into.

The fact that I made it here at all was far from a sure thing. In my neighborhood, I was more likely to go to prison than get an advanced degree. Somehow, however, I made it back to college. After spending many miserable years working myself to death, I knew that I needed to try for a career rather than a job. My sister was wrapping up her BA and my little brother had graduated high school. It was a "now or never" type moment. So, there I was, filled with overwhelming negativity and disbelief as my brother enrolled in classes. While I sat there waiting, he suddenly informed me that my little brother and sister used the last of their financial aid to cover one class for me to get back in the system for my first semester returning at El Paso Community College (EPCC). I failed the first time because of circumstance and a lack of priorities. This time, I resolved to make them proud and turn that investment of my future into something that they would not regret.

I'll be honest, the only reason I ended up really looking at TCU was because the University of Texas at El Paso (UTEP) didn't offer me a scholarship. While at EPCC, I worked my way back up to a strong GPA and joined Phi Theta Kappa (PTK). As part of PTK, I ended up becoming a chapter officer and promotional information for universities began to arrive in my mail. Being from El Paso, UTEP was my assumed destination. Don't get me wrong, I have nothing but love for UTEP and El Paso and always will, but when the prospect of going to University of Texas at Austin, Baylor, TCU, and other schools across the country presented itself—my eyes lit up like a Christmas tree. The decision of which to choose was pretty clear cut. I chose TCU sight unseen, having never been to campus or spoken to someone there. I followed that "light of faith" to an uncertain future.

I had first heard of TCU as a kid. My grandfather was working at UTEP and sneaked me into the Sun Bowl game. At the fan fiesta, I met a player who was apparently destined for great things. He asked if I was a TCU fan. I told him I could never afford to go to his school, but I liked the colors and mascot more than USC's so I was cheering for them that day. He told me not to let money tell me what I could and couldn't do and to have fun. He said it in passing and likely doesn't remember the encounter, but it put TCU on my radar and made me look at life outside El Paso for the first time in my life. I won't name names, but I'm pretty sure he went on to set a record the next year against UTEP.

Years later, when I started looking at where to continue my studies, I was with a friend talking about my pending decision. We were watching YouTube videos and waiting for another friend's shift to finish. Out of the ether, a commercial appears on my screen. "This shirt says more than don't back down," the narrator said, in a gravelly voice, as a Horned Frog T-shirt filled the ad. If nothing else, I have a habit of not giving up right when I feel most like doing so. Those words stuck with me as I inched closer to my decision. Less than one week later, I was having a particularly rough day when I received a postcard in the mail from a student likely working in admissions. It read, "Becoming a Horned Frog is one of the BEST decisions I have ever made, and I hope you'll do the same. GO FROGS!" Patty has no idea I still have that postcard. They probably signed hundreds of them that year. With the postcard was a pamphlet on the TCU family mentality and a keychain (which is still on my keys). That was still the proverbial straw on the camel's back, the final sign needed. TCU was where I needed to be. No one else told me not to back down. No one else encouraged me to join the family. Less than six months later, I was packing up my belongings and moving to Fort Worth. I had nowhere to live, no job lined up, and a car with a hole in the door that barely ran. But I was on my way over the rainbow on a road that felt like destiny, and I would not back down. With my sister and best friend at my side, I set forth on the wildest journey of my life.

Oddly enough, it turned out I had a long-lost grandmother who lived just a few miles south of campus. My mother had been given up at birth, and her biological family found us just after I had made my decision. I had missed out on a life with my grandmother in it, and I was going to be starting a new life mere miles from her and an entire branch of family I did not know had existed. She was a saint of a woman. Welcoming, encouraging, loving, and resilient. She was everything I wanted to be. We bonded instantly. Until her death this past year after her third fight with cancer, she was a constant supportive part of my life from the moment I arrived in Fort Worth. They didn't know it, but TCU had unintentionally given me a priceless gift before I even started classes. Even more of a sign that I was in the right place.

All that being said, I still do not feel like I deserve this. There are so many others who are so much more successful and had experiences that would be amazing for recruitment and the prestige of TCU. I'm not exactly the poster-child type. I'm still poor, currently unemployed, my clothes are ratty, my social standing has not increased, and I'm driving a hand-me-down fifteen-plus-year-old Hyundai. Only now, I'm struggling under an omnipresent menacing mountain of student debt, and I have severe anxiety to go with it. I stepped on campus to register for classes while still not having a place to live and knowing no one. My first memories as a student are deeply unpleasant and will haunt me forever. I didn't even finish my scheduled classes the first week of my first semester because someone reported I had a weapon in my backpack. That weapon was my traditional flute, a recent gift from my newly discovered grandmother. I had been wanting to find a nice corner or a stairwell to play and recenter myself. Instead, I had campus police pull me out of class in front of other students, humiliating me in the process. To add insult to injury, I forgot my newly gifted Australian slicker coat in the classroom and never saw it again. Any goodness I had been shown or hope I held had been extinguished unceremoniously by a single phone call. For their part, the police were good to me. I won't say they did not do their job well. I know now that they had to investigate a report of a weapon. I was angry and hurt by the encounter, but the thought that someone was so threatened by my presence that they felt the need to have this happen was what really broke my heart. I knew I had to spend the rest of the semester with everyone who saw it thinking I was some sort of criminal. From then on, several students pulled their bags closer when I entered class.

I spent the rest of that first semester just trying to get my work up to par. I had to relearn how to write, because apparently my overly casual, community college-level, storytelling style writing was far from up to the task. It took everything I had to pull a barely passing average, but it was not enough, and that was very nearly my one and only semester at TCU. I promptly lost my scholarship and sincerely considered going home with my tail between my legs. I had seen racist behavior, elitist students, and a community that believed I was only there because TCU needed to fill a minority quota. For the record, I did not indicate my race or ethnicity in my application, but I shouldn't have to explain that to people as a default. It became clear that TCU has an image problem. It's a school for rich, White kids with summer homes and daddy's credit card, living in palatial fraternity and sorority houses and partying. It's no place for someone like me, no place for the millions of us who don't fit that demographic. It's no place for a nontraditional student who just wants to earn a degree and be proud of themselves. TCU's reputation was overwhelming at first, and to my eyes it was easily living up to it.

I was feeling guilty, disconnected, and entirely alone. My tribe was ten hours away, my family was still in El Paso, and I was at a private school that I was feeling more and more like I had reached too far to be at. I wanted to fly under the radar and make my family proud but had no idea how to do that. I was going to football games while my parents were losing our family home. I was losing my scholarship while my little brother was struggling for dinner and my sister was working herself to death as most likely one of the best-educated cashiers in the history of working at the Dollar General (likely an exaggeration, but this is my story and it's probably not far off, so I'm sticking to it). I was feeling guilty that so many of my childhood friends were dead, in prison, or on the verge of one or the other, while I was miserable at a place with opportunities none of us could have dreamed were possible. I was letting the weight of my ancestors' disappointment and my family's broken dreams drag me to depths at which no one should have to exist. My existence at TCU had become an existence of spite and resistance. I couldn't quit, but I couldn't enjoy myself either. I wasn't going to let money tell me what I could and couldn't do. I figured that in the best case scenario I would succeed and get my degree, and worst case scenario I was right and didn't belong there in the first place.

Yet, I sit here writing this today as an alum. It turns out that the feelings of a new student did not quite reflect the reality of the larger overall context. The narrative shifted. I am a proud graduate of that very same university that almost crushed me. I bleed purple and my love for TCU is infectious. With everything I've said before, that might be a bit of a curveball. Yes, I'm as shocked as you are—probably more so, if I'm being honest. A funny thing, however, happened after that first year at TCU. Some of my classmates rallied around me and encouraged me to never, ever give up. Even though I felt robbed because my scholarships were gone, and even though my PTK status did not change, I was supported and encouraged to keep pushing. My professors built up my confidence and did their best to keep me focused, even with my ADHD—professors like Dr. Alex Hidalgo, who in essence taught me how to write professionally. While professors like Zaira Crisafulli at El Paso Community College had taught me how to express myself and paint a picture with words, Dr. Hidalgo taught me how to be taken seriously at TCU and in the rest of academia. Simultaneously, a new love was emerging. While I knew I loved history, much of my work before TCU was in culture and archaeology. I had been volunteering at the El Paso Museum of Archaeology for years, teaching classes, acting as docent, and in other support roles. I didn't know it at the time, but volunteering would end up being the most important early decision in guiding my future.

It was there, when I was just having fun supporting a local museum, that I realized I loved telling stories and teaching about culture. So, needing a minor for my degree plan, I naturally chose anthropology. The anthro department adopted and supported me without hesitation. With the efforts and compassion of the entire department, I started to feel less and less alone. Wonderful people like Dr. Dave Aftandilian and Dr. Miguel Leatham took me under their masterful wing and made me feel not only welcome but needed and respected. They subtly shifted my techniques and research into something that I could use to emphasize my expertise rather than fight it. They made me feel like my experiences were a unique asset rather than a barrier to belonging. I would say that the entirety of the anthro department, from the reception desk to each and every professor, created an environment where I felt the most at home I have ever felt anywhere.

Before I knew it, I was involved in several organizations. I became the vice president and then the president of the Anthropology Society, and a member of the Phi Alpha Theta and Lambda Alpha honor societies. Soon after I started to become active and feel comfortable, I talked to my little brother. He, like myself, had dropped out of college and was feeling like he could never go back. He had stopped singing and playing his saxophone, which was absolutely tragic as it brought him so much joy. So I decided to look around and see if there were any singing groups I could join to show him that it could be done. It was then I stumbled on a fledgling organization, the TCU Horned Tones. I auditioned and became one of their original members. I didn't particularly like the singing style or performing. I just wanted to prove a point to myself and my brother. I wanted to prove it could be done. I had no idea what was waiting for me along this path.

When I say that those guys became my brothers, I mean it. I spent more time with them than anyone. We sang whatever we wanted, and I legitimately started to have fun. We sang a weird little song about Chick-fil-A and even performed to a full house while opening for Jessie McCartney (I will admit I had no idea who they were at the time). This couldn't have been a group of more seemingly random guys. A football player from Hawaii, a musician from LA, a gentle giant from Oregon, guys from DFW, Nashville, San Antonio, Houston, and this big dummy from El Paso. I swear we had to be the most diverse group on campus, and I loved every second with them. With those guys, we competed in the International Championship of Collegiate Acapella and put TCU on the map. We sang in front of thousands and for dozens of events. I had gone from wanting to fly under the radar and being miserable to having the time of my life with some of the most talented men I will ever know.

Still, even with that, I knew my days at TCU were numbered. Due to the trainwreck that was my first year, I had lost my scholarship and simply could not afford to continue. I made the decision to visit Chancellor Victor Boschini to thank him for the place he has helped mold. I wanted to thank him for the efforts at the university in the new millennium, turning it into what it is today—a place I love even with all its flaws. I won't disclose exactly what happened in that meeting. However, I will state that his kindness, compassion, and willingness to listen means more to me than I can ever state. I walked into his office unsure of what my next day would bring and left with a full heart and hope for the first time since I had left my corner of the Chihuahuan desert. That decision to express gratitude changed my life forever. After that meeting, I made it my mission once again to make everyone who had ever invested a part of their life in me proud. I made it my purpose in life to leave TCU better than I found it. I didn't know how, but I knew I was going to make it happen.

I had been reminded of a lesson my grandfather taught me when I was a child. "Complaining without looking for solutions is just whining," he'd tell me. He urged me to think about my problems first, try to figure it out, then ask for help to figure it out if I couldn't do so on my own—rather than just complain that there's a problem and not be open to a solution. I had taken that to heart my entire life, but somehow, I had forgotten this in my first year at TCU. I saw the problems clearly, but I wasn't looking for solutions. I was simply trying to do my time and move on. I was broken and whining. It wasn't my place to try and fix a billion-dollar institution. I was going to fly under the radar and keep my cool just long enough to get that piece of paper that says I might be worth the investment my friends, family, and ancestors put into me. TCU is this immovable megalith, and I am one insignificant speck in its 150-year existence. It was not my place to fight this institution, in fact, I believed in my heart it wasn't my place to be there at all. However, what I believed, what I perceived, and what was the reality waiting for me if I only cared to dig a little further were very different from one another.

Soon, I met another student who was Indigenous like myself. She and I got to talking after an Anthropology Society meeting and decided that it was time for an Indigenous Students Association on campus. It was time to give our peoples a voice in a place where we were surrounded by people who would one day run businesses and guide people's education. Cultural education really is not a staple of business schools, which is a shame. What is business without people? How can a business truly expect to succeed and serve their clientele if they completely ignore history and culture? Still, we realized that our presence, our voice, could be the only exposure to our cultures that some of these students would ever get. When would they get a chance to speak to another Coushatta woman or Tewa man? Whether we liked it or not—and I personally did not like it one bit—we were the de facto spokespeople for not only our own tribes but for all 574-plus tribes and their cultures too. We weren't there just to be college students. We did not have the luxury of focusing on ourselves. We were there to show people we still exist and deserve a voice.

While a Native Student Association had existed in the past, it was a distant memory by the time I had been on campus. So the effort began with Morgan John and me becoming president and vice president (respectively) of the newly formed Native and Indigenous Students

Association, and we found our sponsor right away. Dr. Scott Langston was ready and willing to take on that task as we gained our footing. He guided, supported, and encouraged us every step of the way. Together, our little group began to push for change and inclusion at our university. It's a source of pride for me to think back on what we managed to accomplish. I still don't really believe I did anything special, but Dr. Langston gives me credit to this day. For the rest of my days, I will always call him my friend and be thankful he appeared in my life.

I was just starting to hit my stride. I was beginning to feel confident in my classes and like maybe, just maybe, I could pull this off. I found myself signing up for a class that I decided to take thinking it would be garbage: a class by Dr. Theresa Gaul that introduced Native American literature to undergrads. How could I resist? If I was going to be at TCU and make myself known, I might as well go all in. I walked in there expecting the need to be militant and watch as a lady with no tribal connections taught a class she probably shouldn't be teaching. Yet again,

Above: Chebon Kernell (right) showing a medallion made and gifted to him by Albert Nungaray on behalf of TCU's Native and Indigenous Student Association, February 28, 2017. Kernell was speaking on a panel regarding Standing Rock and the Dakota Access Pipeline.

I was wrong. Dr Gaul turned out to be amazing, having endless patience for my interjections and tangents. She encouraged me to voice my concerns and lead discussions when I felt the need to. I learned more than I thought I ever would in that class, and I felt heard there. In the middle of the Dakota Access Pipeline conflict, I was sitting there in a classroom and sharing my perspective on readings with people who one day could oversee companies just like Energy Transfer Partners. In turn, I gained lifelong friends and experiences I will always hold dear.

Meanwhile, Dr. Aftandilian was having me teach students about how to use and make atlatl and letting me have fun exploring culture. We made TCU's one and only most official unofficial Atlatl team with Ba'Leigh Burns and Coyt Ransom. At the time, none of us could picture where we are today. Ba'Leigh ended up being crowned Miss Texas for America (2019), diving with sharks, traveling the world, gained an MS in psychology, and is currently a licensed practitioner counselor associate. She is constantly underestimated and stereotyped, much like myself—a fact I'm ashamed to admit I did not see for too long. Except for her, it's because she's a beautiful blonde who too many expect to be a delicate princess when in reality she's a force of nature. She has this way of steering people where they need to be with sass and intelligence, and it's astonishing every time. She has become an amazing, confident, compassionate, and supportive woman that I have no doubt can take on the world. Coyt ended up joining me at University of Texas at Arlington (UTA) to get his PhD in history and become one of the most resolute and passionate people I know. At first glance, he's easy to underestimate, too. He has this archetypal look to him that would lend itself to the professor role in any given movie involving academics. It would be easy to assume he's a pushover. However, if you look close enough you can see the wheels turning as he puts anything and everything into a context no one could understand in a way everyone can. The East Texas boy I met has always been a bit of an old man type, but it has been wonderful watching him grow from a shy, introverted freshman into one of the most talented historians in Texas. He impresses me every time we speak. The more confident he gets, the more he stands up for himself and others, the more he proves beyond a shadow of a doubt that he is not one to dismiss or underestimate. I am prouder of those two than could possibly be put into words. They have motivated me to be better and not give up on myself. I consider them my best friends and am thankful every moment of every day that I found them. This unlikeliest of trios were, well, *are* a special group and they make my world a better place simply by existing. Moreover, at the same time as those bonds were being formed, the Horned Tones were gaining popularity, NISA was on its way to becoming official, and I was surrounded by people with whom I could spend every waking moment and never get tired. Every one of them encouraged me to go to grad school. They became my friends, my family, my brothers, and sisters. I had gone from "not smart enough" to considering going for a PhD in a very short time.

So why bring up my past in the beginning of this chapter? Why does my childhood or friends matter in my telling of the story of a university? To put it simply, I wanted you to know that I'm beyond used to not getting my way. I'm used to struggle and failure, disappointment, and discrimination—they are an ever-present part of my life. So when there's a small glimmer of hope, and a ray of sunshine in my story shows up, it means more to me than anyone could ever express. That is what makes TCU so special. Those rays of sunshine, those people who kept me going and made the effort so worth it *are* what is so special about this place. I am prouder of the picture of the boys and me standing on stage in front of a massive crowd than any award I have ever received. That picture stays on my wall and makes me smile every time I notice it. I have realized that my crowning achievements at TCU are things that will never show up on transcripts. I played a small role in the installation of a land acknowledgment monument next to the History Department's building and was given the chance to speak at the dedication ceremony. It was a beautiful, cold, and rainy day, and I was proudly standing in front of a full auditorium of very important people, speaking in a hoodie and a bandana. I was also selected to speak at the Senior Speak-Up, which put me on signs around campus. I had gone from being escorted off campus for appearing to be a threat to hugging the chancellor as I walked across the graduation stage. From feeling as if I didn't deserve a voice to having people in positions of power calling me for my opinion. Before I knew it and seemingly in the blink of an eye, I had somehow been transformed by TCU.

My eyes fill with tears and my throat tightens as I write this. Both my grandparents have since passed but my grandfather, grandmother, and parents got to see me graduate, and I had the privilege of seeing the pride in their eyes as I hugged them in my cap and gown. My mother got to meet her mother, my stepfather got to see both myself and my sister graduate (she with her master's from UTA) the same weekend. I was blessed with a venue to show my biological father who I am and what I do. After his first visit, taking him to a football game, treating him to some BBQ, and even getting a shoutout from coach Gary Patterson, my relationship with my father has never been stronger because we sat as equals talking and taking in the most beautiful campus I've ever laid eyes on. I had almost given up on this place and was dragged up from the ashes of my own burned bridges to make something of the opportunity I had before me. If I never went to TCU, I would never have joined the PhD program at UTA, never felt comfortable in my own identity, never felt respected or valued. I would have continued to live my life, constantly wondering if I'm smart enough, good enough, strong enough, Mexican enough, Native enough, human enough, simply enough at all to be worth any little bit of kindness. I still wonder sometimes. However, I find myself leaving an indelible mark on our campus and literally making my own history. That's something, isn't it?

The "memories sweet and comrades true" will stay with me until my final breath. I will bleed purple for the rest of my days. My most treasured friendships, my most valued mentors, right down to my favorite color and expectations of treatment have been shaped by my time on the campus where I at first felt I didn't belong. I have once again found my purpose. It is my mission in life to leave my little slice of earth and humanity better than I found it. I want everyone around me to feel loved, safe, and appreciated. I want to help my friends and family's dreams come true, even if my own don't. I will work until the day I drop dead to make sure that my people have a voice and ensure the generations to come don't have to struggle as I did and continue to do. My dream is to love and be loved, to spread joy and make as many people as possible succeed where I have failed. When we are born, we cry and the world around us smiles, and I will live a life worthwhile so that when I die, I will smile while the world cries. My time at TCU was miserably difficult—hindered by racism, constant reminders of my socioeconomic status, isolating, exhausting—and put me in soul-crushing debt I will never recover from. It's not perfect. It has many wrongs to correct, and it has failed many people in many ways. Still, if you ask me if I love my alma mater: Well, I say this with a full heart, open eyes, and all the gratitude I can muster to any prospective student who may read these words: "I swear, without a doubt, becoming a Horned Frog is one of the BEST decisions I have ever made and I hope you'll do the same."

UNDERSTANDING THE SIGNIFICANCE OF MY HERITAGE:
An Interview with Lauren Denham (Unangan)

Lauren Denham graduated from TCU in 2023 with a major in political science and minors in history and women and gender studies. At the time of the interview, she had graduated just weeks earlier. Growing up in Portland, Oregon, without a sense of herself as Indigenous, Lauren experienced her first immersive exposure to her Tribe (Qawalangin Tribe of Unalaska) by attending a tribal-sponsored culture camp. In her interview, she discusses her changing sense of her own identity, grappling with the effects of her family's history of relocation, and her growing commitment to advocate for Indigenous representation on campus through her coursework and leadership in student government.

Life prior to TCU

I grew up right outside Portland, Oregon, in a little suburb. I grew up going to a public school near me. Being in a public school was a very big part of me growing up and understanding my identity, because there were a lot of different ethnicities and the school facilitated ways to learn more about my diverse community while learning how to embrace my own heritage. I grew up in a household that was not proudly Indigenous. We usually spoke about our Indigenous heritage in a way that felt quite separate, only talking about it from an ancestral perspective, not about how it influenced my personal life. It was the more distant members of my family who are proudly Native Alaskan, mostly the ones who were able to remain on or return to our ancestral homelands after my family was relocated.

As a child, I knew we had family who lived in Alaska, and I knew we were Native Alaskan. But I just don't think the language was there to be able to connect our everyday lives to living an Indigenous life or understanding the significance of my heritage. There had been quite a bit of separation from our Alaskan family, and intergenerational trauma came back up for my great-grandmother, who didn't often talk about being Indigenous. She also lived quite far from my immediate family, so I missed out on opportunities when I was young to learn about her experiences as a Unangan woman. When you are filling out any kind of form, you check Native Alaskan, and you check White. But it wasn't a very big part of our culture and our everyday life at home.

In Oregon, I grew up in a predominantly White area, attending a mostly White high school that still had some strong non-White ethnic identities, but my school district was majority White. This fact formed how I viewed myself, because I didn't have very strong Indigenous representation around me and was able to easily fit into my non-Native community. I look White. I look like I could fit right into any other White person's home. Even my family and the people in my tribal homelands, they don't necessarily look like a stereotype of a Native American, which is most of the imagery available to me throughout my education.

So not growing up in an Indigenous household, I didn't really embrace my Indigenous ethnicity until I went to a culture camp [Camp Qungaayux] on my tribal homelands, which was a grant that my tribe participated in when I was in seventh grade. That's when I went and learned what my tribe was. I'm a member of the Qawalangin Tribe of Unalaska. Unalaska is an island in the Aleutian chain that connects Russia to Alaska. The islands are very small and difficult to get to. So it was a very isolated community that didn't really have a lot of colonial impact until World War II.

My family was relocated during World War II, because the US government had fears that the Aleutian Islands, where my tribal homelands are, would be a target for [Japanese] attacks. The whole island is just littered with big concrete bomb shelters. It's very strange, but beautiful. They were a military family, which is how my great-grandmother and great-grandfather met. He was stationed in Unalaska, and they got married quite young. But they lived a long and happy marriage.

So my family relocated to the Deep South, where my great-grandfather had family. Other members of my great-grandmother's family had been sent to residential schools in Canada instead of being relocated. So we lost a lot of our tribal connection through the relocation experience [brought about by WWII]. There's a lot of intergenerational trauma that still goes on because of this tumultuous time. My great-grandmother never talked about being Native Alaskan to us. The relocation I think really spooked her, obviously. My family who is still alive is trying to rekindle that sense of being Indigenous, which has been special to see. Most of them have returned to the tribal homelands. My side of the family moved to Nevada and then Oregon, so they bounced around.

Post–World War II, a lot of people had separated from the island, similarly to my family. So there was a big push to try to connect youth back to their homelands. We got a scholarship to go back for a culture camp back in 2011. My family and I went and spent a week in Unalaska, and got to meet family who I had never met. It was quite the intense learning experience, especially for a twelve-year-old. Tribal members ran it on the island out of a big camp. It felt like so many people on the island were involved and were so dedicated to having the camp be a positive experience for everyone. There was probably one hundred kids in total. My grandfather is the one who initiated the trip and took Rachel, my sister, and me. My mom and my uncle met us up there later in the week. Culture camp was about four days, and so we spent a little bit of time afterward just being with family and exploring the island.

So we went, and we had different stations that focused on different aspects of tribal life. We learned how to fish, and we learned how to cook. We learned how to mend nets and enjoyed traditional games and songs. It was very impactful in just reconnecting me to just the ancestry that I have and the important aspects of life for my tribe that I grew up so disconnected from. There was an aspect of learning, but also just the aspect of existing in tribal homelands with family who were so connected to our ancestry.

It was like entering a whole new world. We had talked about it a little bit before I had gone, but nobody in my family really knew what to expect, going back to Unalaska during this time, or what even culture camp was supposed to look like. My mother and her siblings were never granted the opportunity to go. For both my sister and me, it was just completely eye-opening into how much we were missing out on and how much we really had to learn to reconnect to our people.

Part of the camp was learning a little bit of the traditional language [Unangam Tunuu], which is very complicated. I started to learn just a little bit about the sentence structure and what the sounds were, because they use a different alphabet than English does. But since then, the culture camp sparked an interest in me reconnecting to my family, reconnecting to the tribal traditions that we have, and advocating for Indigenous representation. If I had had further Indigenous representation in my school experience, it may have not taken me so long to try to go and learn more about my heritage. It could have just been a part of my everyday life to hear about my tribal members and hear about the history of relocation for different tribes and learn more about how that impacted my family.

Life brought my great-grandmother and great-grandfather back to Unalaska for a couple of years. I think my great-grandmother was really the push to get them to go back. I think she really did not enjoy living in the South and wanted to return back to her family. So they lived there for just a year or two and then permanently relocated to Las Vegas when my grandfather was in middle school. There's a piano in my family's house in Unalaska that has her name carved into it on the side, which is so special. They've kept it for generations. My great-grandmother, despite the physical distance, really treasured her heritage and made sure to instill that in my grandfather, even if she wasn't able to share that knowledge with my mother or me.

My mother was born in Virginia, spent most of her life in an island on the Georgia coast, and then resettled in Oregon. My grandfather worked for the Indian Health Service (IHS) as a dentist. He also spent several years in the Navy and attended the US Naval Academy. When he was in the Navy, his call sign was Orca, which he loves to talk about. So that was very special for him to be able to connect his heritage to his service. He got a grant from the IHS to go to dental school. In return, he had several years of service for the IHS, where he bounced around the United States at different regional hospitals for Indigenous folks and spent time there, served there. So that moved him from reservation to reservation around the country. They ended up in Oregon near the Umatilla Reservation in Pendleton and then eventually settled down in Eastern Oregon. My mom is the one who moved my family to near Portland.

My grandfather actually just passed away, but he's very important to me. His name is Alfred Dennis Alleman, and he was a very active member of the Qawalangin tribe. He would travel to Alaska and around the Pacific Northwest just to attend shareholder meetings [of individuals who were one-quarter Alaska Native and who received 100 shares in their regional corporation overseeing Alaskan Native lands if they enrolled before December 17, 1971]. He made sure to keep our whole family informed about all of the tribal news, and he would even save every tribal newsletter and give them to my mom. He was still a shareholder in the tribe when he passed away. So now my mother, aunt, and uncle are all shareholders, because it's passed down through descendancy. He was very proud to be Unangan and really treasured his heritage. While he was very proud, I don't think he really had the complete understanding that my great-grandmother had of what it was like to live as an Indigenous person. He knew it was part of her history and it was an important part of her, but he didn't have the language to describe or the knowledge of traditions to be able to connect to it.

Our tribe is very connected to the islands that we claim as our homelands. My family is still in the house that they've had for generations. With the relocation, our tribe has understood that a lot of our tribal members have dissipated and aren't as connected as the people who necessarily live on the island. So that's why my grandfather was able to be a shareholder from Oregon, was able to have that say in how the tribe is run.

I don't know too much about life on the island right now. I've only been there once. But when I see my family's posts on Facebook, they're often speaking in the traditional language or just using little phrases from the language. There's still very much a traditional lifestyle. They go and hunt and gather berries for many things. They also make it a priority to instill this knowledge in my younger cousins. One of my cousins has the traditional facial tattoos. She's very proud, and the tattoos are just gorgeous. So yeah, I can't speak too much about what the relationship looks like with the tribe and the people there, but from my understanding, they have a much deeper connection than I would due to my physical distance and lack of education.

I've done a lot of personal research, read lots of books by Indigenous people about how they stayed connected to their tribe and what Indigenous representation would look like. I've always just had a heart for social justice, and so seeing a part of my own identity that is not being represented well was extremely disheartening. So I just took it upon myself to really try to

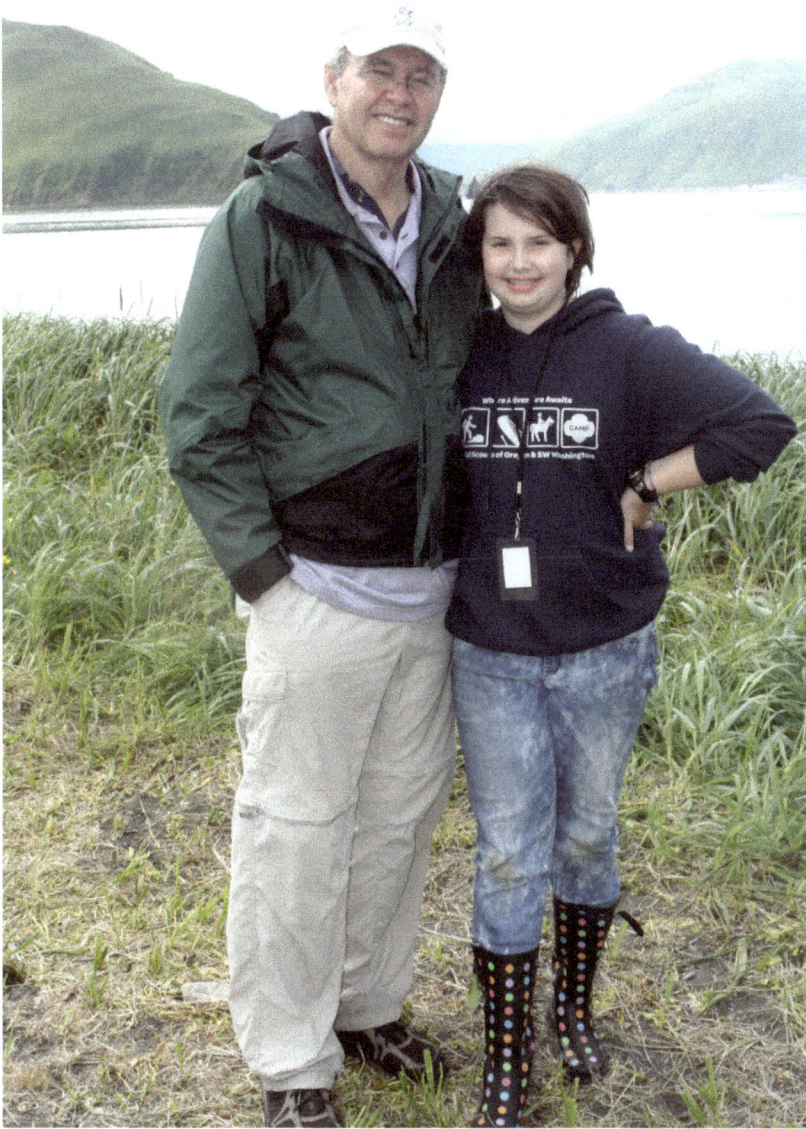

Lauren Denham with her grandfather, Dennis Alleman.

reconnect myself and my family to living a life rooted in social justice and Indigenous representation.

My high school looked very much like Texas Christian University did people-wise. You could basically take my whole high school and put it at TCU, and I think everybody would fit in very well. So that personal transition wasn't such a jump for me. In high school, I was on Student Council. It was a very big part of my identity. I was in our committee called the Human Rights Committee, where I spent basically my whole senior year advocating for Indigenous representation in my high school. I encouraged them when we were talking about different social justice movements to include Indigenous representation. We usually did have the months, like Black History Month, those kind of things, Pride Month. So I was a big spearhead in getting that started at my high school, including Indigenous history in November as a month that we celebrated proudly.

Experiences at TCU

When I was in high school, I didn't identify as Indigenous. It was the box that I checked when I filled out forms, but personally, I didn't identify much with the Indigenous label. Now I do, very proudly. I think it came with personal education and learning. I tried to make Indigenous education, learning about different tribes, learning about what representation would look like, a very big tenet in my personal education journey. This continued into my college career. In all of my classes, I was making some kind of statement about Indigenous representation. My creative writing class, I wrote about Indigenous dance. My art class, I learned how to bead and presented that as my final project. After that and realizing the importance of connecting and just how little representation TCU had, I really took it upon myself to start those Student Government Association proposals [relating to the Land Acknowledgment]. That really cemented my identity in that I feel that this is important for me to be representative of my tribe and my community and take that personal journey.

As I embraced my Indigenous identity during my time in college, I looked around and realized that there wasn't anybody talking about Indigenous representation or Indigenous ways of life around me. I slowly started to bring it up in my sorority. That was a very big part of my experience at TCU, and they really supported me through a lot of the initiatives that I took on, which was very exciting. So I started there in my own community. I started encouraging my diversity, equity, and inclusion (DEI) chair [in the sorority] to talk about Indigenous representation and what that looks like in our chapter. I shared my story a couple of times about what it meant for me to be an Indigenous student within small groups, and that's really where I took hold of that Indigenous identity, and it became such a big part of my college experience. Then, that passion for service and social justice encouraged me to continue to try to make change on a university level through student government. That is another significant part of where I really embraced being an Indigenous student and advocating for Indigenous representation on campus.

When I would identify myself as Indigenous, everyone responded in a very positive way. I think that I spoke about it in a way—simply because I didn't have the understanding—that I was able to come at it from a very approachable perspective, just talking about, "Oh, my family is Native Alaskan, but I'm trying to learn more about it." I think that often formed a very positive experience between me and others. My professors, whenever I did bring it up, were always very receptive. It took me a little bit to be able to find that footing to be able to say, "I am Qawalangin. Here's what this means to me." But it definitely took shape while I was experimenting with it at university.

The first time I ever said "I'm Qawalangin" publicly was in high school. We were working on the Indigenous Heritage Month program. I talked about it in front of my classroom, other Student Council members. There's probably twenty-five of us. That was the first time where I was like, "I am proudly Indigenous. Here's why this is important to me. Here's how this relates to me. This is a cool thing that I'm very proud of." Just because I don't fit the image of a stereotypical Indigenous person or lived a life with a strong Indigenous background, I felt that I was maybe taking away from stories of other Indigenous people who grew up living harder lives than I did or were more connected to their culture. But I had a long discussion with my grandfather, where he said it wasn't our choice to not be involved in our tribe, it was taken away from us during relocation. So it's our responsibility to take that back on.

A lot of the time when I said Native Alaskan, people would respond with, "Oh, so you're from Alaska?" I was like, "No, no. There's Indigenous peoples up there, too, who have lived here long before America was founded." Just having to break down that to that level was sometimes shocking, just people's incredibly limited knowledge about Indigenous history and the differences between the relationships with colonizers across United States and how we all did not have a Trail of Tears experience. But my ancestors were and still are impacted by colonialism, just not in a manner that is as visible or discussed. Even if it wasn't something as discussed as the tragedies that we mention when speaking about other tribes, it's still important to discuss the long-standing impact of colonialism for all tribes.

And coming from a place where I was still learning was interesting, too, because while I have done a lot of personal research, I don't have much lived experience. So it was sometimes hard to try to be a steward for my tribe, while also still trying to educate myself, representing while not having the lived experience. So complicated sometimes. Coming from a place where my first interaction was rooted in advocacy and not necessarily knowledge, almost from an outsider perspective, really allowed me to connect to non-Indigenous people and be able to understand the way that I should approach explaining why Indigenous representation is important. It really allowed me to view the issues from a non-Native perspective and understand the importance of convincing, honestly, non-Native people about the importance of Indigenous issues.

I would say that on an individual level, the Native American presence at TCU is very strong. They try to educate and encourage people to learn about Indigenous representation, while creating a community for Indigenous students. But on an institutional level, it's just not there at all. I'm only speaking from my own educational experience and what was offered during my time at TCU. I would hope that with the growth of the university, more specific courses would be offered. The courses that were offered are quite sparse in terms of Indigenous education. No Native American history class was taught during my four years at TCU. We don't have a specific Indigenous feminism class in the Women and Gender Studies Department. We don't have a tribal law class in the political science department. It's just these sections of our university where Indigenous peoples could be taught about, could be interacted with more, and there's just not that university level engagement.

Just at commencement [in May 2023], I was very excited to hear them read the formal Land Acknowledgment, and it was not included. It was disappointing to see that we have this wonderful acknowledgment but the university is just not paying attention and not including it in the location it should be. I was looking forward to hearing the Land Acknowledgment, especially just to a group that large. My whole family was there, and they were all excited to hear about it, because they had known that I'd worked so closely with it throughout my TCU experience. It was really disappointing for them, too. So next day, I was on the phone, making phone calls to ensure that the future students at TCU will not have to face the same disappointment that I did during commencement. They were very receptive and it seems like the Acknowledgment will be included in future years. It seems like it's a secondary thought at all times, that TCU attempts to be inclusionary of everybody, but the inclusion falls way to tradition or habits.

This is actually why I participated in student government. The legislation that I wrote in the past was all about codifying the use of the Land Acknowledgment. So my first piece of legislation was about its inclusion on syllabi for professors and faculty. It was, I believe, the first time that several people in the House of Representatives had even thought about Indigenous inclusion on TCU's campus. I read aloud the information from the Land Acknowledgment website about how TCU received their land and the history of Indigenous peoples in the DFW area, and I think even the people who grew up in the Dallas–Fort Worth area had never heard about the history of removal and the wars that occurred so close to their home.

So the Student Government Association resolution passed with flying colors. It had 82.6 percent support. At the university level, it failed, because when the bill got to the faculty senate committee, the faculty was concerned about being overly controlling of syllabi. So they decided to not pass the resolution, [tabling it], and it really spoke volumes as to what they were willing to include. We could have all the mental health [resources' phone] numbers on there. We can have all of the [additional] resources available to students. But as soon as it becomes about acting on representation for underrepresented students, it falls to the wayside, and it's not important. It's not typical for students, even the ones who wrote the bills they are considering, to be invited to the faculty senate meetings, which was the case when they tabled my bill. I found out about it through my committee head. I 100 percent think that if I was in the room while they were discussing it, it would've turned out very differently, because they just didn't understand the importance. I stood up during the first vote on the legislation [in SGA] and spoke very passionately about why I was proud to be an Indigenous student and what that looks like at TCU, and it wasn't reflected when another group went to consider it. I was incredibly disappointed, because I felt like including it in the syllabi was a first step and not a major step, because it already should be on syllabi. That's what the Land Acknowledgment is for, for these formal documents that are presented to members of our university. Seeing that inclusion and representation was not a priority was incredibly disheartening and made me feel like they didn't value me as an Indigenous student personally. They didn't see acknowledging history as a significant part of the university, seeing it instead as a burden to faculty.

I did not let that discourage me. I wrote a second piece about including the Land Acknowledgment in the Student Government code, which passed. It did not need faculty approval. So it is now formally included in the Student Government code and is read before every Student Government formal meeting. Just the numbers that it passed by [87.8 percent], students are ready to be inclusive. They're excited about seeing more students of different backgrounds and ethnicities on their campus and having them feel like they're a part of the TCU community. But that was not reflected in the faculty relationships.

I talked about the Land Acknowledgment more in my classes, after I became more familiar with TCU's specific history, and the importance of using it. As I continued through my time at TCU, I definitely saw the Land Acknowledgment used more and more, but it's still not in all of our courses. I took an "Indigenous Movements in Latin America" class as a history course. Not on the syllabus. That first day I kept thinking, "What are you doing teaching Indigenous history and not including the history of what happened to Indigenous peoples right where the university is located?" It was a very confusing moment for me to reckon with.

The Land Acknowledgment means to me that the university understands that it's not a perfect place, that they have a history that is sometimes dark and flawed, and that they have to come to terms with these realities. Reflecting on our impressive, award-winning Race and Reconciliation Initiative, it was so impressive to see the university changes, but they were still not enough. It was a bummer that the Land Acknowledgment wasn't used more widely and more cemented in everyday life at TCU. My connection with it looks a little different than I think it does for most Indigenous students, because I worked with it so closely throughout my university experience. But it means representation. It means that I feel seen in my commu-

SGA
TEXAS CHRISTIAN UNIVERSITY
House of Student Representatives
108th Session
Texas Christian University

Introduced By: Lauren Denham   H.R. 108-09

Introduced: February 15th, 2022   Action Taken: Passed 82.6%

"A Resolution to Encourage TCU Faculty to Include Native American Land Acknowledgements on All Course Syllabi"

Whereas: Wichita and Affiliated Tribes lived in the region spanning from Waco, Texas to Kansas, including the Dallas-Fort Worth metroplex, and the Caddo confederacy as well as other tribes also resided in the DFW metroplex, and

Whereas: In April of 2021, a TCU approved Land Acknowledgement statement was created by Native American Advisory Circle in November 2020 and approved by the TCU Chancellor's Cabinet in April 2021, and

Whereas: The Land Acknowledgment reflects TCU's emerging respect for Native American peoples and commitment to build a positive future by empowering Native Americans on our campus while creating mutually beneficial, respectful relationships with Native American nations and communities, and

Whereas: The Land Acknowledgment helps remind and educate the TCU community about the long and diverse presence of Native Americans who precede and coexist with our presence in this area, and

Whereas: This statement serves as an invitation for individual and institutional reflection and a call to action, and

Whereas: A Land Acknowledgement in a educational setting, like a syllabus, could lead to constructive conversations about the impact of colonization on indigenous people, and

Whereas: Land Acknowledgments are a productive step forward in continuing a relationship with local native American tribes and promoting Diversity, Equity and Inclusion on our campus, and

Whereas: Syllabi are a centralized location that will allow for every student to have the opportunity to view the acknowledgment; therefore,

Let it be resolved by the House of Student Representatives at Texas Christian University:

(1) That the House of Student Representatives at Texas Christian University encourages faculty to include TCU's Native American Land Acknowledgement in all course syllabi.

SGA
TEXAS CHRISTIAN UNIVERSITY
House of Student Representatives
108th Session
Texas Christian University

Introduced By: Lauren Denham   H.R. 108-09

Introduced: February 15th, 2022   Action Taken: Passed 82.6%

CC:

Certified By: _Bella Pettigo_   Duly Approved: _Lawant Heaycutt_

Speaker of the House   Student Body President

nity, and a place that is so important to me values me and my whole history.

In my classes in particular, I think that the non-inclusion wasn't from a place of, "We're not including Indigenous peoples on purpose." I think it was maybe just more the nature of the courses that I was taking that didn't really lend themselves. The goal in political science is often to be neutral, especially when taking an educational stance. So while, unfortunately, DEI should not be a controversial topic, I think often the virtue signaling that often happens when discussing DEI would've become more controversial than actually beneficial when trying to find solutions for furthering representation.

In my political science classes, they only talked about Indigenous issues when I brought them up. I had the "Indigenous Movements in Latin America" course, but it was from a Latin American perspective. So it had a different impact on the class than I think an "American Indigenous Movements" course would have, but there was no related course that was offered. Even on a basic level, my American history professor used the word Indian to describe relationships with Indigenous peoples. Indigenous rights

Above: TCU Student Government Association resolution encouraging faculty to include the university's Land Acknowledgment on course syllabi, February 15, 2022.

and representations were brought up more frequently in my social jus-
tice-oriented classes, like my women and gender studies courses. The importance of representation was brought up, and in that, talking about Missing
and Murdered Indigenous Women, talking about the ways that Indigenous
removal harmed tribes throughout the years, the way that gender interacted
with Indigenous identity were all discussed.

I don't remember that another Indigenous student ever talked publicly
in a course I took. I'm sure that they were around, but I don't have a specific
memory of somebody reflecting on their personal experiences and joining
in when I was referring to Indigenous experiences. But as for my in-class
experience, I often felt like I had a pretty big weight on my shoulders to try
to represent the entire Indigenous experience and not just mine, which was
hard. But it was also rewarding in a way that I know that some of the people
in the course had never even taken the time to consider how Indigenous
traditions may fit into creative writing or art or what that would look like. So
I felt the pressure to represent, but also the power to be the representation.
My Student Council director wrote me a letter, and she said, "You're never
going to let us off the hook, Lauren." I said, "You're right."

I never encountered hostility, just, I think, annoyance about me talking
about it so much, bringing it up all the time. When I was presenting to the
House on my first bill, somebody did ask, "How do we know what land was
Indigenous land?" I got to really get him with a zinger when I said that "it
was all Indigenous land at one time" in front of everybody, which is funny.
But yeah, other than just coming from a place of misunderstanding, never
anything hostile. So I think I'm lucky in that situation, too.

I talked to my grandfather and family a lot while I was at school. I
didn't have that tribal connection, but my family all saw the importance in
what I was doing and so really took the time to encourage me, listened to
all my different forms of the bill, and listened to me cry after it failed. They
were a wonderful support system. Dr. Langston was absolutely wonderful.
NISA was also very powerful. Members of my sorority, my friends that I
had made there, several of them came to the painting dedication [of art
by Comanche/Kiowa artist J. NiCole Hatfield (Nahmi-A-Piah) installed
in the TCU administration building] and watched me read the Land
Acknowledgment. It was very inspiring to be able to show my Indigenous
representation work around TCU to my friends and watch them understand
the importance of representation on campus.

Advice to TCU

Having more Indigenous faculty would have been important to me while at TCU. Seeing that strong example of what I could grow to become someday would've been incredibly significant. I'm grateful for the Indigenous faculty that we do have, but they're not in the departments that I learn from every day. I'm not around them very often unless I go seek them out, which is sometimes difficult on such a large campus.

Receiving the MMIW Scholarship was incredibly powerful. I am only able to attend TCU because of scholarships from my tribe and outside scholarships. So receiving the MMIW scholarship really just cemented that the work I'm doing at the university is being seen, that my tribe, all the money that they're putting into my work is paying off, and that making Indigenous representation and education such a main point in my life was working. It allowed me to continue my education at TCU.

Even though Indigenous representation wasn't always a priority for the university, it weirdly enough allowed me to develop the skills to be able to continue to advocate on a larger scale. So TCU, thanks for being willing to grow and learn, even if it took a while.

I think there just needs to be a more deliberate dedication to representation on all levels for any community that's a part of TCU. I would say most of the ethnic communities are pretty isolated in how they interact with the university, as in they don't receive enough university-wide support and instead only get support from members of the community. But if TCU made representation and inclusion a bigger priority on all levels for all communities, I think TCU would look very different in the communities that are there and the people that are a part of the community within the next couple of years.

I wish for a more robust Indigenous community presence in Fort Worth. I would hope that TCU and the changes that they're making would ripple out into the larger community. I would hope that there'd be more Indigenous students at TCU in a bigger way for them to be prideful in their culture. I think that the key is students just getting more representation, having more opportunities for the Indigenous communities to be involved at TCU, to share their stories, and educate those around them at a predominantly White institution—this is really the solution and what I would like to see.

LIVING MY ANCESTORS' DREAMS:

An Interview with Haylee Chiariello (Cherokee)

Haylee Chiariello, an enrolled citizen of the Cherokee Nation, grew up in Oklahoma City, Oklahoma. She graduated from TCU in 2025 with majors in journalism and Native American expressions and dance as a John V. Roach Honors College student. She was the very first student to earn a Native American degree at TCU. As a student athlete—a TCU Feature Twirler—she occupies a uniquely visible position from which she advocates for American Indian students and Native representation. She has earned numerous leadership roles on campus, including her work in Native recruitment, tribal cultural education, and promoting inclusive campus policies. Grounded in her Cherokee upbringing, family, and identity, Chiariello shares in her interview the opportunities and specific challenges she experienced as a Cherokee student at an institution with limited Native American representation.

Osiyo, Haylee Chiariello daquadoa ale tsitsalagi.

Tsalagi gvn(i)di Tsalagi Nvyah Osani ale Gigage Agaquali daquadoa. Agitsi Tanya Chiariello dudoake agidoda Eric Chiariello dudoa.

Hello, I am Haylee Chiariello, and I am an enrolled citizen of the Cherokee Nation.

My Indian name is Cherokee Jewel (after my grandfather, Jewell) and Cherry Cheek (after my great-great-grandmother). My mother is Tanya Chiariello, and my father is Eric Chiariello.

Above: Haylee Chiariello, TCU feature twirler.

I have just finished my fourth year as a student at TCU. I am double majoring in Native American expressions and dance and will be earning the first TCU Native American degree. This is an incredible honor, and each day that I'm on campus at TCU, it fills my heart to know that I'm carrying on the legacy of the Cherokee Nation. I served as president of the TCU Native and Indigenous Student Association, and I've also had the opportunity to serve as student representative on TCU's Native American Advisory Circle and Race and Reconciliation Committee. Being at TCU has also given me the opportunity to represent my Cherokee culture as a Miss Texas contestant. I've gotten to meet so many incredible people and be a part of the conversations that are happening on campus to highlight and include Native people.

Life prior to TCU

I'm an enrolled citizen of the Cherokee Nation. My family has been in this region since Indian Territory, and my grandfather grew up on his mother's Cherokee allotment. It is our way of life, our language, our food, our culture. Being Cherokee is who I am, it's who my family is, and I recognize that it's my responsibility as a young college student to be mindful of the opportunities to serve Cherokee people and my Native brothers and sisters as well.

My Cherokee family is my life. I grew up living just a beautiful dream of what I think my ancestors would've wanted for our family. During major holidays like Thanksgiving and Christmas, we would gather and really just celebrate who we are as Cherokees. We would remake our pucker toe moccasins and do bead work together. My family are very skilled artisans doing leather work and beading. And my mom is the most incredible Cherokee cook. So Christmases for us looked a lot like grape dumplings and fry bread, and that was always something that just felt normal to me. I always thought that that's how Cherokee families would celebrate. Another big part of my own journey is being a patient of Indian Health Service. I have been a lifelong patient of the Oklahoma City Indian Clinic (OKCIC).

As Native people, we are strong, we are resilient, but we are disproportionately impacted by numerous health issues. And for my family, the health of our eyes became a huge issue. My mom has a degenerative eye disease that impacts Native populations. While I was in high school, during a routine eye exam that is required for all OKCIC pediatric patients, they discovered that my optic nerves were hemorrhaging. That's obviously very alarming. I was immediately referred to the University of Oklahoma Health Sciences Center. Within a span of two weeks, I was diagnosed with hydrocephalus, known as water on the brain, and had emergency brain surgery. I found out later that this condition also disproportionately impacts Native people. I know that what I am doing right now is possible because of those resources that I had growing up as a Native person—it truly saved my life. I don't know that I would be standing here today if not for the Indian Health Service. It's my responsibility to tell my story because it's so important to recognize the relationship between Native cultures and health.

My mom is a true saint. She home-educated my three brothers and me. I grew up with a distinctly Cherokee education, and I think that was perfectly fitting for what the Cherokee people celebrate and what our values are. The Cherokee Nation is a matrilineal society, so our women's perspectives are valued, and they are sacred. My mom's role in the family carried incredible weight, and her voice is very prominent. We grew up having a special understanding of who we are and what our history is. I think that's so valuable, and we don't always see that today. I think for Native people, there's something about us because of our histories, that we care so much about who our ancestors are and keeping our stories alive. It's that sense of responsibility. I'm grateful for the time I was home-educated, because I understand that much more how special it is to be a Cherokee young woman.

I got to TCU as soon as I could, but I did start at the University of Oklahoma (OU). It was a bit closer to home for me at that time. I was very passionate about my degree program, which was Native American studies. That's a really strong department at that school, and I loved the coursework. I've known ever since I decided that I was going to obtain my college education that I wanted to carry on the legacy of my ancestors, that I wanted to study who we are, what our history is, because I believe that that's going to strengthen our future. Native language courses aren't offered at TCU right now. I had the amazing opportunity to study the Cherokee language, which was so rewarding and so fulfilling—to know that I'm having an opportunity to learn the language of my ancestors.

Experiences at TCU

My journey to TCU connects to my background as an athlete. Baton twirling is my first love, and I actually fell in love with the sport because of my family's history. My father is a disabled US Army veteran, and I grew up watching him pick up household items such as an umbrella or a broomstick or a hockey stick, and he would twirl them. This is because while he was serving our country, he was in the Old Guard, performing twenty-one-gun salutes at Arlington Cemetery. I grew up with a really amazing family example. I think it scared my mom a little bit that I was twirling household items, so she found me some batons and coaches.

I grew up going to baton twirling lessons across the country, and one of my baton twirling coaches had a poster of a former collegiate twirler who later went on to win the Miss Texas competition. And I just remember being completely mesmerized by the photos and thinking, "Wow, that is so fantastic. That is so beautiful." And I think I spent the entirety of my first lesson just asking everything about that twirler and what her experiences were. And it was during that time, I was about ten or eleven years old, that I decided I was going to get to Texas somehow, some way. I knew that baton twirling was something that I wanted to pursue in college. Growing up, I just always envisioned that I would get to have the opportunity to twirl at the collegiate level because baton twirling representation is important. Diversity matters, and it's valuable. I felt very confident because of how I was raised that I would be able to carry on my legacy on campus, but it's different going into a different setting and being away from home.

It's been an interesting path to pave because baton twirling is an incredible opportunity for me to be a role model and serve as a representative of Cherokee people in my sport because there's not a lot of Native representation. That's something that I have been advocating for as a college athlete, just trying to provide opportunities to the next generation to be able to share in my sport because it really does change your life. It's incredible for me to think that a young Cherokee girl had the amazing opportunity to perform at the National College Football Championship [in 2023], to perform at SoFi Stadium in Los Angeles, California, as the TCU Horned Frogs got to play in the game of a lifetime. That's something that I get to pass on to my family forever, and even the family that

I perhaps won't ever even meet—the next seven generations. That's a dream come true, and it really is living my ancestors' dreams to know that a young Cherokee woman is getting to have this incredible athletic opportunity. It's so amazing, and I'm so thankful that my family has always reminded me to remember who I am and to remain Cherokee. I wear the Cherokee Nation Seal as a hairpiece in my hair when I perform during Native American Heritage Month, trying to do even the smallest things to honor my people. It's so important.

I fell in love with TCU from the start. I traveled to Fort Worth for twirling lessons and competitions at a young age. I think the one thing that was going to be a little bit difficult for me was figuring out how to pave my path as a young Native leader, but it's all fallen into place. I love that I have the opportunity to be here, serving as president of the Native and Indigenous Student Association. It is quite different from the experiences of Native students in Oklahoma, but it's just as impactful. It's just as important. Every Native student at TCU has just as valuable of a voice as any other student across the country. It looks different, and you have to remain focused and dedicated, but there is a place for Native students at TCU. I think it's even more valuable because I have such a special voice in the classroom. I love being able to have these interactions with my peers and with the TCU community as a whole.

I think it's been surprisingly really special and even much more rewarding that I'm more dedicated to keeping Cherokee presence and culture alive at TCU. I'm having to remain incredibly mindful and connected, but I think that's exactly what my ancestors would want for me: to stay focused, get my education, but always remember where I came from and who my people are. At TCU, there may not be language courses, but I can still speak. I still have a voice here at TCU. What's most important is that in my heart, I am reflecting on what it means to be a young Native student and what I want to accomplish. And I'm having to search a little bit more. It's a little bit harder to find fellow Native students sometimes, but whenever you do make those connections, it's so special. I think that I am strengthened because I have been at TCU. It's so special and so rewarding to know that as a student I had a small role here. Even if it's a tiny, small voice in helping somebody better understand Native histories and Cherokee perspectives, that means so much to me.

Being named a Missing and Murdered Indigenous Women Scholarship recipient at TCU was so meaningful for me, and it aligned so perfectly with receiving an invitation to join the Native American Advisory Circle. I just felt so encouraged because it's scary to step away from a place where you're completely immersed in your culture. I was home educated growing up, and I was just surrounded by my Cherokee family, that was my influence in life. And so I knew that I was going to have a path that I had never experienced before being a student at TCU. But when I was asked to be a part of the Native American Advisory Circle to offer my perspective as a student, I truly felt like I had a space and a voice and that someone like me had opportunities and was welcomed at TCU.

The MMIW Scholarship financial aspect was incredibly encouraging for me and my family. What an incredible blessing. But I have always had an understanding of how meaningful this conversation is. And whenever you're not in a Native circle, people don't always understand just how important it is to reflect on MMIW. I am a young Native woman, and I grew up with an early understanding of the realities of violence that surround and impact Native women. It's something that I have always had to be mindful of, and we know families that have been impacted. Knowing that somebody at our campus understood how important MMIW is—that connected with my soul at a level that is hard to even explain. I just felt like I could continue my mission because someone, somewhere at TCU cared.

I think something that has been awesome as a young Native student is that the TCU community seems to really care. I know that I have had some conversations with TCU leadership where they ask questions, they want to understand, and they want to learn more. That means so much to me because I'm not able to change someone else's understanding, their background, or what they were exposed to before in their life. But if they are open to learning more, to listening, that's what counts. And that's where I can step in and offer my own story and perspective and help point them in the right direction.

And there are some things that are perhaps better understood by people in Oklahoma that I am asked about at TCU. I love driving on campus with my Cherokee license plate. I often get questions about that. And I view that as an opportunity to share my story and to help somebody else understand more about who Cherokee people are. So there's always a few everyday surprises, but I look at it through a positive lens because that's how we develop learning. I think people have a lot of questions, and there's some things that seem very ordinary and just routine to me. Some students come to TCU and don't even understand that Native peoples had an ancestral language. Very limited knowledge sometimes. But I think what has been awesome is that on campus it's always been a really warm reception whenever I have had the opportunity to engage in class settings. I've been invited to speak and share more about Native peoples.

Sovereignty is something that people tend to have a lot of questions about, and sometimes even my non-Native friends will ask me about a book that they read or an article that they encountered on social media that has in some way a connection with Native people. And they ask my perspective on it as a Native person. I always remind them that I am a Native person, and we are sovereign. We each have distinct and individual voices and perspectives, and issues look different for different tribes. I think sovereignty is something that I've talked about a lot on campus. Yes, I am Native, but I am Cherokee and that is my distinct experience. We are individual tribes, and we each have our own histories and cultures. So I view it as really rewarding whenever I'm able to help be a part of those conversations.

I think that sometimes there's some hesitancy to ask questions, too, because it can be scary to ask. Maybe something is a misconception or a misunderstanding or an inaccuracy that they somehow encountered. I think people are sometimes afraid to ask questions, which is sad. More than anything, the legacy that I want to leave at TCU is that anybody I met got to understand a little bit more about what it means to be a modern Native young woman and college student. I think that's where we are right now in today's society. I want there to be a greater understanding of what it means to be a contemporary urban Native. For me, it means that I love TCU, but I also still love coming home and having fry bread with my mom and making our pucker toe moccasins together. I'm a contemporary college student, but I remain connected to my Native heritage. I think that sometimes people are afraid to ask questions, and an important part of the learning process is to ask so that you understand somebody's story better.

In specific classes focused on diversity and representation, if Native American people and cultures are a part of the lesson, I am often asked questions about that. That can be a little bit tricky sometimes because it's not always a Cherokee perspective that we're engaging with. Sometimes it may be Comanche or Chickasaw. It could be any tribe, but my understanding is going to be distinctly Cherokee. I see it as just another opportunity for me to be able to discuss tribal sovereignty.

In most of my classes, I am the Native student in the classroom. And that's an interesting role to take on sometimes. But what an incredible encouragement for me as a student to know that it's so important for me to keep going and to be successful and just remember how far that my people have come. I may be the one Native in the classroom right now, but it's my objective and my aim to see that number vastly increase at TCU. I know our young Native students would thrive if they had the opportunity to be at a place like TCU.

I want to see more Native presence at TCU. To see the faces like me represented on our campus. It would build them, and it would build the TCU community. But I think as far as fellow student presence goes, it's been really rewarding to see what the Native and Indigenous Student Association has been able to accomplish with connections. Since we are a small group, everyone knows everyone. I love that it holds true to what TCU says, you're more than just a number. So our students are able to really connect with each other, to really know each other.

I'm a student member of the North Texas Cherokee community, and that has meant so much to me to be able to connect with that circle. It is a Cherokee Nation community, so it is outside TCU, but they are incredibly encouraging and have offered me so much support, wisdom, and just a reminder of how valuable it is to remain committed to keeping Cherokee presence alive at TCU. The Cherokee Nation tribal jurisdiction is in northeast Oklahoma. Being in the Dallas–Fort Worth metroplex, I'm more removed from our headquarters, but I just am so encouraged whenever I remember that we do have a history in Texas as well, and there is Cherokee presence in the DFW community. There is one distinct memory that is really special to me. I was going through the TCU archives and found an article from the *Skiff* [student newspaper] where Principal Chief Wilma Mankiller came to campus, and she spoke with students. Goodness, I loved that. And at that moment, I felt like she smiled at me. A strong Native woman, someone I look up to so much, our Principal Chief, had been on my campus and had spoken about how important it is to have conversations about Native peoples.

I reflect on that when I just want to connect with my family and when I feel like I'm far away—to know that there are others who have come before me is so encouraging. Sometimes it does take some searching, but I have a resilient spirit in me because of who my people are. And I would encourage any other young student at TCU, any Native student, that it's a different path, but it's still so important for you to stay connected and to remember who you are. Keep holding on because this is our work, and this is our responsibility. It's only going to get better if we stay on this journey together. Cherokee National Holiday is something that my family and I observe and celebrate. It's a big part of what we do together as a family, and that's a conversation [about class absences] that I've had to have with my professors. And sometimes it feels like I'm having to offer a lot of information about something that is just really sacred and special to me and my family. But it's always welcomed, though, with a lot of encouragement and a lot of questions. And so I'm glad that the community wants to understand what it is that Cherokee people do in contemporary settings to celebrate.

As close as Dallas is to Fort Worth, a lot of opportunities to engage in Native cultural expression take place in the Dallas area. And sometimes it's hard to make that trip and to travel. For me personally, it has been challenging to find a buddy and get transportation. You may have one close Native friend who you go to tribal activities with, but if they're not available on that specific weekend, you may not be able to go now. So it's just something that you have to be a little bit more mindful of and find different ways. Sometimes it means that I'll travel to a tribal celebration with a non-Native friend whenever it's appropriate. It is just a little bit of a different experience.

Advice to TCU

If I could go back to first-year Haylee, I wish that she had had a stronger understanding of what opportunities are available with the student association. It's been wonderful to see the growth that we have experienced. And I think a lot of it is the size of TCU. It's a smaller school, and so everything is a little bit smaller and a little bit different, so it takes more dedication and searching, because they're not necessarily coming to you. You need to go to them, but the resources can be available to you if you really, really look.

My brother, Clayton, will be joining me at TCU as a Chancellor's Scholar. It's my hope that my legacy at TCU helps open doors for him, where we are doing more outreach together as Native leaders, and there's less instances of students having to reach for the opportunities. But there's progress happening, and it's so encouraging to be able to reflect on what the Native American Advisory Circle and the Native and Indigenous Student Association have been able to accomplish during my short time here at TCU. I think it speaks to a really promising future for our campus.

I recently have had the opportunity to engage with the presidents of the Native student associations at University of North Texas and the University of Texas at Arlington. And I know in our conversations that we talked about how as Native students, it can be difficult to feel like you have a space. And I think that for Native students, knowing that they have a space is a distinct need. Space is sacred to Native people. And I think that even reaches beyond physical limitations. Whenever we hear the word space, it's easy to just think of a building or some type of physical setting, but it means more than that. It means having a community surrounding you. It means having a circle of supporters. It means knowing that you are known.

I think it is so important that whenever students come to our campus that they know they have a space and that they have a voice. I love TCU. I love TCU, and I love everything that this university has brought into my life. It's been a dream come true, but I know that for some students, it's going to be a journey that looks a little bit different if you grew up in a home completely immersed in your culture. There is a space for every Native student at TCU, and I want to be a part of helping to build that.

And I think what's important to remember is that we do have incredible people who are committed to making sure that Native people are included and represented and seen at our school. And that's all I can ask for in a college experience, is knowing that I have a place and a platform and a voice. I am so grateful to this day for those opportunities.

From an early age, something that my Cherokee mother instilled in me was a love for learning and being a part of the Advisory Circle has been an incredible learning opportunity because Native peoples are sovereign. I feel like I've gotten the most incredible opportunity to engage with leaders from across the country who have had such distinct and individual experiences. And there are few perspectives that are more valuable to me than that of my Native community who have come before me and are cheering me on. I have a space to talk about what I'm trying to promote on campus as a Native leader and that means everything.

Being surrounded by others who share my values, who will also stand and say "Native people have an important voice and place on our campus"—I have loved being a part of these conversations, and some of them have been so thoughtful and so in depth. I always find it so rewarding, and I've been able to create connections with people that I might not have known otherwise. I think our university is incredibly blessed that there are leaders that are willing to commit their time to making our campus stronger and making sure students from every background will feel welcomed and encouraged and supported at our university.

We grew up going to stomp dances and to powwows and cooking traditional meals and making our regalia. And I understand that that is an experience that doesn't happen a whole lot for students at TCU, but I have such a strong understanding of who I am and just how important it is that I continue to remain connected to my culture. I think that's sometimes a struggle for Native students, to recognize how important cultural preservation is. Our journeys are different, we're in a world where we're not necessarily seeing Native representation happen constantly, but we can search and we can find it, and we can still keep that fire alive, and that's been my experience at TCU.

How special it is to know that I will have a Native American expressions and dance degree from TCU. I think that speaks volumes about our university's values. There wasn't a Native American Studies opportunity for me when I came to TCU. That passion never left me when I accepted my role as the TCU Feature Twirler. And whenever I communicated my love for my culture and just wanting to continue my studies of my people, it was so warmly welcomed. And now there will be a degree for a Native American major awarded at our university. What an incredible step forward. I may be the first, but my mission is to not be the last. I know there are so many other Natives who are going to be able to follow this journey because people cared.

I don't believe I would change anything because it shaped who I am and where I am going, and I think that connects to Native values. Life is lived in circles, and I am so grateful for how the Lord has directed my path. We are a faithful family and I'm just so grateful that I'm having this opportunity at TCU. There have been difficult moments for me, specifically it's just hard not being surrounded by your culture.

But I think what has always kept me going is that I was able to find people who really did understand the value of Native representation. Whenever I felt disconnected or was just trying to find my place, my mom would tell me, "You just need one person. You just have to find one person at this moment." And I have found so many "one persons." There have been so many people that have just believed in what I'm trying to accomplish as a young Cherokee woman, and that has meant so much to not only me, but my entire family.

It is so important to constantly seek Native perspectives. Storytelling is incredibly valuable, and as a journalism major, I have been able to understand even more how important somebody's story is to develop understanding. That's incredibly true for Native peoples, because if you look at our nation's history, Native Americans did not have platforms or microphones to be able to tell their stories from their own voices. And so whenever we're making decisions about anything that is going to be impacting Native people, we need to include Native perspectives. That is so important. And perspectives will look different from different generations as well, which I think is what's so incredible about the advisory circle. While there are graduates of TCU included in our circle, there's also people from the DFW community and other Native leaders from different backgrounds, and I've been included as a young Native student.

I think it's so important to include Native people in the conversation about events or developments that are impacting them, and include Native people from different generations as well, because we have different stories and experiences. My own story looks vastly different from my grandfather's, but they're both valuable, and they both need to be heard. Both stories carry an incredibly special place in strengthening our future. I want TCU to keep listening and to keep seeking Native perspectives because I think that's really going to help our community become stronger.

I feel like whenever I am in conversations that are really encouraging, I can already see the future for TCU in ten years. I think it would be beautiful to have a powwow on our campus. I think it would be beautiful to have a student organization that is really recognized on our campus, that every TCU student somehow has been able to connect with the Native and Indigenous Student Association because the organization is that big and that prominent and that successful. I would love to see involvement with TCU Athletics. Natives are athletes, they're performers, they're so successful, that's a part of our history. How beautiful it would be to see our people thriving, to see our young ones involved—that's something that Native people value so much, to see the next generations successful and continuing our culture by being bright leaders.

I think if I saw these kinds of developments happening, it would make me even that much prouder of where TCU is. I know that would take a tremendous amount of work, but I do think that we have the leaders that are committed to making this happen. And the last thing I would add is I would really want TCU to continue to lead on with a Native perspective and value. What is happening right now on our campus, that means so much to me. We are having conversations, and there are people on campus that care about making sure Native Americans are included and are welcomed. I want to see that stay. I want that to continue to grow because it's meant so much to me, and I know that it would mean so much to the next generation of Horned Frogs as well.

I would've loved for first-year TCU student Haylee to have been able to connect with some of the leaders that I know now and that I've been able to have personal connections with. A mentorship opportunity would've been incredible. Part of the responsibility for young Native leaders is to pave a way forward for the next seven generations. But we have to do that with a mindfulness of who came before us, what their values are, what their journey is, and what they need because they got us to where we are now. It's important that we continue to serve them. They're a part of our story.

And I think that kind of mentor presence at TCU would be a beautiful connection and would speak to the university's commitment to truly supporting Native student experiences. We're so closely connected to the voices of the generations before us, so it means the world to have a mentor. I relied on my own family members and Native leaders in the DFW community. And I was later able to connect with leaders at TCU. So I think it'd be wonderful for a young Native student to walk into TCU and already know that they have a person who is on their team and is going to be their ultimate cheerleader.

CREATING COMMUNITY TOGETHER:

An Interview with Dr. Wendi Sierra (Oneida)

Dr. Wendi Sierra (Oneida) joined the faculty of TCU in 2020 and is an associate professor of game studies in the John V. Roach Honors College. In fall 2024, Dr. Sierra assumed the role of TCU Native American Nations and Communities Liaison. Among many scholarly achievements, Sierra has worked with her Tribe to create a language preservation video game, A Strong Fire, *which received funding from the National Endowment for the Humanities. In her interview, Sierra recounts her experiences in academia as a Native scholar and teacher. She offers ideas to increase knowledge of contemporary Indigenous cultures among non-Natives and create community and support for Native students, faculty, and staff at TCU.*

Dr. Wendi Sierra ní yukyáts. Onʌyotaʔa ·ká · niʔi ·, ano:wal niwa-kiʔtaló:tʌ. Shirley ne: yutatyats aksotha, Cheri ne: yutatyats aknulha. Kheyaʔtakenhas ukwe:hu:we̲.

My name is Dr. Wendi Sierra. I am Oneida, turtle is my clan. My grandmother's name is Shirley, my mother's name is Cheri. I am helping the Oneida people.

Above: Wendi Sierra moderating the keynote session of TCU's seventh annual Native American and Indigenous Peoples Day Symposium, October 2, 2023. *TCU Marketing and Communication, photo by James Anger.*

Life prior to TCU

I am currently an associate professor of games studies in the John V. Roach Honors College at TCU, and I came to TCU in 2020. I am a first-generation college student, making me the first person in my family to have a bachelor's degree, a master's degree, and a PhD. My family moved around quite a lot when I was very young. I was born in Maryland, and over the course of the next eight years we moved to Germany, Virginia, and then Hawaii. When I was in third grade, we moved to Plano [Texas], and my family has stayed in Plano ever since. I do still have relatives, great aunts and second cousins, in Wisconsin. My great-grandma is the one who originally moved away from the reservation. There just weren't a lot of job opportunities available on the reservation. And so she took her whole family; they moved when my grandmother was young. I think my grandmother was in first grade when they moved. They weren't the only family that moved; the economic state on the Rez was not good at the time. To have a better chance at supporting a family, her parents felt like they had to leave. A lot of Oneida people left Green Bay and moved to Milwaukee, so there was a big Oneida community—and there's still a big Oneida community in Milwaukee—but that was sort of the first move away. When my grandma grew up, she continued to move around. But a lot of my grandma's siblings stayed up there and many eventually went back to Green Bay.

As a child, I knew I was Oneida and that was discussed in my family, but certainly when I was younger it was challenging to learn a lot about what that meant living so far from the reservation. I won't say what year that I'm born in, but in those years, there were not internet resources to find out information or share knowledge. And even as the internet grew and there were more internet resources and more ability to share, the Oneida, like a lot of nations, have been hesitant to put a lot of cultural information on websites. And so if you didn't grow up in community, which I didn't, your access to specific resources was really, really limited. At the same time, being Oneida has always been a part of my identity. My family has gone to powwows for as long as I can remember, but they often weren't the Oneida powwow because Oneida was so far from us. So we would go to the Alabama-Coushatta powwow fairly frequently because that was close to where my dad's parents lived. We would go to Red Earth in Oklahoma fairly frequently, since that was only a few hours up the road. We would do other things like that when we had the opportunity.

I'm not sure I ever heard the word Oneida in my K–12 schooling. I do think that Iroquois were briefly mentioned, which (from talking to other people) seems to be fairly common. I think when people have heard of Haudenosaunee or Iroquois, it's because history textbooks sometimes reference the idea that the Founding Fathers may have based parts of the Constitution on the Haudenosaunee Confederacy. But that would've been like a footnote. It's not a major focus, and there's not a lot of deep learning that goes on there. On top of that, I remember learning in seventh grade in Texas history that some of the Native Nations of Texas were cannibals. That was in a textbook that I had in seventh grade. So, what I learned in my public education about American Indians was both extremely limited and not great. I think I didn't realize so much when I was younger how much my mom did to supplement the education that I was getting. We had *The Legend of the Bluebonnet* [by Tomie dePaola] as a picture book when I was a kid, just to have anything, even if it wasn't about Oneida. To have anything that didn't depict our people as cannibals living on the coast. Like I mentioned, we went to powwows. My mom really integrated a lot of stuff into what we were doing. We did have *Kalihwisaks*, the tribal newspaper that we saw fairly regularly and heard stuff from. And then wherever possible, I think my mom consciously or subconsciously was bringing stuff to us and having conversations. I remember when *Pocahontas* came out and my mom was not happy about that movie, and particularly the savages song. And so we had a lot of discussions as a family about, "What is this and what's going on? Why are they doing this?"

I think that certainly when I was younger, and I'm talking when I was elementary, middle-school aged, a lot of what I was learning was more sort of pan-Indian stuff, just because that's all we had access to really, not living near the reservation and not having access to any internet necessarily. But as those resources have become more and more widely available, then we've had more access to those. There's my Auntie Carol Cornelius's book [*Iroquois Corn in a Culture-Based Curriculum*] and there was a book that came out, *Glimpses of Oneida Life* [by Karin Michelson, Norma Kennedy, and Mercy A. Doxtator] that had interlinear translations of stories, and there's an interlinear creation story for Oneida as well. COVID, while it has been terrible, has also meant that Oneida has been putting a lot more stuff online, particularly the

Tehatiwʌnákhwaʔ Language Nest has started putting all of their language videos, all their language lessons online. So that's been a really great source for me to find more connection there.

Growing up, particularly in high school, I definitely had perceptions of TCU, and I hung out with the alternative crowd that was sort of my group. We're talking like the '90s, so it's grunge, things like that. And there was no chance that I or any of my friends were going to TCU. That was not for us. That was where the preppy kids, the upper-class kids, that was where they went. That was not where we were going.

I always knew that I wanted to be a professor from the time that I started college. I was not a great high school student, but the one thing that I was always really good at was English, was reading and writing. And so I thought to myself, well, where do people value this? And the only answer that I could come up with was being a professor, even though I didn't know any professors, had no idea what being a professor was like, only had sort of those media images of the huge office with all of the bookshelves. And from that, I decided to be a professor. So I went to community college in San Antonio to start off and then ended up at the University of Oklahoma, where I studied English and religious studies. I was always interested in a good story. I did minors in classics and Russian as well. I wanted to do everything, I wanted to learn everything. In my master's degree, I moved from literature into rhetoric, and that's when I discovered that some rhetoric people research gaming, and having been a lifelong gamer, I was really excited by that. So I sort of moved even further away from literature in some ways into technology studies. I did an interdisciplinary PhD at North Carolina State University, and my dissertation was on gamification and game design. And that led me to my first tenure-track position, which was at a small liberal arts school in Rochester, New York, where I was sort of the faculty member in charge of all the new things in English. I taught digital rhetoric, I taught visual rhetoric, I taught some of my games stuff. I taught writing with New Media, which was all about using social media for writing and things like that. And then that led me to TCU.

Experiences at TCU

Living in Rochester, I was very far away from my family. And so I had been looking to come back to the DFW area, particularly after my daughter was born. It was very important to me that she be near my family, but I was also in a job that I was really happy in despite being sort of the all-purpose New Media person in the English department. I got to do a lot of things that I liked, and I had a lot of autonomy. So I wasn't going to just jump on any job that came my way. It had to be the right job for me to move. When this position came open, two things appealed to me. One, they were looking for game studies, which is the area that I had been steadily moving toward. Two, they were interested in someone that addressed elements of diversity, equity, and inclusion in their teaching. Because I had begun making games with Oneida, with my tribe, that was right in line with where I was going and what I wanted to do.

I also really enjoyed the interdisciplinarity of the Honors College, the idea that this was a place where I wouldn't necessarily feel, at least in my teaching, that I was being pulled in multiple different directions. I play in Native studies, that's one playground where I do work, I play in game studies, I play in rhetoric. Sometimes it's difficult to feel like there's a cohesive center to all that as I'm bringing together so many disciplines. The Honors College and my teaching offered me the ability to make those things make sense together.

Then through my work, I've been working on making language games with Oneida. And so that's enabled me to connect with the school, with the Cultural Heritage Center, with the language center. And I've also been connecting with speakers and with artists and with musicians. Gaming is an interdisciplinary field, you need people from all these different areas to come together to create a game. So I've been able to leverage that work into more connection as well, which has been great both for the game and for me personally. I am very much currently a language learner. I can conjugate some of my verbs. I know my conversational phrases, but I'm still in the process of learning the language. But that's also been a great joy for me. When I talk about my game, *A Strong Fire* [astrongfire.com], I often tell people it's a language and culture game because we're teaching you words in Oneida, but a lot of Oneida people will conflate language and culture. They see them as one thing. To really understand our concept of ka'nikuhli ýó, the good mind, you need to understand it in Oneida because you lose a little bit of it in translation. You lose the focus on relationships that is just built into the language, and it's an important part of that concept. So I think of *A Strong Fire* as a language and culture game because it's doing both, it's sharing the language and the culture.

In that game, we tell the Sky Woman story both in a fully Oneida version and in a mixed language version where you are hearing eight words in Oneida over and over and over. And we split those between words that we think that the kids will grab onto. So we have a'no·wál in there, which is turtle. We have Yotsitsya'ahs, which is Sky Woman. We have the nouns, but we also have the verbs that convey value. So Ka'nikuhli:yo, having a good mind. Asheya'takenha, helping her or to help someone, because Oneida is a verb-based language. We try to balance between conveying values through the words that are chosen and words that we think will be enjoyable for kids. And there are some mini-games to reinforce the vocabulary that you learn after you listen to the story.

My daughter actually knows several words in Oneida. My daughter's nine, so she has been playing my language games, both the official National Endowment for the Humanities–funded language game that I made, but also all of these little ones that I create practice demos that only live on my phone. She's been playing these for years; she was my first play tester for these games. And as I mentioned, we just have more access now to Oneida resources. She knows the clan names in Oneida—our family is Turtle Clan. The other Oneida clans are Bear and Wolf. A'no:wal is Turtle, ohkwa·lí is Bear, othahyu·ní· is Wolf. She thinks that Wolf is the coolest. When we go to powwow, she gets a wolf painted on her face instead of a turtle. She bought a little stuffed wolf at the last powwow that we were at. And she tells me othahyu·ní· is cooler. Her username in some online games is othahyu·ní·. And I'm like, "Okay, Turtle just carries the weight of the world on its back. But that's fine. Wolves are cool." I think that in some ways I'm trying to do some of the same things that my mom was doing with me. I'm getting picture books to fill in what she's not seeing elsewhere. So *Fry Bread: A Native American Family Story* [by Kevin Noble Maillard] is one that we love. *Rabbit's Snow Dance* [by James Bruchac and Joseph Bruchac] is a Haudenosaunee story that even has—I think technically it's actually Mohawk, but Mohawk is very similar to Oneida—some

Mohawk in the book. So we read that. I try to supplement what she's not getting in most media, what she's not getting in her schooling, with what we read and watch at home. But it's also different from when I was a kid because there's just a lot more access to resources. I am able to give her more specific stuff on Oneida and even to give her language resources that weren't available when I was young.

For the most part, people at TCU have been very well-intentioned. But what I have encountered, and it's not necessarily surprising given the area that we live in and given the culture in America, is a combination of just an overwhelming lack of knowledge and even some misinformation. There's an organization I really like called Reclaiming Native Truth that did a survey and found that overwhelmingly people in America are kind of aware that they don't really know much about Native peoples, and they're also kind of aware that their schooling was deficient in this respect. So this is not just a TCU thing, but it has been very prominent at TCU. And I think that it shows itself in a variety of ways. For example, when I mention things like going to powwow, people have a variety of different responses to that. I've also gotten some unexpected questions about things that I'm wearing, that kind of thing. This has come from all levels of the TCU community, from students, faculty, staff, admin, the whole way through.

The two common misconceptions that I feel like I run into frequently are one, that Native people are just mostly gone. They're not really here anymore. And two, that American Indians are a monolithic group, with essentially one culture across all nations. I think that most people don't have a lot of education about Native Americans, and the education that they get is often strictly historical. And so it leads to these two ideas. Regarding the idea of a monolithic culture, I do feel like I've done a lot of work educating about Oneida culture, which is very different from the sort of stereotype that people have in their head of teepees and dream catchers and horses. We're an Eastern Woodlands tribe. Those things aren't part of our culture, but it's certainly what many non-Native people are most familiar with.

I've also tried to directly address this idea that there just aren't Native people anymore. In a class, I asked students, "What are the nations that were native to where you grew up?" And most of them didn't know at all. A couple of them had learned a tribe or two in their

K–12 education. And then I asked them, the ones that did know a tribe or two, "Where are they now? That tribe that was originally in the area where you grew up, where are they now?" And overwhelmingly, students told me that they were all gone. And so I had students both Google what tribe lived wherever they grew up, and where is that tribe now? And we did a little activity in class on it. And when we did it, I told my students, you're not responsible for your K–12 education. You didn't choose that. You had no control over that. It was a thing that happened to you. But now, particularly as you're setting forth on your college experience, now you're responsible for your learning. Now you can make choices about it, and particularly as you're exposed to understanding places where that education may have been deficient, it's on you to correct those or not. I've heard about students that don't know about our TCU monument, that don't know about the Land Acknowledgment, that don't know about our Indigenous Peoples Day Symposium. It's very easy for students to just completely miss all of the great work that we're doing, to not see it or hear about it at all.

I certainly think it's worth noting that I'm in the Honors College, so all of the students that I'm engaging with are Honors students, so it's a small subset of the TCU population. But in general, they have been really eager to learn. They've been very excited to hear about the topics. In fact, I am retooling one of my courses. I taught a course called "Technological Dystopias" that was looking at sci-fi dystopian stuff with a technology focus, which as you might imagine, is a very, very male dominated, White-centric genre. And so the big texts that we read fit that bill totally. But I worked in a lot of short stories from Indigenous authors. And actually, in the comments, I got from students, "We want more of this. We want to learn more about this." So based on student feedback, I retooled the class. When I taught it again, we had a focus on Indigenous Futurism and Afro-futurism in the course. So we just did a light touch on the classical sci-fi, but then we really delved into Rebecca Roanhorse and things like that and looked at the game *Coyote & Crow*. We looked at Indigenous Futurism as a different way to think about this idea of technological dystopias.

I've also had the experience where I think that my students are hyperaware of their lack of knowledge, and they really want to lean on me as the expert. I taught a Native representation in games class, and I scaffolded it with: here's an example of something, let's talk about why this is problematic, here's an example of something, let's talk about why this is great. I had them read a book, *Seven Myths of Native American History* [by Paul Jentz]. And we also read a chapter from *"All the Real Indians Died Off": And 20 Other Myths about Native Americans* [by Roxanne Dunbar-Ortiz and Dina Gilio-Whitaker]. So we did some non–game related reading to try to get them up to speed to be ready to tackle this. And then we hit the point in the class when I wanted to turn it over to them and say, "Okay, here's a game. Let's look at what's happening. Let's look at how the characters are depicted. What are they saying? What's the story? Now, what do you think? What are the good things about this? What are the bad things about this? How do we talk about this representation?" And they really wanted to lean on me to be the one to tell them right or wrong. I've taught courses about feminist theory, and students will not wait to tell you what they think is right or wrong. They are ready with opinions on that, but in this case, they weren't. And it was really surprising to me, and I feel like I had to do a fair amount of both extra supporting and pushing to get them to want to offer a criticism. They were so hyperaware of how much they didn't know, and they were aware of me as an Oneida person, so they just wanted to say, "Well, you do the interpretive work, we want to leave it to you." We got to a good place at the end of the semester. But their hesitance was certainly surprising to me and not something that I had encountered, as I said, when I've taught about women in games. Students are ready with opinions on that, but on Native people in games, they held back much more.

I am repeatedly struck by the realization of how much was baked into my childhood, that I didn't necessarily identify at the time. Again, going to powwows frequently, knowing what fry bread is, knowing about my tribe and how they're different from Cherokee or Diné or Pacific Northwestern Tribes. This is a general awareness that was a part of me growing up that just lets me sort of feel like I instinctually knew some things, and I've been coming to the realization that this knowledge actually isn't common. Actually, very few people know these things. To actually get to the issues that I want to talk about, whether that's Native representation in games, or language reclamation through games, or even teaching about culture through games, whether it's in research presentations or teaching, I do have to backtrack and start with some basics: How many federally recognized tribes are there in America? What does it mean to be a federally recognized tribe, and why are there some Native peoples who are not federally recognized tribes? What is blood quantum and why is it different for different nations? Why are there many Native people that might not be on any roll and what are the politics behind why that is? What are the different big cultural groups, and how are we not a monolithic group? So yeah, I really feel like, well, I've got to teach a crash course of Native Studies 101 before I can get people to the things that I want to talk about.

Overwhelmingly, people here don't know about Oneida. If they have heard the word Oneida at all, they've heard of the silverware, which is not related to the tribe in any way there. Sometimes they know Iroquois, as I mentioned from K–12, sometimes you learn about Iroquois. And so I frequently talk about how Haudenosaunee is our word for ourselves, and Haudenosaunee means People of the Longhouse. I like to joke that that's not saying people of the ranch home. But the longhouse is a metonymy for our community, because a longhouse is an intergenerational and often a multifamily dwelling. And so People of the Longhouse is people of community. In fact, my game, *A Strong Fire*, comes from an Oneida saying, "A good heart, a good mind, a strong fire." And that fire refers to the longhouse fire. And it's, again, a symbol. If you have a strong fire, that means you have a strong community. So People of the Longhouse is referencing our relationships to each other, it's referencing our values, our way of life. Whereas Iroquois—the best etymology that I can find is it's a bastardization of an Algonquin word that was an insult. So I do find myself doing a lot of education and backfilling frequently.

In [my first] three years, I have, to my knowledge, had one Native student. I think that a big part of that is that I teach in the Honors College, and so it's already a very small portion of TCU's population, and those classes are highly fought-over. I'm always hearing from students that wanted in my class and couldn't get in. But I don't run into Native students in my classes near as much as I'd like. The one Native student that I just recently had was in a world-building class that I taught, where among other texts we used *Coyote & Crow*. She chose to be in the group that read and analyzed *Coyote & Crow*. And she told me that she called her mom and her grandma and told them about this game rule book that she was reading, and how excited she was. And then in the final project, they had to create their own fictional world and then write a little bit about it. She was able to bring some of her Cherokee culture into what she was writing about and create some little pieces of the world that she was working on with the rest of her group that reflected that. It was a cool experience for me because, well, *Coyote & Crow* is an example of Indigenous futurism, a tabletop role-playing game made by an intertribal team with a variety of different traditions represented. When I looked at it, I looked at the Haudenosaunee stuff and how the game imagined our future. And when she looked at it, she looked at the Cherokee stuff and she looked at, "Where are the Cherokee in this imagined future?" It was really cool because again, we're different cultures. I have my own cultural perceptions, and then I have the general Native Studies 101 stuff in my mind. But she was able to point out some stuff to me that I hadn't seen, and I was able to point out some stuff to her. It was a really great experience. I certainly wish I could have more Native students in my classes because it was, like I said, it was really fun for me. I think it was fun for both of us.

In my teaching, absolutely, I've been affirmed at TCU. And some of this is because being in the Honors College, I get to set my teaching agenda for the most part. I have some loose guidelines I have to follow, but I have a lot of flexibility because we're not trying to meet any sort of requirements related to a specific major in the Honors College. I've been able to do some direct and highly visible things. Like my "Video Games and Representation" course, it's a combo of a brief Native Studies 101 and then explicitly looking at Native representations in games. It's been a great course. I've mentioned I've had some trouble drawing students out, but I've gotten really good feedback from them, and I've gotten a lot of excitement from that. I also work units into other courses. And then I've also done things like in my Games and Learning course, where we don't necessarily explicitly look at either language learning or cultural learning through games, but when we read critical scholarly pieces, I intentionally choose examples. We've used *Coyote Quest*, which is a really cool browser-based game. We've used *When Rivers Were Trails*. I have a variety of different approaches in my teaching that are everything from teaching a class that's entirely on a Native studies topic down to intentionally selecting specific examples for a class that otherwise maybe isn't necessarily about Native issues.

I also frequently will give my full Oneida introduction, which I began this conversation with, as a teaching tool. In my Oneida introduction, in addition to just giving my name, we go in smaller and smaller relationships because you're situating yourself within the community. You start by naming your nation, which for me is Oneida. You identify yourself as a member of the tribe, and then the next smaller down relationship would be your clan. I identify myself as a member of a Turtle clan, and then the smallest level of community is your mother's line, because we're matrilineal. So I identify my grandmother and my mother to fully situate who I am and where I belong within this community. I give that introduction, and then I talk about those increasingly smaller circles, and the reason for that, the cultural background for that.

In my research and the tenure process, I definitely felt very supported, but I certainly also felt the tension of being very interdisciplinary. There was one person on my tenure committee that knew about games but didn't necessarily know about anything else. There was someone on my committee that did work in Native studies and Native literature but didn't necessarily get the game stuff. In a certain light, the ways that I was trying to weave these different fields together was the biggest challenge, as the academy remains very disciplinary. To me, though, it feels very holistic. And I think that's just a part of my worldview and a part of that Native focus on relationships. It's all about relationship building and identifying your obligations and your blessings. And so being interdisciplinary, to me, just feels like living that truth, taking from a variety of places as I need, and giving back to a variety of places as I can.

One place where I have struggled is trying to get others involved. One of the things that I've been working on at TCU is something that I'm calling *Turtle Island Games Collection*. It's an on-campus collection of games with Native representation. Actually, there's a [Nintendo] Switch that's in the library that's available for faculty to check out. There are a couple games on that Switch that feature Native people. There are other games that we have on other systems. And this is something that I've been very excited about because I think that showing particular Indigenously created games counters so many of the misconceptions that people have: one, they show we're still here, two, we get to display our culture as vibrant, three, our languages can be part of these games to show they are still out there. You see all of that when you see a game made by a Native person. So that's something that I've wanted to share with more people, and it's been tricky getting that off the ground. Sometimes TCU feels a little siloed. The work that I'm doing is support-ed, but it also exists in a bit of a vacuum. I don't know how much of that is COVID-related, because most of my time at TCU has been heavily impacted by COVID, and that's changed a lot of relationships. But that's been something that I think has been a challenge.

I also think that for sure there's an additional emotional service load I carry. And this is something that is well-known in academia. If you are seen as a representative for a minoritized group, you are dispropor-tionately called on to do emotional labor. And that's certainly been true here. And I don't think, again, for the most part that people—whether it's students, faculty, or admins and staff—have necessarily been aware of when they've been doing things that have maybe required extra emotional labor on my part. I am frequently asked to be a voice, and it's sometimes hard to think about balancing that because I certainly recognize the value of the perspective I bring. I recognize that anytime I get to stand in front of a group of people and give my Oneida intro-duction, that increases the number of people that get to hear the Oneida language, the number of people that have heard of Oneida as a nation. And that's very important to me. But it can be a lot. I really appreciate when there's an opportunity for these types of things to be about me as a scholar and an Oneida woman instead of just me as an Oneida woman. I've been invited to give guest lectures and courses, and I love it when I get to be invited to give a guest lecture about my work on language reclamation games, or studying Native representation in games, or how to teach about Native culture through games. When it's something that's very obviously about me as a scholar and not just me as someone with this genetic connection, those are the types of experiences that I really like and I really value.

And then I think one of the other things that is very true is that, at times, it has been hard to protect my own emotional well-being, partic-ularly in summer 2022 with the stuff about the residential schools that I have known about forever. Residential schools and the casualties from them hadn't really been a part of the public conversation or conscious-ness, but it's been something that I've had an awareness of for a long time. But both nationally and in the TCU community, all of a sudden other people were discovering this awareness of a really tragic part of our (fairly recent) history. And that's a really difficult issue to talk about because that's people that I relate to, and some of the choices my family members made were in a direct attempt to avoid residential schools. And so those conversations are really emotionally rough. When we have a focus on Missing and Murdered Indigenous Women Girls Two-Spirit (MMIWG2S)—again, this is a very emotionally deep subject for me to think about. I feel like I have done some work to try to protect myself emotionally from some of these conversations. Related to that, my constant fear is that the only thing that people know about Native nations is a victim story. And so I often wonder, "How do we talk about these important issues (MMIW2GS, Every Child Matters), but not just entrench those conceptions and those ideas?" I feel like I have to push very hard to do things that are celebratory, that are talking about our cultures in a way that is forward-thinking and resilient. That's surviv-ance, basically. Talking about the culture in a way that does survivance [a term created by Gerald Vizenor (Anishinaabe)].

As one of a small number of Native faculty on campus, there is sometimes a sense of well, you should weigh in on this. This is a big issue. You're a Native person, you should talk about this. And I think, again, it's coming from a good place. It's coming from, "Well, we want to lift up Native voices. We want to let Native people share their perspec-tives and their experiences." But sometimes those who ask this of me don't think about the trauma that comes with those and how someone might not want to perform that in a professional setting or might want to choose when they want to engage with that. I certainly recognize that it comes from a very well-meaning place. It comes from wanting to foreground Native voices, and that is a good thing, but it can have consequences for the people you're asking to speak, and that has to be considered as well.

I think that a lot of this comes down to feeling like one of a very small number of representatives. And I think that if there were a larger community—if more Native faculty and staff were hired—there would be more voices. People would be better able to engage when they emotionally feel like they can engage and not feel pressured to engage when it might be putting their own well-being at risk. One of the things that I always think about when I'm asked to do something, whether it's read the Land Acknowledgment or give a talk or answer a question, I always think about, if I don't do this, who will? Will no one do it? It will just be a void, and I want to be open, and I want to share my perspective, and I want our faculty and our students and our administration to have the opportunity to learn about these things. But it's asking me to sometimes perform things that are highly personal, that are my family and my family history. That's not what I got a PhD in. That's not why I was hired into this position. And navigating when and what and with whom I share things has been tricky because people want to know. "Did you know anybody that was at a residential school, do you have family members that were at a residential school?" And that has nothing to do with why I was brought here to teach. Again, it's this sort of constant back and forth about what am I willing to share and when am I willing to share it. I try to find that line, but I don't know that I always succeed as well as I hope to.

As I said earlier, one of the things that makes finding that balance tricky for me is sometimes it feels like if I don't agree to do a thing, maybe nobody will. Maybe they just won't talk about this issue, or maybe they won't be able to get another Native person to be a voice on this issue. Sometimes, maybe, I lean even a little more toward doing things that I might otherwise pull back on, because I feel that sense of obligation. Frankly, if there were a larger community, if there were more faculty and staff, that would be less of a concern because there would be other people that could answer that call. There could be other people that they might go to.

Advice to TCU

I think that that one of the things that TCU has been doing fairly well, at least from what I've seen in the last few years, is that we are making a lot of good partnerships. We are doing a lot of outreach; I certainly don't want to diminish that. But at the same time, a community partner doesn't have an office on campus. They're not available in the same way that a faculty member or a staff member is available. And it is still somebody coming from outside TCU, which I think just creates this separation. It wasn't until I got to OU that I ever knew I had a Native

American teacher. Even at San Antonio Community College, I didn't have a teacher that was Native. And so I think that community partners are great and fantastic, but there's something different about having somebody that's in the TCU community that just provides a different level of perspective that is important. There's a different level of commitment when you hire a person and you bring them into your community and you say, "As an organization, we are going to support you and develop you, and we want you as part of the work that we're doing," versus a guest speaker that you invite in once for an honorarium. I don't want to necessarily say it's easy to invite guest speakers because certainly you have to build relationships, you have to build trust, and that's valuable work that I don't want to undermine. At the same time, it's letting that expertise always live outside of TCU. It's letting that expertise always be somewhere else, and it's not bringing that expertise into the community in a way that faculty or a staff member would.

I think that, in general, finding ways to build more of a community on campus would help me feel more supported. And that doesn't necessarily mean exclusively a community of Native people, but I think that people that are interested in talking about and learning about these issues. A community of practice that does a mix of learning and sharing together would be great to see to prevent some of this siloed feeling. I think that that could also potentially make more visible some of the good work that's being done at TCU, because I think that there is great work, great outreach to the community, and initiatives, and things like that. But to me, those also feel very siloed. They feel very easy to miss if you're not explicitly looking for them. So thinking about ways to build more of that community would be helpful.

It's important to realize that a connection with Indian Country broadly is an unending conversation. And conversations take work. There's not room to rest, because if you rest, you lose the ground that you have gained in terms of building trust, building reciprocity, and building collaboration. The relationship has to constantly be foregrounded. It has to constantly be thought about. I think that putting official resources and sustained resources behind initiatives, behind scholarships, behind the Native American and Indigenous Peoples Day Symposium, and behind the Native and Indigenous Student Association are the things that are going to help continue to grow and expand the good work that we've already done.

And then, and this echoes what I said earlier, expand the number of engaged students, faculty, and then administrators. I explicitly say "engaged" because while I absolutely want to argue for bringing more Indigenous students to campus and having more Indigenous faculty, I also think that there's an opportunity to expand the number of non-Native students, faculty, and administrators who are engaged in this project. So raising awareness of what has already been done and raising awareness of what's currently being done and getting more cross-campus support of that, I think, is important.

And hire more faculty. More faculty teaching more classes. And frankly, more faculty teaching more classes to raise awareness with the campus population so that then when we want to roll into having more Indigenous students, it's a more welcoming environment. Somewhere, there are more places where thoughtfulness and compassion are being practiced. I think that not just with Native students, but in general with any minoritized group, there's a tendency among a lot of colleges to want to rush to recruitment. Let's just get them here. Let's just get as many as we can and get them in the door. And I don't think that that necessarily sets those students up for success if the environment hasn't already been made welcoming to them.

And so starting with expanding the number of engaged students, faculty and admin, and hiring more faculty to teach more classes would do good work to make this a more welcoming space, which would then make it inviting for those Native students to want to come here. My biggest takeaway, then, is that I think that we have done good work with outreach to the community, and I absolutely think that has to be maintained. But I think within our own community, we have some work that we could do that would both strengthen the TCU community and also feed that outreach that we want to be doing in really good ways.

An obstacle to achieving this is general American culture, which doesn't know a lot about Native cultures, and what it does know is mostly wrong. It's just going to be a lot of work reteaching the same ideas because as we have both new students coming in fresh, but also faculty, staff, and administrators coming in, we're going to have to be doing that Native Studies 101 work constantly because people aren't getting it elsewhere. So I think that's certainly a challenge. I also think that TCU is a really big place, and everyone has competition for their time. And so I do think that for the people who aren't teaching Native representation of video games or Native spiritual traditions or Native literature, one of the other few classes that we have, finding the ways for them to feel like this is something that they should be connected with, that they should put their time into. Again, whether we're talking about students or faculty, I think that time is always going to be a challenge.

I would love for us to have a minor. A minor would mean that we would have a variety of courses in different departments that students from across campus could take. A minor would mean that we had committed faculty and committed students. I think that that would be a really great goal for us to have. I would love for us to have a yearly powwow. I've done some consulting work locally, certainly engaged a lot with faculty, staff, and students at TCU, and I'm always shocked that people either don't realize that powwows are real—I've heard that one quite a bit—or that they don't think that non-Native people are allowed to go to powwow. That's very common as well. I actually started comparing it to Pride. I said, "Non-LGBTQIA people are welcome at Pride. Are you going to be surrounded by that culture and that music and that iconography? Yes, you are, but as long as you're an ally and respectful, of course you're welcome. The more, the merrier, let's go. It's a celebration." And I think that powwow is very similar. If you go to powwow, you're going to hear Native music, you're going to see Native dancing, you're going to see all kinds of Native art. You're probably going to see more Native people than you ever see when you're walking around Fort Worth, Texas, and you're going to have great food, and it's a celebration. You are welcome, so long as you are respectful. I think a powwow would be a fantastic way for the local community and the TCU community to be together and to interact around something that's joyful, that's a celebration. Because I really feel like our TCU population needs to see that celebration. They need to see that vibrant, thriving culture in a way that's different from a lecture, in a way that's different from an evening keynote. Those are great things, too, but powwow is just different. And then I would love to see more community engagement through curriculum but also through student groups and events.

I think that if we had those things, if we had a minor, a yearly celebratory event, like a powwow, and more community engagement, what would happen in turn is we would create a space that felt affirming and welcoming for students, faculty, and staff. And we would get more applications from Native students. We would get more Native faculty and Native staff because we would have created a space where that felt open and comfortable. It's just three things. Check them off.

I think to the non-Native people at TCU, I would encourage you to take charge of your own personal education. As I've said already, I recognize that the K–12 system is not great about teaching Native cultures. And I certainly don't put that fault on teachers because I understand the stresses and the challenges that K–12 teachers are working with. I don't necessarily hold teachers accountable for that, and I certainly don't hold the people that went through that education system accountable for that. But there are so many fantastic resources out there with just a very tiny amount of Googling. And in some ways, I feel like we're in the midst of a renaissance of Native artistry and pop culture. One of my favorite bands, The Halluci Nation, mixes electronic music and dubstep with traditional chanting and drumming, and it's amazing. *Rutherford Falls* is hilarious. The most recent *Predator* movie, *Prey*, you can hear in Comanche. There's so much out there. Whatever you're interested in, Native people are doing an awesome, awesome work. What was it I just recently read? Stephen Graham Jones, *The Only Good Indians*. You like some Stephen King, you like some horror, there's something out there for you. So go explore it. Recognize that you've got gaps in your knowledge and then do a little reading, go to a local powwow. That's something you can Google—powwows in Texas—and find a list. There's a lot, basically every month from March to November, everywhere from El Paso to San Marcos to Dallas. So go to a powwow, have some fry bread. Engage, not just in learning some facts, how many tribes are there, where are they located, what happened to them, but engage in learning something celebratory and cultural as well. That's what I would say to non-Native people.

To Native people at TCU—in some ways, this one is a little harder because it's such a smaller population. But I think that what I would probably say is strive to find that balance between representing and being your authentic self and protecting your own well-being. Because while you have a great perspective to share, you don't owe anyone your own well-being. You only owe that to yourself. And so just try to find that space where you can educate and share when that feels comfortable and when you need to find that space for yourself.

TO SIT IN TWO SPACES:
An Interview with Sarah Tonemah
(Comanche and Kiowa)

An enrolled member of the Comanche Nation, Sarah Tonemah worked as the costume technician/master draper for the theatre department at TCU for eight years, from 2013 to 2021. In her interview, Tonemah explains how her involvement with TCU's Native American and Indigenous Peoples Initiative coincided with her deepening understanding of her multiethnic identity. She details her efforts to "scrape back as much of my Native heritage as I can," sensitively treating the fissures stemming from religion and culture that occurred in her family's history during her father's lifetime. She also speaks candidly of the marginalization she experienced in some TCU contexts.

Life prior to TCU

I'm an enrolled member of the Comanche Nation of Oklahoma, granddaughter of Rowena Aesnap and Harry Treat Tonemah Sr. My grandfather was Kiowa, full blood on the Kiowa roll. His son, my dad, Harry Treat Jr., is also an enrolled member of the Kiowa Tribe. In my family, most of the women chose to enroll in the Comanche Nation with my grandma and most of the men on the Kiowa roll with my grandpa. I grew up in Wichita Falls, about twenty-five minutes from the Oklahoma border and about an hour away from Lawton, Oklahoma, where my parents grew up and met. I was raised in Texas, about an hour and a half away from Meers, Oklahoma, where most of my family grew up, went to school, and went to church with the other Kiowa and Comanche people.

Above: Sarah Tonemah moderating the dedication of TCU's Native American monument, October 15, 2018. *TCU Marketing and Communication, photo by Amy Peterson*

I heard about TCU from a young age, because I was born into the Christian Church (Disciples of Christ), which is affiliated with TCU. We went on mission trips, church visits, and church youth trips to the football games starting when I was seven or eight. I applied to TCU, was accepted, and envisioned that I might go there as a music major. Then, I switched directions to be more art focused and ended up going to an arts conservatory in the northeast.

I did not attend many powwows or those kinds of ceremonial events growing up. But I've definitely connected to my heritage through other kinds of ceremonies. I come from a very big extended family on my dad's side. When I attended funerals or weddings, there were traditional music and traditional practices involved. That's something I just grew up with. My mother is White—English and Scottish, a little bit Irish. I grew up in a mostly White city. People knew my dad in our city of 125,000 as (probably) the only Native American man there. My sister and I were often the only kids with any connection to our Native heritage in any of our schools growing up. That's very much been a normal part of my life.

I was the costume technician/master draper in the theatre department at TCU for eight years. I was responsible for patterning all of the garments for our productions, fitting the students, dyeing fabric, and planning the construction of the costumes. I was an informal instructor in the studio space for up to thirty college students at a time. While at TCU, I was affiliated with various groups on campus like Women and Gender Studies, Comparative Race and Ethnic Studies, and the Native and Indigenous Student Association, of course. I've served on several committees—search committees, hiring committees—which was just such an influential part of being there. I didn't get any credit for it; it was just a wonderful part of the job, I thought.

In terms of how I navigated being Native at TCU, which is mostly non-Native, it really wasn't very different than what most of my life has been. Most Native young people that I knew growing up were family, directly related to me. It even seemed to be that I found out I was related somehow to ones I met that I didn't know. My grandpa was very involved in the Indian United Methodist Church. My dad grew up going to all the church events, and still to this day, people know his name as part of the church because he left an impact in terms of leadership and creating curriculum. When I meet Kiowa people, most have heard my grandpa's name. He left quite a legacy, which is my own understanding based on how they've reacted to his name.

My sister went to TCU. She graduated with her undergrad in education and her master's in special education but had left TCU by the time I got there. She's definitely been interested in some of the work that I've been doing but hasn't dived as deep into her rediscovery of her heritage. Like I said, I think that we grew up trying to assimilate into this White culture because it was just easier. When you're young, it's hard to be different. We were always proud. There was never a shame brought about it. I think we just didn't like to be singled out. We were often, I don't mean to say tokenized, but we were the only ones in the room, in the school, who would show up in the demographics at the end of the year as "American Indian/Alaska Native." We knew the two people listed were us. During periods studying Native Americans in the curriculum each year, they would let us wear regalia or whatever, just showcase it. It was always exciting, and there was always a bit of awe. I definitely felt very special. Then I think I quickly just switched gears to assimilate more. Like I said, not because I was embarrassed. I think it's just hard to be young and to feel different. That act became something I carried with me through college and every workplace after. In the last few years, I've been fortunate to have meaningful talks with Scott [Langston, former TCU Native American Nations and Communities Liaison] and other mentors throughout my life about finding my place as somebody who is connected to their culture but grew up as an urban Native or who is part White. I haven't always felt like I know where my place is.

I've now realized that my two races have allowed me to sit in two spaces very comfortably because I've been doing that my entire life. I've been able to navigate Brown spaces and then switch it off quickly and live life in White spaces—effortlessly, just not even realizing it. I think that what I thought was so confusing and something that made me feel so different is actually a gift that I have, to be able to walk in both of those worlds and understand those perspectives. That's something that has partly come out of working with NISA and students, part of it being support from staff at TCU, and part of it just growth, individual growth, at this point in my life to be able to realize that about myself.

My grandparents were very involved in their church. I went to a powwow once with my aunties. But I never went much with my dad. And

I never thought about why I didn't until I was an adult. I think you live your life how you live your life, and then you just have this moment where you're like, "Why do we do these things?" I had never thought about why my immediate family didn't attend many powwows. This journey of cultural discovery has been a journey for my entire family. Like I said, my mom is White, and my dad is not. We don't talk about race around the table much. We just exist as we are. I am lucky to have an extremely close immediate family. I grew up having dinner together every night together, and all four of us still talk daily to each other on the phone.

But we never talked much about the fact that my dad is very dark and my mom very fair, and how that impacts us. My grandma had five other kids, and she was in her mid-forties when my dad was born. He was a surprise. But I say this because a lot of this [choices about how his parents and family lived as Native people] had already been set in motion, already set in place: the way things were done, the way they were living life as Native people in the Oklahoma of the 1950s that my dad was born into. And so, because they were older, whenever my dad was grown up enough to ask those complicated questions about tradition, religion, and race, I think he relied on his siblings for that kind of understanding. I think about my dad a lot in terms of what it must have been like to have grown up in a rich cultural community but then to live over half of his life as an identifiably Native man in his mostly White, non-Native community.

I've watched him closely as he straddles his different communities. He doesn't often draw too much attention to his heritage. I know it's not a lack of pride. He's one of the proudest people I know. And I don't mean that in a bad way. I know that pride sometimes is not the best virtue, but I mean it in terms of being proud of where you come from and who you are and being unwavering in that. I have a feeling that his not drawing attention to his heritage has something to do with focusing on similarities with those around you instead of our difference. It makes life more pleasant. I think many of us who live as minorities in their communities know this to be true. It doesn't mean you're not proud of who you are, though.

I don't necessarily know that I have, but I think back on it often, whether I've experienced racism before. I do think there may have been some indirect things when I look back on my life. Opportunities or certain instances, interactions with people, groups I've worked with—they may have included stigmas or questions about who I am. Because I do volunteer the information [that I'm Native]. I always thought it was just a special trait about me. I think it's exciting. I think it's unique. I like to be unique.

In terms of my dad, though, I've witnessed ridiculous things people say to him that are so ignorant and annoying. It's horrible that he has "gotten used" to this kind of talk. I've heard people ask him if he lives in a tipi, can they call him "chief," does he know how to do a rain dance, or mispronouncing our name as Tomahawk. Asking him, "How much money do you get for being Native American?" and "Can you get us some peyote?" Or people saying, "You're welcome, we lost a bunch of money at your people's casino last weekend." Let me be clear, he's not one to be talked down to or treated unkindly. And he has taught my sister and me to speak up when it's time to speak up. There is still so much that people don't understand about what it means to be a contemporary Native person in this world. But in order to be heard, you definitely need to pick your battles.

My mom's side of the family is just very "White." And I don't know if this is my own experience, but it's very different from the Brown side of my family. And not just in terms of language, but in terms of social practices, body language, the way we measure time. Indian time versus a very punctual White-lace-glove kind of family on the other side, honestly. I think that anytime I had questions about my Nativeness, I would ask my dad. Or my Whiteness, which even now I'm still learning about—I'm so excited that I recently found out that I am Scottish—I would ask my mom. Family is very important to both sides of my family, and heritage too, and knowing where you come from.

In the past few years, culture and race have been something our family of four—well, now, my husband and babies, too—sit around the table and talk about more. We're all actively trying to be open-minded about growing, about teaching my children who they are and where they're from and how all of these things make up who they are. At Thanksgiving, maybe three years ago, I asked my dad "Why have you never danced at a powwow?" I literally started thinking that anytime I've ever danced, he's never danced. He said, "Because it's a pagan tradition." He said, "I'm a Christian man, and my parents raised me to be a Christian man. I don't feel that that is something that they would approve of. They told me that they didn't approve of that. My sisters went and danced, and they took you. You can always go, and you are welcome to go and learn about those things. I don't feel comfortable with some of the dances that are being performed there. I don't believe in that."

I remember a story about his sister who dated somebody who was some kind of dancer. She took the chairs that said Tonemah, written really big on the back [to the powwow]. It became such a thing that everybody knew that she had gone. To this day, he said of his parents, "They would roll over in their grave if they knew she did that." My dad and his siblings went to public school and lived in the city. I remember a cousin telling me that growing up among her Native friends, those things made her feel different. My dad and his siblings got a quality education. That's something that he said that his parents made a priority and were unapologetic about. That is something he and my mom have always made a priority for my sister and me, too.

At times, I've felt a little removed from my cultural community. But I think some of that was on purpose. I think he's said that he and my mom, for whatever this means, have tried to make choices for my sister and me so we could have better opportunities. Maybe the pendulum swung a little far at times. And so, I'm over here trying to scrape back as much of my Native heritage as I can. I've had talks with my dad before where I've said, "This is really hard for me. It's hard for me to exist in these groups of Native people where I feel so different. I went to a private college, and I've had opportunities that not everybody has had." I said, "I'm struggling. I don't feel connected to them. I feel like my experience has just been so different." He got upset with me, and he said, "I'll never apologize for giving you these opportunities." He said, "This is part of your story. This is your life, and you use these experiences to help our people and come back and bring your gifts to our tribe." However uncomfortable my story has been at times, he's reminded me that there's always been the intention that I would gain my own perspective to bring back to our community.

I notice that if we go to certain ceremonies or as I'm starting to attend more events just for my own learning purposes, that when we mention our family name, people still associate it with the church. I think my parents' Christian upbringing and my grandparents converting to Christianity when they were young adults really impacted where I am now in terms of my connection with my culture. There are a lot of people who straddle culture and religion and walk in both of those worlds really well. That's somewhere I'm trying to exist, too, but it is tricky. I have a lot to learn. I think certain Native traditions were probably withheld or not kept because of my family's comfort level with what my grandparents allowed in their household and instilled in them in terms of what God wanted for their lives. My extended Native family were all raised Christian like me. But many cousins of mine are Christian and participate in ceremonial events. It's safe to say there is a wide range of beliefs in my extended family in terms of their faith and belief in who the Creator is. Many are learning their traditional language, and some use our Comanche and Kiowa languages more than others. For sure, Native hymns in church are something that I grew up with. Even in our household, music ties me back to my community and its people.

Getting together with people that knew my grandparents, knew my aunties, my uncles, showing me pictures, telling me who they are—that's something that has been a tradition in our family for a long time. It is an unspoken tradition. It seems like every time we get together, since I can remember, someone shows up with a shoebox full of black-and-white photos. And somehow, every time they're different. There are hilarious ones of my cousin when he was prom king in the seventies, all the way back to ones that are just so crispy, I feel I shouldn't even touch them. I love to talk and learn all about who everybody is. I ask, Where were they living? Why are they wearing this? How did they get there? This spoken knowledge seems to be where I'm drawing a lot of my cultural connection—just through family, extended family time together, talking. Me asking questions.

More so now, I'm asking questions with urgency. Because a lot of the members of my family who know the answers are getting very, very old. There's a lot to learn and a lot to hold onto right now. Sometimes, my aunts tell me stories that are completely different every single time. I do my best to decipher what they're talking about and know my ancestors. I feel like that's something that we all need to know. I'm not always sure that my non-Native friends know where they come from in the way that I know where I come from. I'm very proud of that. It's something my parents, from a very young age, made sure that I knew. They've always made sure I knew my ancestors' names and who I've come from. At least as far back to the ones whose names I can pronounce.

I think the greatest takeaway [that I have learned about being Native and White] at TCU, was finding a community of people who were biracial and watching and learning how they navigate those things on and off campus—just realizing that it's not as much of a curse as I thought it was. Feeling that made me feel more out of place. It's just like everywhere you go growing up, forms say "pick one, pick one, pick one, pick one." Or check the box that says "other" because you could not check two boxes, which is so dehumanizing. Isn't that crazy? I remember as a kid, how that made me feel. I remember at a young age asking my parents "Which box do I pick?" I can honestly remember the first time I saw "Native American" on that standardized testing box. I was probably midway through high school. Until then, "Asian Pacific Islander" was the closest or "other," which I hated checking. I just remember being so excited when I saw the Native American box. And I still get excited when I see that. I'm saying that even from a young age, I've been staring at this paper like, "Where do I fit? Where do I fit? Where do I fit? Which box do I check?" My parents said, "Whichever you want." And I think my sister and I together were just like, "Yeah, we're going to be the two Native kids in [the demographic breakdown of the] school, so we're going to check it."

I think with growth, I've learned that that my combined race is more of a blessing than a detriment. And so I find myself adapting to those situations when I'm in those spaces in life. To be honest, still to this day—and I don't know if it's because of my education, the careers that I've chosen, or where I've chosen to live—I still have to seek out Brown spaces. I still often feel "other" in those other spaces, too. I know I can be White passing. I think mostly I'm passing as just as a "What are you?" or "We know you're something Brown-ish, but we're not sure." But I've always considered myself, firstly, to be Native American. I've never considered myself White first, even though I think I fit very easily into those spaces. And that's something I think people are surprised about. As I started this journey of really working to rediscover myself, I did have some people in my life who asked, "Why now? Why are you talking about this now?" Not people that knew me very well, but I did get a few "Why are you all of a sudden Native?" I think it probably made people a little uncomfortable. Probably because, that "otherness," all of a sudden I'm drawing attention to it.

Recently, it has just felt safer to explore my heritage more openly. Not just for me, but for others, too. We have our boarding school elders, and then we have their children (our parents), and then you have my generation. So whatever age that is, we're all in the same place. We're all searching and reconnecting, because there was a whole generation where it wasn't safe to talk about your Nativeness. And so, especially in social media, it feels more welcoming, and it's very exciting right now too. It's exciting to connect with people and talk about what's going on. It was an incredible blessing at TCU to be able to work with students who broadened my horizons, in terms of what it meant to be Native. Like I said, most of my experiences with other Native young people were within my family or tribal nations. So most of the cultural traditions were the same. Even if some cousins had married and they were from different tribal nations, we all had very similar traditions and beliefs, because we are all from Oklahoma. There's just some bigger similarities.

All of a sudden at TCU, I was meeting students now from the Pacific Northwest nations, and the Northeast, and Canada, and California. I was able to just sit in a room with these students and realize that I always thought we were so different. I had been so intimidated by these differences that I never noticed how much we actually had in common: through lines of a having sense of humor, and a value on heritage and family and community, or meals and food and creation, things like that. I thought, "Wow, what you're sharing is so similar to what I know, but we were raised so far away." Even the students who had grown up on their reservations and were completely inundated in Indian society and their upbringings, we had those similarities, which were so exciting to me. I wasn't a student, but I was learning every time I got together with the NISA students and soaked up as much as I could. I have since worked on projects where I realized that there are still some big differences, and that's important to acknowledge, of course. It's complicated to navigate sometimes, but like my father, I like to focus on what we have in common more often.

In terms of my identity in college, I remember that on the first day of school I was asked to go out with this group of girls who were all Black and Brown. And that was so different for me. The diversity at college was very different for me. I felt intimidated. I know that really speaks to where I came from in terms of the cultural shock of being a

Brown person in a White world, and then feeling out of place when I was finally among a group of Brown and Black people. The cultural shock eased quickly in college, and I'm so thankful for the experience of being in a diverse city. But then at TCU, I think I was able to really hone into who I am more specifically. And I think that comes with age, too, and maturity, I hope.

I don't know whether my family talked about identity unless we asked them. I'm talking about it very freely [with my four-year-old daughter], but I have no idea what I'm doing. It really is a complicated subject. She's very smart and very inquisitive. So every statement prompts another question that I have no idea how to answer yet. I think as Native people across the planet, we're still trying to figure out what our identity is, what we want to be called, and how we want to be addressed and named. I was working on this culture guide for a large company recently, which was really exciting. They asked me to put together some text about understanding the Native customer. I asked for a postmortem when I was finished with the project, and my supervisor asked, "What would you have done differently?" I told her, "In an ideal world, if someone were to ask me about my culture or heritage, I could just say Kiowa and Comanche. I wouldn't have to choose Indigenous or Native, or these umbrella terms. I could simply name my nation and people would understand." That's the dream. And obviously, they can't make a specific guide for every single nation and tribe because that is such a huge task. But I do wish that all of us would have our own individual guide because it's such a vast culture. It's ridiculous to lump everybody into the same group. In an ideal world, we would all just be able to name our tribal affiliation and people around the world would be familiar enough to understand. It would be lovely.

Experiences at TCU

When I came to TCU, my Nativeness was definitely a part of me, but it wasn't something that I spoke up about too much. For seven of the eight years I worked in the theater department, I was the only person of color in a faculty/staff of about twenty to twenty-five people. Like I said, that in itself didn't feel any different than what I'm used to, but I definitely don't think I felt comfortable calling attention to my race. It wasn't because it wasn't welcome. I think I just was trying to focus more on my job, I guess. We also didn't have many Native students in the theater program, so I wasn't really sure if that perspective was needed at the time. My closest partners in work, though, were so excited and interested in celebrating any part of my heritage that I wanted to share, which was exciting. In that way, with my fellow costumers, the department felt inclusive.

Then, a couple of years into my job, around the time of the George Floyd event and Black Lives Matter movement, when everyone seemed to be talking about race—which was also just a time in my life where I finally felt comfortable talking about my race and my heritage—I felt more of a safe space to talk about my Nativeness openly. People were listening. And I began a journey at TCU toward my own self-discovery into what it means to be Native and White in this particular generation, when our elders are dying, and many communities are trying to preserve our languages. I was also contemplating how to hold space as a Native designer and what that means.

I think I invited my sister to attend an event [at TCU] around this time. I was blown away that there was any kind of Native presence happening on the campus I'd been walking around. I went to a very small private art school. It was a four-year college, but it was just art; it was very laser-focused into your medium. We didn't have a lot of clubs, unless they were art-based. There weren't many race-related community get-togethers. It was very diverse, actually. Still, I never found another Native student that I know of, and I was very involved in campus events. So I was just thrilled [when I went to the TCU event]. I still get like that anytime there's some kind of Native event happening, I just get so thrilled. Even if it's a Dallas–Fort Worth (DFW) community event or a gallery showing, I try to show up. My sister and I were so excited, and I think we introduced ourselves to Scott [Langston], who invited us to get involved.

When I was in my theater faculty staff group [at TCU], I didn't necessarily always feel that my Nativeness was celebrated there. But within my smaller faculty groups in the costuming area, I had colleagues who just outright championed me. And anytime there was an event, or an opportunity, or a gallery show even, they said, "Let's go. Let's drive to Dallas. Let's be on this journey together. Let's learn together." So that was a really special part of my life while at TCU. It's an amazing feeling to be supported and surrounded by people who were excited to learn with you. And like I said, I think they were being influenced by the Black Lives Matter movement and all wanting to be good allies and advocates for our students, too. So we were all just learning from each other. And as I go forward [after leaving TCU], I'm trying to be pickier about what I'm looking for in the workplace. I dream of a space that supports that diversity and learning. Not asking for perfection, but just a place that's open to learning about different experiences and perspectives.

I don't think I went into the job [at TCU] expecting that I would have any special role or be expected to offer any special perspective. Normally, people shy away from anything that would have to do with Native American representation in theater anyway, because it's really tricky to do, and there's not a lot of material out there that's inclusive. Plus we didn't have students to appropriately cast anyway. We talked often in our greenroom with faculty and staff throughout the years, heated discussions, about how best to represent our students when everyone around that table was White. There were several opportunities to hire someone who wasn't White during my time on staff. I sat on a lot of those committees, and that never seemed to happen, which was disappointing.

In terms of casting and the shows we were doing, everyone was trying, but we just were missing the mark. We started to diversify our students as they came in, really, really seeking out talent on purpose that was different than anything we'd ever had. Not just because they were Black and Brown. Just really, really trying to remove some of our biases to changing the expectations or prerequisites so that we were more inclusive. This was easy to do on the recruitment level, but not as easy to do when hiring somebody at the faculty/staffing level. So we would end up with really diverse casts, and the students then want to do plays by Black and Brown authors. But we don't have Black and Brown directors and designers. How do we get visiting artists who can represent these kids? There was a lot of conversation. Sitting outside of the table as a young female minority [who was staff, not faculty] made it just a very interesting space to be.

I had incidents during my time at TCU, but not on campus, where I was fighting those battles in terms of representation of Native peoples, and it's really hard. It's hard because these spaces have boards and leadership that is non-Native, and they often view things differently. For example, there are topics that if I talk to Native people about, we can unanimously agree that it is offensive. But non-Native leadership will say, "But, actually, it's not." I've been met with a lot of responses like, "But, actually, we tried this on a test audience, and everyone thought it was funny." Or "Actually, I'm part Cherokee and it's actually okay." Or "It's always been read this way, we can't change it." There's this listening that's not happening.

Uncomfortable change needs to happen in theater, and it's tricky. Theater needs to diversify. We need hairstylists who know how to style all kinds of hair, and makeup artists who know how to work with all skin tones. Costuming departments need to work to make sure they are matching skin tone to tights and undergarments in the right colors. TCU costumers do a great job of this, by the way. Where does gender identity and proper representation come in? In the theater world right now, there are a lot of places really celebrating this change. But I think TCU is moving at a slower pace; it needs to continue to have those difficult conversations and put a plan in motion.

Before I left TCU, I was surprised to hear that our department added a prerecorded land acknowledgment to play before each of our theater performances. We had just come out with ours [the language on the TCU Native American monument that was often used as an informal land acknowledgment before the university approved one]. The department knew of my cultural background, and I always thought we kind of had an understanding that if there was a project involving a Native American and Indigenous topic, I would be involved. But one day, a colleague said, "Oh, this acknowledgment was added." I honestly thought it was great! But I had no idea and was hurt and frustrated not to have been involved or even told about it. I felt it was a missed opportunity by the departmental leaders to not involve Native staff. And that really illustrates how I feel like I was treated overall in the wider department. My cultural connection was not recognized.

But I think it's really important to say again that while I didn't feel that inclusivity in my larger department [outside of the costuming groups], I did feel it in other spaces throughout the university. I felt so celebrated, to the point where I was overloading myself because I wanted to be a part of every event, I wanted to talk with and meet these people doing big things. I still had my everyday commitments, but I felt so uplifted in these other spaces. The students were excited, and the leaders were excited. The faculty and staff were advocating for change and having these rich conversations. That is for sure happening on TCU, absolutely. People (a lot of the same people in different capacities) just working their butts off trying to do right by the students and put into place this institutional change that will be part of the footprint of TCU. I'm just so thankful for that. Beyond the department, I had never felt more supported. I would go to an event, and people were so excited that I was there and would want to hear my perspective. But these people were like-minded. We'd all picked these groups. We'd all had these shared experiences. There are all kinds of things I sat in on. I was invited to some think tanks, a people of color network, diversity mixers. I was asked to the table. I was listened to.

After attending my first NISA event with my sister, I was just so excited about what was happening on campus. I wanted to see what else was going on. I think one of my natural gifts is planning and helping with events and coming to community with people. I was excited that there might be a place for me to do that. Like I've said, I wasn't necessarily being fulfilled culturally in my smaller spaces, so NISA felt like a really exciting opportunity for me. I felt like I'd gotten into the groove of my day-to-day job and was looking for something more. I inserted myself into the agenda and just kept raising my hand at meetings. I was busy, but I was honored to be a part of anything I was asked to contribute to. What was the most touching about my involvement was I felt like it was a space where I didn't have to be an expert. I just had to simply show up with my own experiences. I really appreciated that because, like I said, I'm still learning. And I have a very specific type of story in terms of where I come from and what I know.

On a personal level, participating in the events felt very validating. I felt that in standing up there, emceeing [at the dedication of the Native American monument on TCU's campus], I was very seen as a Native person on campus. It was an honor to be a part of that. I was so proud of the work, of the fact that we were bringing that monument to campus, and so thankful for the type of program that it was. Everyone who helped put together that program really listened to what the Wichita tribal leaders wanted in a dedication, but also what the students, faculty, and staff wanted in a dedication. For example, I think we had agreed that a meal [for the dedication participants and local Native attendees] was very important. And I still feel like that. Community and eating and sharing a meal has always seemed like something that's a through line, culturally across all tribal nations. The fact that we sat down together felt like home and like being with family, really. It was a very special day, even though it rained on us.

The art project [taking part in the selection of Comanche and Kiowa artist J. NiCole Hatfield's two paintings placed centrally in TCU's new administration building] was extremely special to be a part of. I'm still trying to figure out how to work within the capacity of my training as an artist and my cultural identity, and where those two things come to meet. Developing a relationship with J. NiCole was really thrilling. It felt like something big was happening, and it felt very tangible to me because it was art. The monument, too. They're both very visually powerful pieces. And those things, to me, because that's my world, feel so strong and impactful. The most touching part of both projects was hearing the community reaction. There were whisperings around it, people notic-ing it in my staff meetings—that was really cool. I would hear students that came through my studio talk about it, not even knowing that I was involved but seeing it as they passed by. That was really exciting.

And then my dad was almost in tears about seeing his great-great-grandfather [Comanche leader Quanah Parker, the subject of one of Hatfield's artworks] on the wall at this institution. I didn't know she [Hatfield] was going to do that. It felt incredibly special. The art pieces were touching for a lot of people. The students' reactions to these paintings were very powerful. I heard some say they couldn't believe this would happen. I think that has a lot to do with TCU being a White institution. It is a huge deal to have works like this permanently, or at least for a while, hopefully, in these spaces where changemakers are seeing them and being reminded on their path to their class or to their office that we are here. They remind them to not forget about us and to serve all the students of TCU, all the faculty and staff there, including even their smallest demographics like Native and Indigenous people.

I helped with a couple of the symposiums, but the one where we brought SOAR [Beyond Youth Inter-Tribal Drum and Dance Troupe, based in Dallas], the youth drum circle, was really neat. Having [Apsáalooke hip-hop artist] Supaman perform was a highlight too. I like to think I'm young, but I don't know what students listen to. I remember at the luncheon honoring Supaman as our visitor, we had Native students who had never come to a NISA event come to take a picture with him and to show their family who they got to meet on our campus. That's something so special that they're able to connect with. I just get giddy seeing the students' reactions to those kinds of special moments. I'm glad those things were able to happen.

My experience with NISA and all the support and encouragement from Scott [Langston] and other mentors I've had along the way were all positive takeaways from my time at TCU. [I remember] going into the DEI office and crying one time to Aisha [Torrey-Sawyer, director of Diversity and Inclusion Initiatives at TCU]. We had gotten to know each other through some events, and I was really struggling in my spaces. "This is so hard," I told her. The topic of change, speaking up as often the only Native person at a meeting and being talked over or ignored—things were weighing on my heart. I was also getting more and more involved with tasks on campus, and things were taking a lot longer than I thought they should to get changed.

Around that time, I had heard someone in the upper administration giving the feedback to our group that we were never going to get the same amount of support, the amount of funding, the amount of backing as other groups on campus because the Native American population is so small. That was really eye-opening to me because we're always going to be smaller. We've experienced cultural genocide. There's a reason that we're a smaller population, and that just was heartbreaking to me. And I think that until TCU can figure out how to completely get that idea out of their head, we're not going to have a lot of progress.

I asked Aisha, "How do you handle this? How are you standing upright? How are you—your mental health and your spirit—not crushed at the end of the day, just swimming upstream?" Pick your battles, she told me, and realize that it took years to get to where we are, so it will take time to make change. I was really thankful for her guidance. I've had conversations with other faculty I consider mentors and great allies about how to navigate change at TCU professionally and healthily. Advocating in my spaces on and off campus, as the lonely advocate at times, felt exhausting. But I started to understand that it was and is part of my responsibility as a Native artisan to speak up when it is needed, when I have the capacity.

Advice to TCU

In terms of TCU funding and support for Native and Indigenous students, I understand the idea of serving your students that are there, but it's completely unfair to have these smaller percentages of students unsupported. And it's scary [for them]. I can't imagine. That wasn't my experience. When I went to school, there was a cultural split for me, so I did feel supported by the White community I could lean on. I know not everybody has had that experience. I listened to students like Shara [Francis-Herne (Akwesasne Mohawk, TCU MA graduate 2019)]; I can't imagine how scary it could be for someone who relocates to this mostly White space for the first time without a commitment of support. How hurtful it must be to be met with, "Well, but you're such a small percentage." I won't share who it was that said this, but the point is I do remember hearing that. Everything just kind of shifted. I thought, "Whew! If this is where we are, and this is collectively what we think, we're not going to get the help we need, are we?" Big picture change takes strategy and planning, and there are so many things at play. But I think TCU has to shift their minds collectively—the administration, at least, the people who are making the decisions—so that we can get more funding and more of a specific student-focused liaison for our Native and Indigenous students. A professional in position with a willingness to continue to learn, to visit different nations, to ask questions, to develop relationships with patience, kindness, openness. And to just be ready to fight for our students in a professional way.

I think there's definitely a lot of learning that needs to happen regarding the general student population's understanding of Native identity. Many of my theater students grew up in the Texas school systems. They had Texas history, which included some information about the Comanche people. I noticed the Comanche are more recognized than Kiowa people. And then, they had some general knowledge of Plains Native Americans, and what that means. I can imagine a Native student coming from California or from the Pacific Northwest and all these assumptions being made that they belong to the Plains tribes that students learned about in Texas history. I don't live in a teepee now, but my ancestors did. I can imagine that [misunderstanding] would be even more shocking [for Native students from other parts of the country]. We are taught about the way Native peoples used to live. I believe most

TCU students have kind of archaic understanding, the history book-taught knowledge—however accurate that even is for the peoples that were around here in general Texas history—but not an understanding of contemporary Native people. I think TCU does a really great job of illustrating and focusing more on contemporary people through NISA and the special programs they sponsor, though. When I first started, we posed a question to the students [in NISA], and something that they really wanted to focus on was that we're contemporary people. So I think having that be a focus of the panels and the learning we have been able to bring here has been really beneficial.

To a Native staff member at TCU, I would say to find your people, find your support groups, and attend as many of these outside events as possible. The school-sponsored events, the ones that are celebrating culture, celebrating differences—that's where you find your people. I really did feel so supported and heard in all of those groups. I had no shame. I'm sure it was completely inappropriate to walk into the DEI office and introduce myself. I also think, though, that if you're wanting to make change that you need to be ready to work, because it was an avalanche. As soon as I said, "Yeah, let's do this, let me get involved," there was no shortage of opportunity for the work. But at the same time, I hope that others have the foresight to take a step back when it's too much. If you're someone who's looking for an opportunity to make change and to grow an institution that needs to change, this is a great place to be. There are definitely allies there, but there is much to be done.

I think a lot of seeds are being planted. I hope that the legacy [of what has been happening recently as part of the Native American and Indigenous Peoples Initiative at TCU] lives on and that things are put in place so that for whoever comes next, it's there as a permanent part of the institution. That means that curriculum, guest artists, and guest lectures are all on the books. Perhaps there is a grant to make sure that guests come back, and we are having continued dialogue. My hope is that NISA will be a constant, not reduced down to nothing. I love seeing these visual reminders of Native people on campus, but I think it really comes down to the people, the students.

[My advice to TCU's leaders is that] I think we need to refocus. We need to redirect our understanding of why our Native and Indigenous students need the support. It's not because it's a smaller demographic, but because it is a demographic of students on campus and a demographic that is so culturally vast. I think it is so important to understand that a table of five Native and Indigenous people can be representing all different parts of the country and many different cultures. I would love to see the administration take time to meet with those students face to face, hear who they are and where they come from, and find out what they need. We did have an opportunity to sit down with the new provost, which was good but felt very fleeting. I hope NISA can have many more in-depth conversations in the future with her and our administration. There is no way, unless our leaders have come from a school with a huge Native population, that they come in with any kind of understanding of what a Native student may need. Just taking that time to acknowledge even the small amount of students and staff and faculty that are here, to really make them a priority, would be the first step. It would be a very easy task, since we are, after all, such a small group of people.

In thinking in terms of working in a department [at a university], I think who has a seat at the table is very important. I like to see all kinds of groups represented. I have my own biases that I'm working on, and I'd love to be in a place that is open to understanding and giving grace to me while I'm learning. I think that's really the only way you get things done with people is if you're giving grace. If you're just continuing to get upset about missteps we're taking, then we're not moving forward. Sometimes, we all can get scared away from change. But I think it's exciting. And I don't always see the forest for the trees. I'm realizing that about myself, which has been such a great part of being a part of TCU and understanding the logistics of how things are done—slowing down and realizing things take time. Being part of a group that's excited for the possibility of change and rewriting the norms in terms of what are the credentials that you need to get a seat at the table. Because that looks different if we want different types of people at our table. That's something that I think is really important.

In terms of day-to-day work, I don't know that I would go back to academia, even as much as I enjoy working with students. I am very interested in the idea of preserving traditional dress and traditional costuming. I'm a pattern maker, so I understand that lot of that knowledge is passed down verbally and is not written down. Our traditional dressmakers are dying. Every time knowledge gets passed down, you lose a little piece of that information, and dress is changing. Just in my own lifetime, what ceremonial dress looked like from then to now—the very contemporary ribbon skirt—is changing due to the access to materials. I'm not a historian, but I'm incredibly passionate about preserving this before it's lost. I would love the opportunity to do that that kind of work: to collect garments, pattern them, and keep and preserve them. I love when I can get my hands on things, turn them inside out, and see how and why they were made.

But honestly, it's such a huge task. It's intimidating to me. Every time I entertain it, I shy away from it. Even if I were to do just Comanche dress, that's a big chunk of knowledge to work on. I have great capacity to do it. That's what I do every day, make these patterns, write them down, and fold them up. That's what I do. I guess being faculty and having the support to do that research would be something that could be really exciting to me. I'd love to sit at a table where I'm not seen as a novelty, and my work is seen as a valuable in helping us all learn about how we as a community have been impacted by Native and Indigenous people. Wherever that community is, it would be a really great group to be a part of.

PART III:
BEING IN RELATION WITH NATIVE COMMUNITY PARTNERS

HOW TO TALK ABOUT MMIW:
Pedagogy and Partnerships between Indigenous Community
Organizers and University Faculty
by Jodi Voice Yellowfish, Nino Testa, and Theresa Strouth Gaul

In this chapter, Jodi Voice Yellowfish (Cherokee, Muscogee [Creek], Oglala Lakota) and Dr. Nino Testa, who at the time of the interview was associate professor of professional practice in women and gender studies at TCU (now visiting scholar at the Women's Institute of Chatham University), reflect on their experiences working together on an ongoing pedagogical effort that is part of TCU's Native American and Indigenous Peoples Initiative. Voice Yellowfish cofounded and chairs a Dallas-based advocacy organization that addresses the crisis of Missing and Murdered Indigenous Women in Native communities. Her work with Testa and other TCU faculty and students on MMIW pedagogy and projects provides the opportunity for the two of them to reflect on what they've learned. The essay uses a dialogue format that emphasizes their collaboration and mutual learning. It culminates in suggestions for "best practices" for community-based organizations and educational institutions to employ when undertaking such collaborations. Dr. Theresa Strouth Gaul, a cofounder of NAIPI, former director of Women and Gender Studies, and professor of English at TCU, contributed context and synthesis in this essay.

Opposite page from left to right: Jodi Voice Yellowfish. *Photo by CINPHOTOS*; Nino Testa.; Theresa Strouth Gaul.

Introduction

In a book dedicated to critically evaluating the efforts of a university to acknowledge its connections and responsibilities to Native American and Indigenous peoples and the land, it is important to take time to consider the role of pedagogy in such an initiative. At TCU, NAIPI has incorporated various forms of teaching, including programming, workshops, and curricular projects. A significant portion of the work in the TCU curriculum has coalesced around MMIW, through an ongoing partnership with the Dallas-based organization MMIW Texas Rematriate, which advocates for Native communities, supports the relatives of missing and murdered Native and Indigenous people, and cultivates networks of care for the Native community in North Texas.

In this essay, we focus on TCU's pedagogical efforts to educate faculty and students on MMIW as a means to identify generalizable principles and "best practices" that may be helpful to other advocacy organizations or institutions of higher education in approaching this topic or engaging in such collaborations. This is not to say TCU was fully successful or even should be considered a role model in its attempts. Nonetheless, the process of engaging in this pedagogical initiative showed both university and community participants what is necessary and important to know and practice.

While there has been somewhat of an increase in public discourse about MMIW in recent years due to the tireless work, advocacy, and activism of Native American and Indigenous organizers, there has not been an accompanying surge in discussion regarding how non-Native communities and educational institutions should ethically and intentionally learn from and support the efforts of Indigenous MMIW advocates. Nor have principles emerged for Native organizers to consider when deciding whether and how to engage non-Native communities in education and advocacy efforts. Even if they are well-intentioned, misguided attempts to address MMIW in university-level curricula can incorrectly frame it as a new phenomenon or can sunder violence against Native women, girls, and Two Spirit people from the histories of gendered violence that have been a foundational tool of ongoing colonization.[1]

The impetus toward this pedagogical work at TCU began in 2019 when the university began awarding an annual MMIW scholarship of $5000 to one undergraduate student each year as part of its ongoing NAIPI. The idea for this scholarship emerged in a 2019 TCU NAIPI workshop titled "Partnering with Native American Communities," which featured Jodi Voice Yellowfish discussing her work as cofounder of MMIW Texas Rematriate.[2] The workshop panel also included Chebon Kernell (Seminole), a cofounder of TCU's NAIPI, and Shara Francis-Herne (Akwesasne Mohawk). At that time, Francis-Herne was a TCU graduate student who has since gone on to work with the Sovereign Bodies Institute, an organization that centers Indigenous knowledge to advance culturally informed and community-engaged research on gender and sexual violence against Indigenous people.

TCU's MMIW scholarship "seeks to honor missing and murdered Indigenous women, girls, and two-spirit people and raise awareness about this issue, educate future leaders who will address this and other Native American issues, and provide financial support to undergraduate students at Texas Christian University who demonstrate commitment to these issues." In establishing this scholarship, TCU took on a responsibility to provide instructors with "tools to meaningfully and appropriately engage this difficult topic" in full recognition of "the sacredness of all missing and murdered Indigenous women, girls, and two-spirit people." This recognition requires an "understand[ing] that this is not merely a topic of study and research" but an ongoing crisis in the Native community.[3]

After the establishment of the scholarship and continuing through the time of the writing of this essay, Voice Yellowfish has consulted with TCU's faculty and collaborated in an effort to organize a pedagogical support structure for faculty who plan to incorporate MMIW as a topic or MMIW-focused projects in their courses. Working inside TCU to organize the activities were Dr. Nino Testa, a second coauthor of this article who was at that time associate director of the Women and Gender Studies Department, and Dr. Scott Langston, TCU's former Native American Nations and Communities Liaison and cofounder of NAIPI.

Voice Yellowfish led two pedagogy workshops for faculty at TCU sponsored by the Women and Gender Studies Department: the first in 2019 included cofounder Snowy Voice (Cherokee, Muscogee [Creek], Oglala Lakota), and the second in 2021 included vice chair Christy Swimmer McLemore (Cherokee). Both workshops had the goal of helping faculty teaching across the curriculum conceptualize the inclusion of MMIW in their courses. In addition, Langston produced a resource guide for faculty to use and tracked the progress of faculty's engagement with MMIW.[4] A range of on-campus and virtual programming during the pandemic, including TCU's Native American and Indigenous Peoples Day Symposium in 2021, featured speakers from Native communities and organizations who are affected by and advocate on this crisis.

Over the course of the six years since 2019, at least thirteen TCU faculty incorporated community-engaged MMIW materials and assignments into their courses.[5] Reflecting on these experiences, we use this essay to highlight successes and challenges in such ongoing collaborations between university faculty and Indigenous community partners. It is important to us, in keeping with TCU's NAIPI goals and scholarship in the field of Indigenous feminist studies, to strive to avoid some of the potential harm and risks of this kind of curricular project. Introducing MMIW into a course without establishing foundational terms and knowledge risks participating in a dangerous erasure of ongoing colonial violence. If local Native organizers are asked to participate in learning that lacks proper framing, their labor may be exploited for little purpose. Indeed, they may be tokenized without having their urgent work supported in any substantive way.[6] Acknowledging these dangers, Voice Yellowfish and faculty at TCU worked to center Indigenous ways of understanding and responding to MMIW while asking members of the TCU community to grapple with their responsibilities in engaging with the crisis and identifying opportunities to support the work of Native organizers.

In this chapter, we have two goals: to reflect on what is necessary to scaffold a discussion of MMIW in a college classroom or other communal learning environment and to identify practices for MMIW advocates to consider before initiating similar projects with settler universities. As Voice Yellowfish explains, "We aren't talking about MMIW; we are talking about how we talk about MMIW" in this essay. Recent literature on the teaching and learning of MMIW as a topic in the classroom presents two prominent themes, which have organized our curricular work and grounded this conversation: the need to center trauma-informed, Indigenous methods in curricular initiatives and the imperative to confront the limits of settler university spaces and curricula as sites for decolonizing projects.[7]

With these themes in mind, and given the urgency of MMIW, our conversation underlines the need for all curricular and programmatic campus initiatives to (1) prioritize the needs and requests of local Native advocacy organizations and (2) articulate the responsibilities toward these local relationships in the learning outcomes of courses, units, or lessons that thematize or engage MMIW. As an illustration of what this might look like, we cite the example of how we arrived at the theme of our 2021 Native American and Indigenous Peoples Day Symposium, "Missing and Murdered Indigenous Women, Girls, and Two-Spirit People: From Awareness to Action." The decision to focus on MMIW emerged from the aforementioned 2019 workshop featuring Native leaders. TCU pursued this theme precisely because local Native organizers asked faculty to do so. At every stage of the planning, local organizers had control over the agenda for the symposium, including the invitation of the keynote speaker, Annita Lucchesi, founder and director of Research and Outreach of the Sovereign Bodies Institute. As a result of this event, MMIW Texas Rematriate developed an ongoing and mutually beneficial relationship with Lucchesi and the Sovereign Bodies Institute, which has included several collaborations on missing persons cases that have resulted in the recovery of those missing persons. Conceiving of TCU's relationship with the Native community as rooted in responsibility to redistribute resources rather than as tokenizing of Native knowledge opened up immediate material benefits to MMIW

Texas Rematriate and demonstrates the mutuality and reciprocity that must be present in such collaborations.

We have chosen to structure what follows as a dialogue between a community partner (Voice Yellowfish) and a faculty/staff member within a university (Testa) in order to honor the collaborative framework of the ongoing initiative. Moreover, we have intentionally centered Voice Yellowfish's perspectives so we share her expertise as an activist and educator with readers. The exchange below is not an exact transcript of the conversation we had; rather, it is an edited reflection informed by our research on pedagogical practices related to MMIW. We leave in references to prior conversations we have had about this topic to demonstrate that this is an ongoing process of learning together.

Dialogue

Jodi Voice Yellowfish:

I like the idea of focusing on how to talk about MMIW as opposed to actually discussing MMIW.

Nino Testa:

Me too. I think this is a really fruitful way to frame our conversation, and I think that's going to be helpful to people.

Jodi Voice Yellowfish:

Yeah, I'm so used to having to go into a non-Native presentation space and know exactly what to say. And because of that, I already know the questions that are going to be asked because they are usually the same or very similar. I already know because it's a really concise specific topic, but then the background can be so broad. That's what we are going to want to see come out of this chapter, I think, is to understand how to digest all that broad topic information that surrounds the crisis. Because I think that can be overwhelming, and those overwhelming feelings can take away from what you're about to learn, which is about MMIW.

Nino Testa:

I really like the framing that you came up with as well, because for me, on the instructor side or the program planning side, we were thinking about, "How do we engage instructors?" It really did feel like we were saying, "Here's a topic that you need to learn more about before you're going to be equipped to teach it."

And as we continued the work, it became clear that it wasn't just learning about the topic. It was about how to engage ethically in this conversation as a learner—and also in solidarity with local Native communities—as opposed to as an expert. I think this can be challenging for a lot of instructors, even the best feminist teachers. The work needs to move beyond reading and discussing a text on a syllabus.

Jodi Voice Yellowfish:

It's definitely a concept that's foreign to me, that instructor side of things—to feel comfortable with saying or believing, "Oh, I read this, and we can go through it, and now I'm teaching it." But there's also an art to that. There's an art to facilitating conversation AND unpacking uncomfortable history, because not many people can do that. I became accustomed to folks not knowing that it's going to get uncomfortable, and then having to walk them through that. I don't think I was prepared or knew that that would be such a big part of the awareness around this crisis. But I think everyone that does MMIW/Missing and Murdered Indigenous People (MMIP) work in some way—whether it's on the advocacy side or you're on the ground with cases—I don't think anyone was prepared for that. I think that's because we haven't had that opportunity to have those frank conversations and actually teach in the process. So it's brand new, and I think that's just a new concept for academia anyway. This brand new thing that we're all learning in real time.

Nino Testa:

And then there's the relationship between global or national or very macro-level discussions about a topic and, as you're saying, the work that communities are doing locally. I think that gap is oftentimes the challenge that faculty don't know how to navigate—understanding they aren't just teaching about an abstract phenomenon. There are people literally right here who we need to be engaged with. Learning from and supporting their work was a big part of our learning about this, as you're saying, in real time.

You mentioned the discomfort that some non-Native people have learning about MMIW. What aspects of your work most make people uncomfortable?

Jodi Voice Yellowfish:

I think there's a couple. This is very broad, in a general sense: understanding and feeling about things around racism. I was really surprised to see that in my personal experiences of how it's been, the racism side of things has come out around the idea of accountability, because accountability to some can look and feel like an attack. But wanting the best accountability practices from law enforcement or government agencies should be positive. It should be like, "Oh, this is going to help me do better." But often it's felt more like, "Oh, you're doing this because I'm White." However, power and authority, law enforcement and government agency positions, don't necessarily mean White. People often equate power to race, which isn't necessarily wrong either, because history has shown us that. But in the present day there is so much to unpack in regards to power and how communities handle that aspect of their existence. So that was a conversation I wasn't expecting that early on.

It's always an uncomfortable thing when you bring up race anyway. But when I offer historical examples of racism, then people are like, "Okay, that makes more sense in how race is an issue." Because even with history in general, we have to unpack that history in terms of how we got to this point. When we bring up positions in history, that doesn't necessarily mean if you're non-Native or you're White, that there's blame. It doesn't mean that. It just means, if it comes up within the scope of MMIW/MMIP work, then we're just asking you to understand. Be open to seeing how race is a part of this. Before I started doing this side of discussing this topic and work, I never really thought that that was going to be such an issue, because it makes me uncomfortable as well.

Nino Testa:

That's such an interesting example, too, because it relates so much to the challenge that I think we just named with faculty, which is navigating the gap between these expansive topics like histories of colonialism, histories of violence or racism, and actually sitting and talking to a person who is experiencing violence. That's a big part of what we tried to emphasize in the MMIW pedagogy workshops. It wasn't just about the stats or the data, and this is not a history that has passed.

Jodi Voice Yellowfish:

Yes, and I think I was talking about the broad sense, but when it's specifically academia, or a university setting, this comes up because students usually want that quantitative aspect of anything. And this topic does not have that. So to have somebody understand that lack of quantitative information, you have to start going backward a little and unpacking some stuff, to understand that there is no government data or count of MMIW cases, because it just hasn't been there. We still don't have the infrastructure to present day-to-day work adequately enough to provide that.

I can see the frustration when I say that, especially if I'm able to talk to students who are doing a project that has particular guidelines or requirements. Like when I helped a class with a project they were doing that involved making informational posters for an advertising agency-type project. The assignment directions were like, "You have to make this for a company. This is how you're going to work." And that was really hard, and I could just see the frustration of the students and the sense of "How do you expect for me to get this information, this data?" And then when you talk about, if you're going to use a photo or a name, the need to ask the family for permission—that was just something that blew their minds. You could see the puzzled looks and thoughts like "What? I can't just research this in a book and online?" That's definitely something I know is super uncomfortable. I can see how it's stressful as well, being in that student setting and how you can have an instructor or a professor that's like, "This is what you have got to do now." And you can just see confusion and frustration in them.

Nino Testa:

And perhaps that was a failure on the instructor's side if we are talking about what the faculty's responsibilities are before engaging MMIW. Before bringing in a community expert, what should a faculty member have to do to prepare for this collaboration? I think at least part of that needs to be preparing students to think beyond a grade for an assignment, because they're so structured to do that: "What are my requirements? What do I need to do?" In this case, the desire to get a requirement right actually has a potential to do harm or to mislearn, to misunderstand what we're trying to engage with. Assignments like this, it seems, should explicitly thematize or prioritize Native understandings of data, the sacredness of names and images, and the ongoing consent of those impacted.

What else, in your experience, should faculty be doing in advance of engaging substantively with MMIW?

Jodi Voice Yellowfish:

A basic vocabulary is a place to start because the simplest of ideas of how we work are really foreign in academic settings. The lack of quantitative anything, any data, anything like that. But also why it's that way.

And the use of words like *relative* and *sacred* are not something that traditionally non-Native students are going to have to deal with in a class project. But even though it's going to be different when you're learning this, how you implement any of what you learn into not just the classroom setting but in your life and the work that you do, that's where it's going to show up later on. Because the understanding of data being sacred comes from this concept of what relative means to American Indian people and Indigenous people.

It really stuck with me when a student said via an after-presentation survey that the term and idea of *relative* was so foreign. I thought, if a student is in social work or any kind of medical field, anything like that, how do you not have that sense of care? But that's something I feel is innate to Indigenous people. We're relatives in so many ways. Even how we talk about our own family systems. I'll mention very nonchalantly, "Oh, I've got to pick up my grandson." And people are like, "Wait, grandson? What are you talking about? You're not . . . "

And I'm just like, "It's my nephew, but . . . " And there's a lesson of how we are.

I think that responsibility is on the folks on the MMIW side as well. It's so ingrained in our community and how we work that we go into this other phase of talking about this crisis. We forget we must unpack how we got to the "concept" of relative and explain how this young lady that's missing right now is seen as our relative now.

Nino Testa:

Can you share a little more about that understanding of *relative* and how it impacts your work?

Jodi Voice Yellowfish:

So thinking about *relative*, I go over this when we do just our organization presentation and we introduce MMIW. The very first thing we do is break down the name: MMIW, MMIP, MMIR. And people are like, "Well, what is the R? I get P for people, but what is R?" It is *relative*, and we have to break that down. Every tribe has a different way of how we connect. But especially here in an urban setting, we're a relocation site [for the US Bureau of Indian Affairs' Urban Relocation Program beginning in the 1950s]. We're not necessarily the same tribe with the same kinship terms and terminology and all that. But because of this shared struggle and overall culture, we're still able to connect and call somebody *brother* and *sister* and *auntie*. Some of our work at MMIW TX Rematriate now is uplifting kinship in a space where it's not necessarily your ancestral kinship ways, but everybody needs an uncle, everybody needs an auntie. When I break that down, I can see the light go off, "Oh, okay." You have that lightbulb-go-off-moment. It's so simple, but it makes sense.

Now, we closed a case [of a missing Indigenous person] last week, and it was somebody that I grew up with. I remember that one got me. That one was just, "Ugh." I was like, "This one sucks. I don't want to do this one." But I was the one that was first speaking with the family, and there was some mix up with our schedules, with our group. And I asked, "So who's going to do this intake? 'Cause I'm already talking. I don't want to do the intake."[8] And that reminded me, this is why we do this work. Because we know that we're not going to get the care from law enforcement or whoever is going to help this specific family and case. Because I had that pain in my heart over someone I knew, I was reminded that I cared and would do my all in that moment.

And that's something, too, the care we give shows up in the follow-through. And because the Dallas Police Department closed that case based on a tip, and we thought, "Are you trying to tell me that we have more protocol to close a case than the police department does?" Nobody had laid eyes on them [the missing person]. How does that work?

So there's that care again, because we have that care as a relative, we want to make sure we follow through. And so it's almost like our best practices come from that relative and kinship care. And we don't see that coming from the places that are supposed to keep us safe, like the police or whoever. So, yeah, you have to give the example to help somebody who doesn't live that kinship way in their everyday life.

Nino Testa:

Thank you for sharing that. And was he found?

Jodi Voice Yellowfish:

Yeah, yeah, yeah.

Nino Testa:

I'm so glad. Thank you for talking through that experience to demonstrate the depth of the term *relative*.

Another concept that is central to engaging MMIW is the concept of the *sacred* and of *sacred data* in particular. You've mentioned that that's a roadblock for student learning and engagement, as well as faculty understanding. It feels like challenging a model of knowledge that is based in the sharing of data, and the "right" to access data is central to understanding this concept.

Jodi Voice Yellowfish:

Yes, I can see that. I feel like challenging that dynamic really comes with challenging power. Because if there's a young cis[gender]-het-[erosexual] White male in this class, I can tell you, they already think they have more power than I ever would. But they're not the ones doing this work and seeing how often the work is needed, or how often it turns bad and how many people are still presently lost all the time. But I can see how challenging the norm is challenging your power, because it's just something so foreign to you.

I haven't really used the term *sacred* in presentations, until just recently, until really that student I mentioned earlier was like, "I just never understood this *relative* concept. It's so new." But that student was like, "It's such a beautiful concept and it works." And it made everything make more sense for her.

Students often feel that things should be black-and-white and in numbers. One thing I've learned to stress when I do any kind of education and or presentation in the past couple of years is that if you want an easy way to research and find numbers, it's never going to be right because of history. History hasn't given us the opportunity to even see this crisis as a crisis until recently. Not even a whole decade, we're inching up on a decade, maybe, of the terminology associated with MMIW and this overall crisis. It's new, this understanding that we've been dealing with this. So I think that kind of helps students understand, "I know you want numbers, but it's not going to happen."

So the easiest way to learn is by understanding a case. And then going into the cultural side of it, why you have to respect that it's a person and not just a name and a number. And you're not just going to give "a name and a year they were murdered." That's not them, that's not that person. And it's disrespectful to be that way. And so you have to kind of, not sneak those things in, but ease your way into that, to soften the blow of, "You can't just research this and get the answer." It's not that way. So it's showing it's sacred, but you have to end with the aspect of sacred. You've got to go over these little hills to get to, *this is why it's sacred.*

Nino Testa:

Would you recommend for faculty who are not Native to try to introduce the concept of the *sacred*, for instance, before inviting a Native
MMIW advocate to visit a class or discussing the topic at all?

Jodi Voice Yellowfish:

I think it would be good. I think it would be helpful to introduce it,
but just very basically, like: "Many cultures—or even if it was for our
organization—this organization really believes in kinship. They do this
work because being a relative is sacred, which means that anything
surrounding that case is sacred." It's very simple, but you don't fully
get it until you're in the conversation. So that little bitty intro of, "What
is *sacred*?" But then you hear it. Even if you're getting familiar with it,
just by reading it one time, it's not a shock when it comes.

Nino Testa:

What is important to you that students understand about something
being sacred?

Jodi Voice Yellowfish:

I think understanding the sacred would be understanding that you
can't always see and touch the sacred. You can't always just say,
"We have sacred sites and do ceremonies." You don't have to be
at these sites. You don't have to be in ceremony to incorporate the
sacred into your life. So I feel there has to be an understanding of
that, that you can't see it, you can't always touch it, but it's always
there. And it's a matter of whether you're going to be open and
respect what's there.

So if you're living your life that way, like the folks that are doing the
work in our organization, we're able to go in with a different kind of
care. 'Cause even if you're in the medical field, you work in a hospital,
you work in a clinic, or you're in law enforcement and you are called
to very violent situations, people who deal with rape cases or domestic violence, you can see the sacredness of each person. But if you
don't approach the situation in the right way, relatives of the missing
person are not going to share anything with you that you need to

help locate the missing person. And I feel like that's what separates our work from black-and-white, filling out a report—us spending time to respect the sacred that is a person.

We go in, and we respect that we need to talk to maybe the elder in the home, or respect that this person that's dealing with domestic violence has a baby. Things that can be often ignored. You can see the issue, but you're dealing with this one individual. The sacredness about that person can be the role they have, which is a mother or a father or a grandmother or grandfather. So it's those kinds of things. The sacred is everything about a person, not just what you can visually see. It's just there.

Nino Testa:

Thank you for sharing that. I think that helps tremendously. And I think it hopefully also gives students and faculty a way of approaching not just MMIW but the work more broadly that you're doing.

And this is a point you have made many times before: that MMIW is not just about MMIW. MMIW itself is connected to all elements of contemporary and historical Native life and experience.

Acknowledging this, what are some of the other things that a faculty member would want to think about before engaging this topic in a classroom?

Jodi Voice Yellowfish:

I feel like, with our existence, our entire existence has been left out. Even in history, our history hasn't been shared in the most truthful way. And what has been shared puts us in a place where we're constantly playing catch up, especially with society understanding our history. What's been taught isn't necessarily the truth, but it's from a conqueror's point of view. And so to conquer people, that's a very violent thing in many ways in the moment, with battles, massacres, things like that. Can you literally say everybody's been massacred, even if there was a massacre? There's still this survival and carrying on of culture. I feel like it's a very vital thing to share our culture and our vibrancy of song and dance and language and food, art and film and music. There's so many things that can highlight that today. So

Members of MMIW TX Rematriate at TCU's seventh annual Native American and Indigenous Peoples Day Symposium, October 2, 2023. Front row (left to right): Jodi Voice Yellowfish, Diana Parton, Tana Takes Horse, Ruth Thunder Hawk; back row: Michael Tongkeamha. *TCU Marketing and Communication, photo by James Anger.*

I think it's very necessary to touch on that. Even within our work, we have to say, "Even if somebody's found, that doesn't mean the case is over. Their journey's just starting."

I like the vibrancy of the living, because I wouldn't be here speaking about it if we weren't thriving in some way, or we hadn't survived to the fullest that we could be. And now, we're in this renaissance of our culture—being art. I'm in a lot of art spaces now, because of the work I do with the City of Dallas Arts and Culture Advisory Commission. I always tell people, "I've never seen myself as an artist," even though I do sing or dance or do beadwork. My family members, my mother makes all of my dresses, things like that, and I know she doesn't view herself as an artist either. So there's been this protection around our culture being seen as art, because if it's culture, there's this different kind of respect to it. But now, like I said, we're in this kind of renaissance of this art where our regalia has morphed very organically into really high fashion. Or our culture with song and dance has really changed into different performances of how you can share your culture. And you're not sharing ceremony or the things you hold very intimately sacred, and you can do it in a very healthy way.

I think it's really vital to share that now, because it is changing. We're finally, I feel, healthy enough to want to do it. For so long, we were in survival mode. Colonization leaves an entire group of people in shock, and you don't function properly when you're in shock and you're in crisis mode and you're trying to survive. And people historically are like, "What do you mean survive? The government stopped doing this at this time or this time. Or you get support, and or you have reservations too." Things like that. But things were literally beaten out of us. And I think now is the most important time to highlight that our culture is vibrant and still very much alive.

Nino Testa:

What I love about having you and your organization present in classes and at campus events is that your framework is such a powerful model of the life of the community that goes into your organization. Students don't just learn about "crisis," they get to learn about your programs like Auntie Time, Uncle Time, and Two-Spirit Relative Time [safe and confidential opportunities for relatives in the Dallas Native community to talk with and support each other]. They learn about how the organization is embedded in a larger community, and that it's not just a community that only focuses on MMIW. They get to see the organizing, the advocacy, and the community support and networking, and how the idea of the sacred is woven into the work that's done as opposed to being an additive thing. I understand the very real danger of only focusing on trauma and violence in relation to Native people—and some folks have asked us why we keep focusing on MMIW for this reason. But even as your organization is centered on MMIW, it is also so full of life.

Jodi Voice Yellowfish:

Yeah. One part of that is that every time I go and speak or things like that—it's a little thing I feel like, but maybe it's not such a little thing—but I try to wear my ribbon skirts, and I try to wear jewelry. Or

I try to, in our presentations, have art in some way on the slides that people can see and refer to. I have said at different times, wearing my skirts make me feel stronger. I've told people, too, that when my daughter was younger, we did a ribbon skirt class and she made a little painting of a ribbon skirt. I asked her to talk about what she likes about ribbon skirts. And she said, "I feel safe."

So it's about how important culture is, and it may just seem like fashion, like it's a way of expressing who we are, but there's so much to it because we couldn't be ourselves for so long. Literally one of the most powerful governments in the world didn't want us to be who we truly are supposed to be. So there's a lot of fear around just expressing yourself. I think it's really important now because even from when I first started doing the work, I didn't see as much art surrounding MMIW. And there's so much art now in so many forms.

Nino Testa:

So we've talked a lot about what faculty should be thinking about and what prep work they should do before engaging MMIW, but what would you like for Native organizers or community members who are doing MMIW work to think about or to know before they initiate collaborations with academic audiences or maybe even other non-Native partners?

Jodi Voice Yellowfish:

I often share, especially with folks that I'm close to or work with closely, especially within our organization, that once you start to speak, you get asked to speak all the time. Once you do and you do it with ease, you're asked all the time, you're asked to speak, and not only to speak and to educate, but you're asked to speak for people and for your community. And that's a big responsibility, and it can weigh heavy.

I feel like oftentimes we have this "I need to do this" feeling, like you can't say no to the opportunity. But I tell, especially the members in our organization, that you don't have to, because I want people to be cognizant of the fact that you can be tokenized. And that's a very real thing. I used to have to say "no" to a lot of things, because I wasn't actually being heard. I was asked to open an event with a prayer, or,

"Can you do this?" I'm like, "No, I don't want to pray in public." And that event planner would be like, "Oh, well, we're doing this and we're going to talk about this." And I would have to hit them with, "Well, why can't I talk about that? And why am I not in that conversation?"

So that's one thing I want people to be aware of, that it's okay to plan and to work with the organizers of an event, and see their intent and see how the whole entire thing is going to work. And is it going to benefit your work, or is it going to exploit it in some way? Because we do have to deal with that trauma porn. Some planners do want to just look at us as victims, and that doesn't always get empathy. It just gets sympathy, and that doesn't always help or uplift our work.

But on the flip side of that, we still must tread with caution, but you have to be open to working with non-Native people. And that's something that I know a lot of MMIW leaders and organizers and groups shy away from. I kind of feel like, especially with TCU, people [in the Native community] ask, "How did y'all get to do this? How are you doing it?" And I have to tell people, "You have to try, and it's kind of trial and error. You won't always know everyone's intentions or if it's going to work, until you try. But in the end that can be your sign not to go back, or you don't do it again. Because you must build and grow in a healthy way."

I think one thing, too, with that victimhood that I mentioned earlier, sometimes our own people, they can live in that space. It's hard to get out of because it requires a lot of healing. I've seen a lot of people go into spaces where they feel like they're owed something, but we're not necessarily owed anything that can be gained in that specific setting that will effect change and or contribute to our overall healing and well-being. What might one gain out of going into a university setting with an accusatory tone or very angry stance? Anger is often warranted but must be harnessed.

We can't blame people for something that their ancestors did, but you can make them aware of how they may be benefiting from it all. That is different and requires education and acknowledgment first. I think that's something that Native organizers need to remind themselves of, especially in the university setting. What professors need to be aware of is that if you don't do your due diligence beforehand, you may be working with an angry individual who students cannot learn from or that they are just not fit to teach on that specific topic.

Nino Testa:

Tokenizing comes back to the responsibilities of the faculty. Faculty members need to ask themselves, "What are my goals in not just covering the topic, but especially inviting a community member to come and talk about their work? How can this be mutually beneficial to the organization?" We should be asking ourselves how we prepare the space given the realities that you have been outlining.

One really important point that we have talked about connected to tokenization is that faculty shouldn't be asking an organizer to come in and give this whole history. It's not your job to come in and teach centuries of history or Native experience or colonialism. That's prep work that needs to be done in advance to then invite you into the space to share your expertise, not ask you to rehearse everything. And that could be for any topic—you're not coming in to speak on all Native American life or culture and you're not going to tell us everything. That's not your job.

Jodi Voice Yellowfish:

Yeah. Yeah, definitely. I think one thing to know is that if you're inviting someone into your space to educate on a topic, be sure to do the research to see if they are connected to a community that they're saying they are connected to. If they're saying they worked with this tribe or that tribe, look and see who they worked with and that they didn't cause harm in that community. Because you could have done the work, but that community may not have wanted you there. You could have been run out of that community for all somebody knows. I think you need to be able to actively say that you're either working with this community or this tribe, or you're from this tribe or this community in some way.

I always tend to say with the Dallas Native community that "I was born and raised here. These aren't my ancestral homelands. My family came on relocation. But this is why I'm doing the work here, because 'I am of the community.'" And I think that that helps so much in understanding why we're doing the work here. I think that almost clears it up, and lets you lean into the work easier. It helps the students understand where I am positioned in history and what my point of view is, and how I also may simplify or only touch on certain aspects of history to get to the crisis of MMIW, as that is my focus.

Nino Testa:

What are your thoughts on classes or groups of non-Native students going to, for instance, an event that you organize or a powwow or some other community event? This has become a central part of many community-engaged pedagogical initiatives, but it seems to carry the possibility of being harmful.

Jodi Voice Yellowfish:

When our organization does presentations, we have a whole segment on how you can help. And that's so important to go over with non-Native people, because especially with our work. We don't want to come in with that angry tone I mentioned before, but we want to invite you in a healthy way that we can build and grow and not just, "You have to do this. We don't want to do that."

We *always* say before we start explaining how you can help, "This is going to be a little uncomfortable, because we're going to ask you to check your privilege." And that doesn't necessarily mean race, doesn't mean check it because you're White. It means, you can see as a male, as a cis-het male, as an employer at a job, as an instructor, as a professor—and that can be a female professor—that you have this power in many different ways. I can always see, especially in students, I can see them literally writing down word for word what I say. *Also* don't center yourself in the crisis. You're not going to go in and be a savior and solve the crisis that is MMIW. You're not going to, because we have to lead it, and we have to do the work. I often feel like people have never heard that or been told anything like that. I knew the words "White savior complex" when I was a kid, and that's not a normal thing for lots of children.

But when we talk about things like events, if it's open to the public and it says it on a flier, or you're invited or you see an event page for something, it's usually something that's community and people can attend. It's not necessarily sacred, so it's not a ceremony, and you can participate. You can go and be in those settings because there is a kind of audience-type aspect to it. You can go in and watch and learn.

I know Annette Anderson [another contributor to and coeditor of this volume], when we spoke before together at an event here at TCU, somebody had asked this question. Annette would tell them, "I tell all the university students to come to attend." But she added, "But I remind them if I see you, I'm going to put you to work. And that's how you start to help, 'cause we need to get to know each other. We must trust each other." And she said, "That means me seeing you take out the trash or wash the dishes." And she said, "That's how you start." I don't think that's something that as a university student you're expecting. You're expecting to go in, and be in it, and intern and do research. So it's different. It's definitely different.

Nino Testa:

One thing that I thought was really powerful in a past conversation we had was the distinction between non-Native people who you have worked with feeling very open to sharing flyers for events, but when you ask them to share a flyer about a missing person they feel uncomfortable doing so. I was hoping we could reflect on that. It seems relevant in the context of student assignments as well, that this isn't just consciousness-raising only for the purpose of educating a closed community of a university or a class about this abstract concept. We should be doing it in the service of people who are missing and of an organization and of a community who's working to support the families of these folks.

Jodi Voice Yellowfish:

So I think I started really thinking about that, especially in this setting, after I helped with the poster project with the advertising class I mentioned earlier. I started really thinking about that, because I know that was hard. It was hard for students to find images and art, and the whole concept of calling somebody to see if they can use this photo, even if they found it online and wanted to share a name. I feel like after that, I know some students took the easy way out, making just a very broad campaign of raising awareness. And it's nice, your intentions weren't bad, but does it really help anything? And so it has to be made more specific, but you have to go about it the right way.

We get asked for help from people in South Dakota. We had two people just in the past month asking about, "I don't know a local MMIW group. Can you help us?" So we've had an online presence where people are finding us. And I always think, seeing flyers made for cases and stuff, and if they're done in the right way and in the safe way, they are crucial. They're vital to helping find people. And so I don't see why you would want to share a very broad campaign poster over an actual missing person's case flyer that shows we're working with the family directly, or we wouldn't make it. We only make flyers if we're working a case. And when I tell people that, they're like, "Oh, okay." When you break down what goes into just making that flyer, then it's like, "Oh, so you can't do it unless you have a case number. You can't do it unless you're connected to a police department. You can't do it . . ." That's how we do it. And so just that understanding of this is what you should share.

It's nice to share the artwork and the campaign posters, the very broad stuff. That's just awareness, but we're beyond awareness. If I'm talking to you and you're learning from me, you're beyond awareness. And so you should want to be as involved as you're comfortable with, and everybody's comfortable with sharing something online. So it's like, "Yeah, you see that flyer? You should share the flyer." So I think that's my biggest thing about it. I don't see why you would rather do this than that.

Nino Testa:

One thing that comes up in classes that perhaps can go underexplored if faculty are not dedicating enough time to the conversation is the important differences in the experience of Native people living on reservations and those living in urban centers like Dallas. Without thinking through the histories of these experiences, students might really misunderstand the structural dynamics of MMIW.

Jodi Voice Yellowfish:

Yeah. I think it's really important to understand that, because we're dealing with the same thing but in very different scopes of law enforcement and government. And even just today, I spoke at the Young Leaders, Strong City Summer Camp. I just had enough time to barely touch on the MMIW work that I do. These are high school students, and this young Black man was like, "How does it differ?"

Literally wanted to know the difference between reservation and city logistics. He asked specifically if I worked a case that was on a reservation. And so the understanding is there, if somebody in high school is asking, a young man at that. It tends to be more female students that want to know about cases, because I feel like they feel more at risk for these things to happen. But this young man was asking, "What does this look like?"

So it's definitely out there in the world that there is a difference, and it affects our struggles of working cases on tribal land. And I tell people that it's even in our organization's name: "It's Texas. We cover a lot of area, and Texas is huge." And I tell people the very basics, that there are three reservations in Texas, and we've helped with two cases on Alabama-Coushatta Indian Reservation, and how that looked. Places vary, the odds are stacked against you depending on the tribal government and the tribal police department. And, fortunately in Livingston on the Alabama Coushatta reservation, their tribal police department, because of tribal members, is more open to understanding that they need to be a little more proactive.

Some reservations deal with tribal police that are okay with, "Oh, well, we can't do that, because we don't know if it's a non-Native or a Native person who made this happen." And you have to break down the fact—which is something I feel like could be some of that pre-work—if a non-Native person comes on tribal land and raises hell and commits all these crimes, tribal police cannot prosecute because of jurisdiction issues. That gives people free rein to come and do what they want and just get out of dodge as quickly as possible. Because there's going to be so much red tape to get to the FBI to do the work. So tribal police have to do some work, figure out if they can do it, see if the county, or if county police can do something. If they can't, they have to pass it on. And there's all this time that's gone by. In my experience working in coalition and learning from groups and organizations in Oklahoma, even dealing with runaway cases gets confusing because of Indian Child Welfare Act–type issues that arise.

So I think if faculty and students had a grasp of that before we actually started talking about this crisis, we could get further into it. Then we can talk about something like tribal law and order and how things in the Violence against Women Act (VAWA) have changed, and how there are efforts to change these things. And educating about VAWA is how I really started doing this work. But I don't get to say that, because I have to talk about all these other things, and then get to the work and the crisis. I have to give you the basics of jurisdiction and why the FBI has to come in and do a case, and tribal government and police can't, or why we have to understand ICWA. It's important and I can do it, but I would much rather talk about what we currently deal with. You can support the reauthorization and understanding, if this person is doing this work in Congress or something, and it takes forever to get there. So it's like, "Oh yeah, and this too." And that's always a last thing and it turns into an afterthought.

Nino Testa:

Again, establishing this context allows you to really share what is most needed in your work right now. That sense of scale of the specifics of MMIW that you're talking through is actually an opportunity for students to understand larger structures, and how the work that you do is embedded in those larger structures. Also, to me, spending time on this context demonstrates a sense of care on our behalf before we invite a community expert to class.

Jodi Voice Yellowfish:

I think it's just that we're not there to teach history. If you had a basic understanding of the jurisdiction stuff, then I could go into VAWA, I could go into ICWA, because those are things that as urban Natives that we work on, because we can utilize those. We don't have to deal with those jurisdiction issues in the city. There's so many other topics that come up, and it's like, "That's what you can help me with." And sometimes we get lost in the history, because we know it well, and we can teach it well. We can talk about it, but then it's like, "Ah, I forgot [to get to MMIW]." But it is so easy to teach some history because we've lived it and literally are products of this very desired history people crave.

You can actually, as a social work student, as a nursing student, you can help us teach about ICWA, because we [Native communities] have the highest number of trafficking victims, because we have the highest numbers of foster kids. And that has come up at a TCU event. We've presented to nursing students on what the Indian Child Welfare Act is because it came up in conversation with MMIW work on campus. They were compelled to step up and thought, "Hey, I can get them to talk specifically about Indian Child Welfare Act now, because we need to understand it in my field of study and work and nobody's teaching that to me." So it's like if we're getting lost in all the history, we don't get to the action of how you can be engaged.

Conclusions

The conversation recounted above surfaced several points emerging from the pedagogical collaboration between TCU faculty and MMIW Texas Rematriate that we wish to offer as potential best practices to guide collaborations between Native community activists working in the MMIW crisis and higher education institutions. These are not exhaustive, and they represent only our current understanding of the work we have done. We hope these principles will be helpful for a broad range of potential collaborations.

For Native advocates and organizers:

- Tread with caution but be open to working with non-Native people if you can identify the possibility of reciprocity.
- Know that once you say "yes" to speaking in educational settings, you will receive more and more requests. Remember that you don't have to agree to every opportunity, especially those that will tokenize you.
- When you first work with organizers of an event, carefully evaluate their intentions. Know that it is okay to walk away after that first event if it doesn't help or uplift your work.
- The classroom setting will likely not be a space that contributes to your own personal healing and well-being. Ask yourself how your presence in that space can contribute to your long-term organizing goals and let that direct your approach to working with faculty and students.
- Share the vibrancy and complexity of contemporary Native culture and life with students whenever possible.

- Know that it is appropriate for you to ask students and faculty for what you need and to tell them what they can do to support your work or build trust with your community.

For non-Native college or university faculty/staff:

- Ask Native community leaders who they would like to invite for lectures, panels, and events. Use your resources to bring these people to campus and ensure that community partners are centered in the event and have the opportunity to connect with the speakers in ways that are meaningful to them.
- Perform due diligence in checking potential speakers before you invite them to class or campus. Are they connected to a Native community? Does the local Native community view their work as positive and/or effective?
- Understand that the timeline and pace of an academic semester, a community organization, and an ongoing crisis in a community differ and may even be at odds. You will need to devote more time in your syllabus to this project than you first think you will. Are you ready to do so?
- Educate yourself on the historical, political, legal, and social contexts relevant to MMIW (such as ongoing colonization) and familiarize students with them before the class visit or event. This will allow your expert visitor to get right to the point in sharing their expertise on the issue. It is not their job to teach centuries of history to your class.
- Establish a basic vocabulary with students in advance of the visit. *Relative* and *sacred* are especially important terms to understand in MMIW work.
- Prepare students for the fact that government data on MMIW may be unavailable and/or unreliable and explain why. Help them understand that facts and numbers are important to the extent that they help us empathize with and work on behalf of others as sacred human beings. Recognize that MMIW organizers may be reluctant to share sacred data with non-Native people. This is an opportunity to challenge the way students may understand the "right" to access or circulate data.

- Do not formulate "awareness" assignments that encourage students to circulate sacred data or images/names of missing or murdered Native people without the ongoing consent of local organizers and impacted families.
- Encourage students to think beyond the grade on the assignment and focus instead on the learning they will take with them into the world. Structure your assignments and grading in ways that cultivate this attitude.
- Be ready to help students consider how they can extend their learning outside of the classroom or campus into action supporting the organization and the community.
- If you or your students volunteer with an organization, be ready to assist their efforts in whatever way they indicate is needed or desired. By doing so, you will build trust over time.
- Ask organizations what they need, and then do the work they ask you to do. For example, if an MMIW organization asks you to share flyers and graphics about missing people, do this consistently.

BUILDING TRUST:
The Dallas–Fort Worth Native Community
and Texas Christian University
by C. Annette Anderson

Annette Anderson (Chickasaw and Cherokee) is a licensed clinical social worker (LCSW) and a council member for the Indigenous Institute of the Americas, a volunteer intertribal organization dedicated to preserving Traditional knowledge for future generations. In the essay that follows, she shares stories of growing up in Oklahoma and Texas, her life's work advocating for Native children and youth, and the history of the Dallas–Fort Worth Native community. She offers reflections and advice to non-Native organizations or educational institutions regarding how to respectfully interact with Native community partners, drawing on her extensive experience working with TCU in its Native American and Indigenous Peoples Initiative, including serving as an inaugural member of the TCU Native American Advisory Circle.

Chokma, Saholhchifoat Annette Anderson, Chikashsha Tsalagi saya.
Hello, my name is Annette Anderson, I am Chickasaw and Cherokee.

Above: Annette Anderson speaking as a panelist at the keynote session of TCU's seventh annual Native American and Indigenous Peoples Day Symposium, October 2, 2023. *TCU Marketing and Communication, photo by James Anger.*

Tribal History

For the people whose families originate from one of the Five Civilized Tribes (Cherokee, Chickasaw, Choctaw, Muscogee [Creek], and Seminole), our relationships with these Tribes were directly impacted by decisions made by Congress in 1887. The Dawes Act was a direct result of US federal policy designed to remove entire American Indian Nations from their homelands. The federal government wanted our land, with rich soil and bountiful wildlife. The Indian Removal Act of 1830 had led to the Trail of Tears and to our entire Nation being forced to move to what the government considered worthless and uninhabitable lands in Oklahoma. The Dawes Act had many purposes, but its essential goal was to strip peoples of their identity as Tribal Nations and implement colonial policies that forced individual land ownership through land allotments. Our Nations were required to create constitutions and forms of Tribal governments that met US government approval. These forms of government did not reflect our Tribal Nations' traditional values and worldviews.

Additionally, Bureau of Indian Affairs (BIA) agents were notorious for their biases as they interviewed Tribal members to determine Tribal status, who would or would not be enrolled on the Dawes Rolls and receive their family's land allotments. These interviews were documented and kept in what they called enrollment jackets. Factors that could impact Tribal enrollment included whether a person qualified as a spouse through "Christian marriage" and how that translated into the circumstances of a child's birth. Some Tribes allowed enrollment only if the person stayed on their own assigned allotment and did not move. Families who left to find better land were removed from the rolls. Families with multiple Tribal affiliations were forced to choose only one. Some Tribes honored only descendants from the matriarchal lines. Some families lost their Tribal enrollment through the arbitrary decisions made by people outside the culture.

Personal Story

The long-term impact of the Dawes Act policies played an instrumental role in the remorse, sadness, and trauma my father experienced during his lifetime. My biological grandfather was Chickasaw and Cherokee. His father was considered a prominent leader in the Chickasaw Nation and his Cherokee mother worked in this leader's home as a maid. Unfortunately, my grandfather's birth was a result of an affair between two people who were already married to other people. No BIA agent would add this child to the Dawes rolls, especially when the father had a "Christian" marriage and there were children by that marriage.

My father was ten and his sister twenty when their father, my grandfather "Blackie" Anderson, died of a heart attack at age forty. He was a well-respected wildcatter on the oil fields in Oklahoma. He married my grandmother, who was of English descent, at a time when "Indians" didn't have the right to vote and mixed marriages were clearly frowned upon. My grandmother divorced my grandfather after the children were born. The extended family was sworn to secrecy about her having been married to an "Indian." That translated into dad and his sister not being allowed to speak about their father. This silence was a rigid rule with Grandmother, especially after she remarried to a retired sheriff who was very prejudiced against what he called "Blacks and Indians." It was only when she died that the family was able to speak openly about this history.

Blackie's mother, my great-grandmother, was very aware of the importance of her child being enrolled in the Chickasaw Nation. She received a verbal promise from my great-grandfather about that enrollment. At some point after the birth of my grandfather, his Chickasaw father gave his mother the roll number for Blackie. It wasn't until I went to college that my aunt discovered that they had been lied to. The roll number given to my aunt was incorrect. I spent many hours reviewing the Dawes Rolls and enrollment jackets at the National Archives at Fort Worth. After reviewing many of these interviews and learning about the power of the BIA, I am convinced that no matter how prominent my great-grandfather was in the Chickasaw Nation, or however well-intentioned he was, it would have been impossible for him to influence the BIA on this matter.

My father always identified as Cherokee, but he never revealed we were Chickasaw until I was in college. It was my aunt and my Uncle Jelly who finally told me the truth about my Chickasaw family. I know who they are because my Uncle Jelly was a close friend of my grandfather Blackie and had direct knowledge about my great-grandfather, who had been a judge at the Tishomingo Courthouse. As a family, we regret not being able to restore the family connections within the Chickasaw Nation for my father.

Oklahoma Education (1962–1975)

I grew up during the school year in Tulsa, Oklahoma. Tulsa Public
Schools educated and promoted our knowledge of the Oklahoma
Nations. We learned about the Nations that originated on the lands
and those who were forcibly moved to those lands. There were always
strong threads of Native culture; understanding geography and history
concerning the Tribal Nations was standard. We learned about when
a Tribe came to Oklahoma and the many renditions of geographical
drawings that showed the change in land area over time. Tulsa Public
Schools required field trips to the Gilcrease Museum, one of the best
collections of famous Native painters and sculptors. I even found a spell-
ing test from third grade with all the Tribes written alphabetically.

I started kindergarten in about 1962 and graduated high school
in 1975. Outstanding literature was being published, like Vine Deloria
Jr.'s *Custer Died for Your Sins* (1969) and *God Is Red* (1973). These were
incorporated into our school assignments. N. Scott Momaday and the
book *Black Elk Speaks* were very popular. I attended the famous Four Moons
ballet in Tulsa (1967) with Yvonne Chouteau (Shawnee), Rosella Hightower
(Choctaw), Moscelyne Larkin (Eastern Shawnee-Peoria), and Marjorie
Tallchief (Osage), my ballerina idols. High school years were exciting, with
the Red Power Movement, Alcatraz, and more. Even the American Indian
Movement came to the Tulsa Library when I was a teenager.

Cultural Education

I spent my summers in various parts of Oklahoma, depending on where
my maternal and paternal grandparents lived: Nowata, Poteau, Talihina,
Eufaula, and Krebs. My father's friends were Kiowa, Cherokee, and
Cheyenne; some worked with him at Dowell, now called Dow Chemical,
and others he met through his hobbies of gun shows, pawn shops, and
photography. My mentor and the man who helped me enter the powwow circle was my dad's friend Ken Anquoe. The Anquoe family started
the Mohawk Park powwow in Tulsa.

Outside of public schooling, I learned my culture by observing and
listening to elders while tagging along with my dad. He visited the pawn
shops on the weekends in Tulsa, Oklahoma. He studied the artifacts,
precious items people sold because they were out of money. Turquoise

jewelry, leatherwork, beadwork, fans, paintings, and regalia were all at pawn shops. That is where I learned to tell the difference between Nations by their leather pieces, silverwork styles, and beadwork stitches. By the time I graduated from high school, I was doing beadwork and some leatherwork and could tell the difference between fake and authentic regalia and jewelry. I liked it when he recognized an artist or a piece of jewelry and would convince the pawn shop to make a trade or gift it to him in exchange for his ability to repair cameras, lawn equipment, and other items.

College Years

Oklahoma State University (OSU) was my first experience of people assuming my heritage by the color of my hair and eyes. You realize this when overhearing conversations or people trying to engage you in jokes or commentary about your culture. They have no idea you will be offended, because you have light skin. That's when you realize you must form new alliances to survive.

OSU was my first experience of feeling lonely and craving a Native community. Thank goodness the Creator chose my first college roommate. She was a full-blood four-foot-eight powerhouse Choctaw. Her friendship helped me adjust during my first year. Her nickname was Faye-Faye. The first day I stepped through the door to our dorm room, she looked like she thought it would be a standoff between the Indians and Custer. She was hanging up her Tribal flag on the wall. I complimented her Choctaw flag. She looked so confused and then broke out a huge smile. That is all it took; we became good friends, and that friendship helped me survive college. Even though I attended an Oklahoma college, I had no Native American professors at OSU. I do not remember seeing a powwow anywhere on campus, and there was no Native American Heritage Month that would draw people together. It was also a challenge in my sociology and psychology classes, where discussions were very biased by race and gender.

Another memory from OSU was an opportunity to earn extra money by helping with a summer dance program. The grant was written to "expose" Native American children to college. I was a ballet and tap dancer in my spare time; my dance instructor was an enrolled Muscogee

(Creek) Citizen and wrote the grant. It was easy to convince me to help with the program. Children from the Muscogee (Creek) Nation were brought to OSU. When I accepted the position, my understanding was that I would help teach ballet and jazz while they were on campus. However, what happened was completely different. After receiving the list of activities on the first day, I realized that the grant writer wanted to teach these "Indian" kids how to do "Indian" dancing!

I had no idea what that meant, and it never occurred to me to question what was planned because the woman who wrote the grant was part of that Nation. It turned out she had hired someone from a Plains Indian Tribe to come and teach powwow dancing. When this poor man showed up, half the kids turned and sat facing the wall. They were the kids who attended church. The other kids, the stomp dance kids, were curious, but they also knew this was not a part of their upbringing at home. All the mess-ups led to some great conversations, which turned into friendships. Everyone took it in stride after a lot of teasing, and best of all, it led to my first invitation to a social stomp dance between the Seminole Nation and Muscogee (Creek) Nation.

Indian Child Welfare

I started my master's in social work at the University of Oklahoma in 1979. I was selected for an Indian Child Welfare Act training grant administered by the Department of Health, Education, and Welfare. I believe it was the first year the grant was offered because the knowledge base that led to the need for specialized training was the same need that resulted in the passage of ICWA in 1978. Over a quarter of Indian children were being removed from their homes and placed outside the family/Tribe and with people outside the culture. We were losing our most valuable resource, children. This grant allowed select social workers to receive specialized training on American Indian cultural values, Traditional child-rearing practices, boarding school trauma, multigenerational trauma, placement preventive services, and much more.[1] Our professors were all Native! I remember two special people who helped teach the courses, Jo Ann Dodson, and Antonia (Toni) Dobrec. They also helped me see the importance of understanding and sensitivity when working with Native families as well as families from other cultures. The coursework was all focused from a Native lens rather than the Eurocentric models that are sadly a central component of Child Protective Services, both past and present.

When I was in social work school, the courts in Oklahoma were starting to dissect and understand ICWA. The law was in effect, but no one knew which Tribes would want to enter into agreements with state courts for help with ICWA cases. My social work placement was with Judge Alan Couch at a district court in Cleveland County. I had the opportunity to listen in on many of these discussions. I only fully appreciated this opportunity once I started writing my story, forty years later.

The ICWA grant required federal oversight of my work in child welfare for five years. That is how I first met my mentor and friend Gregory Gomez, MSSW (master of science in social work). Gregory worked at the Federal Building in Dallas, Texas. He oversaw all the students on this grant in a five-state area. I never realized Gregory's relationships in Dallas–Fort Worth would intersect with all my relationships in DFW today. He likes to tell the story of our first meeting. It was one of my most embarrassing moments. I was supposed to have an on-site meeting at the campus with the person who had "federal oversight" on the grant. The meeting was to ensure I was in school and complying with the conditions of the grant. I was an hour late for this oversight meeting because of a complicated, court-ordered home visit that had become volatile. I couldn't leave the situation until things had calmed down. Once things were settled, I raced to the university to meet this person.

I walked in to find what, in my opinion, was this tall, intimidating Indian guy with long black braids, beadwork, and turquoise bracelets. I was scared to death. I started stammering, apologizing, repeating myself, and blabbering, "I am so sorry!" He had this deadpan look, and I thought he was mad. He stopped me in the middle of my blabbering and asked, "Were you doing what you were supposed to be doing?" I stopped, and I said, "Yes." Then he said, "Well, that's where you were supposed to be." That marked the beginning of our friendship.

He was the first to tell me to always put my name on any document I created. I never found my writing valuable, but he said people steal stuff from our culture, including our writings. Knowing Greg, I don't think he believed it would keep my work safe; he probably thought at least the thief would know who he stole it from, ayyyyyy (a common saying used at the end of teasing). Sure enough, when I didn't listen, that came true. Someone used my PowerPoint at an event without asking or giving credit for the work. Lesson learned. He also taught me that I should not complain or describe people I have met as "difficult," "impossible," "prejudiced," etc., until I had invited them to sit down and share an Indian taco or fry bread with me to discuss our differences. He has provided a lifetime of learning, fun, and friendship that has lasted until today.

Coming to Texas

I married my college sweetheart in 1980 and followed him to Houston after he got his first job out of college at Texas Instruments. I transferred to the University of Houston, School of Social Work. It was so different from OU. First, in Oklahoma, at the time I attended, our focus on minorities and culture was related to Black culture and, in my case, American Indian culture. New concepts for me at the University of Houston were working in urban settings, private practice using a medical model, and working with Spanish-speaking populations. If I had learned about Texas and our Indigenous roots, I would have realized that the focus on Hispanic cultures also overlapped with the Indigenous people in Texas. I was still on the ICWA grant and had to continue my commitment to at least five years of working in child welfare.

This time, my graduate practicum was in adoption and post-adoption at a nonprofit named DePelchin Faith Home. The organization was started by Kezia DePelchin as an orphanage during the yellow fever epidemic in Houston during the 1800s. She was noteworthy for this quote: "I have faith in Houston that they will take care of the children of the yellow fever epidemic." So that is how it got the name DePelchin Faith Home. The funny thing about working at DePelchin was the number of times people told us they were members of the "DePelchin faith" to get help. I truly admired this agency; they were always at the cutting edge for the needs of children. They listened to the research on infants' and children's needs for attachment. During the early years of DePelchin, orphaned babies stayed in a hospital-like clinic; then, studies said children needed loving attachments to caretakers. Then researchers said the best place for children to be is with one set of parents, so foster care, adoption, and post-adoption were prioritized as a goal for every child that had to go into out-of-home care. We were a voluntary child placement agency, meaning the birth parents came to us looking for a good permanent family for their babies and children. When I was hired as a full-time worker, I participated in one of Texas's first placement prevention, in-home therapy programs. It was beautiful to find success before children had to separate from their parents.

In my first year as a student, I performed social work duties in adoption, and I realized several Native American children had been adopted through this agency. These children were adopted a long time before my involvement with the agency. Some were teens, and others were young adults; their families had served as foster homes. I observed that these kids didn't have any references for their identity. Only one young adult knew they were Navajo, but that was all they knew or understood of their culture. As a Native person, it was very upsetting to meet these young people who had no idea what Nation they belonged to and had no reference for their identity except through TV, movies, and books. These were not children on my caseload but represented the national statistics of Indian children who were placed outside their culture many years ago, which resulted in the ICWA. I started researching the agency's history on Indian Child Welfare (ICW).[2] DePelchin was a member of the Child Welfare League of America from the late 1950s to the late 1960s. This national group and its member organizations made possible adoptive placement of American Indian children across the nation, but usually as far away from their origins as possible. Sadly, DePelchin had a part in these adoptions.

A pivotal point in my practicum happened when I was assigned a case that I was sure involved an American Indian child. The interactions and history of the biological mother and my intuition made me suspect the mother and infant were Tribal people. The law was only two years old at the time, and even today, many people don't know that voluntary child placements also have some protections under the ICWA. I seemed to be the only person with that knowledge or concern. I did ask the birth mother and had my intuition confirmed. She was a Tribal citizen, but her infant was not yet enrolled.

When I approached my supervisor about my concern, the reaction was, "Oh, we don't have to follow that law, do we?" with an additional insinuation that I might be okay with looking the other way. I had mentioned on a few occasions that I was Chickasaw and Cherokee, but I realized when this situation came up the assumption was that since I looked White, I must think White. The only social workers who understood my concern were the Black social workers who also had concerns about biracial placements. I realized that although I had made my culture very clear at the agency, I was being treated as, "You look White like us, so why are you so upset about this? Let's not say anything." I made it evident that I could not and would not turn my head but essentially received no support or validation to follow up appropriately with federal law.

I believe Tribal children need to be with families from their Nation. My anxiety about the situation led me to seek help outside the agency.

I called Gregory Gomez, my supervisor on the grant, in Dallas. He fit everything I needed. He was Apache, a social worker, and a federal employee in the Administration of Children, Youth, and Families. He still had oversight over my internships and employment. I called him, and we discussed the situation. I needed him to validate me as a Native person and to remind DePelchin of their legal obligations. He arrived a few days later and brought what I have heard him call his "dog and pony show." He came to the agency prepared to educate my supervisor and staff about our culture and to deal with these infants and their future placements. That was my first opportunity to see Gregory in a face-to-face dialogue with people outside the Native culture. He was very gentle and conversational. He was polite and soft-spoken, with a touch of big smiles and some Native humor. I was prepared for a confrontation and had built up a lot of anxiety about what would happen, but the outcome was remarkable. He promoted me as a person, as a Native woman, and as knowledgeable on ICWA. He had this way of massaging the conversation so that by the end of our talks, people acted like, "Wow, aren't we lucky to have this person here at the agency? Let's do what's right and feel good about it."

I learned so much just by watching and listening to him. I continue to contact him with complex ethical issues, organizational dilemmas, and cultural protocols. I can always depend on him to have a worldview reflecting his experience as a sun dancer, pipe carrier, world traveler, and knowledge keeper. That afternoon, we dressed in regalia and went to the gymnasium to do the round dance with all the kids. I agreed to write the first-ever protocol for voluntary Indian child placement so that if a family comes to a voluntary adoptive placement agency, the organization can fulfill its obligation to all Indian children. I put my name on that protocol, and someone quoted my name in a book years later. Here is another thank you to Gregory Gomez.

Move to the Dallas Area

When I moved to Dallas in the mid-1980s, my first contact with the American Indian community was through Sandra Blackbear Ramirez. She was a nurse working at the Department of Family and Protective Services. She was not a social worker, but she was the only identified American Indian person at the state agency. She was one of the only people who could provide consultation and guidance when Native children entered the Texas Child Protective Services system. Somewhere, she had heard, maybe from Gregory Gomez, that I wrote a voluntary checklist for ICWA adoptions. She asked me to provide training on ICWA, and that was when I first met other friends of Sandra's in the Native community.

My first Dallas job was at the downtown Dallas Family Guidance Center (FGC). FGC was a United Way sliding scale counseling agency. I worked as a psychotherapist, then was promoted to supervisor and moved locations to Plano. After a few years, I worked for the Plano Child Guidance Center, which merged in 1996 with the Family Guidance Center and was renamed Child and Family Guidance Center. In 1987, I started part-time private practice which led to full-time private practice in 1992 in Plano. Native children or Native families would become my clients, and I would use my knowledge to assist with identity issues; many were a result of adoptions. Once, I was referred a child who wanted to learn from a man about his culture. He told me there were no men anywhere in his life; all his Native fathers, uncles, and grandfathers were in jail or prison. I knew someone in the community who would be a fantastic resource, so I reached out to this well-loved and respected elder in the Native community named Larry Larney. I didn't know Larry well then but always saw him at the powwows and other gatherings. After getting appropriate permissions, I talked to Larry about the situation, and he gladly offered to meet with the child. I met his wife, Peggy, and son, Brian. Peggy and Larry significantly impacted the Texas Native community through their help with bowling leagues, basketball, and stickball. They supported everything and were the glue and backbone for the Dallas Independent School District (DISD) Indian Education Program and the activities and organizations that developed over time in the Indian community. Peggy made outstanding progress at dismantling Indian mascots in the DISD school district. She took this on before offensive mascots were on the radar of the broader community and the media. Peggy and Larry had influence and power in the Native community but were also respected outside the cultural boundaries. When I met Brian, he would have been considered a youth. What I quickly realized was his early accomplishment as an American Indian artist. Choctaw from his mother's and Seminole from his father's, Brian brought to life his father's love for stickball through artwork and his mother's work in Indian Education. Brian has incredibly detailed authenticity in his paintings. He continues to be my children's favorite artist. In December of 2012, Larry Larney passed away. In my opinion, a large crater was created in the heart of our community.[3] Still, Peggy and Brian pursued a dream of Larry's: to make Texas have a "day" for recognizing American Indians. American Indian Heritage Day in Texas was proclaimed by the state legislature in 2013. The last Friday in September is the official day to celebrate our heritage in Texas schools.

Founding of the Indigenous Institute of the Americas

In the mid-1980s, Gregory Gomez, his wife Cathy Gutierriz-Gomez, PhD, and Eddie Sandoval, MS (master of science), MEd (master of education), had started collaborating on their vision for the Indigenous Institute of the Americas. After completing my five-year grant obligations, Gregory moved to Alaska, working for the Feds, and then returned to Dallas, where he and his wife Cathy had their two children. I know we ran into each other around 1986 because Gregory found a cute picture of Cathy and me both pregnant, and Greg was standing between us. It is one of those photos he puts on Facebook occasionally to tease Cathy and me and give our friends a laugh.

Life got hectic and complicated for both of our families. I lost touch with Gregory for several years. Only later did I realize that life had turned upside down in 1992 for the Gomez family. The Mesquite

Independent School District kicked their youngest son out of kindergarten for having long hair.[4] This was a stressful time; the Larneys and other Native American families reached out and helped the Gomez family. After much prayer and talks with legal consultants, Gregory moved his family permanently to Albuquerque, where students can wear their hair long without repercussions. They didn't want their child traumatized by lawsuits and to experience further prejudice in Texas.

I crossed paths with Gregory Gomez again when he came for a gathering of the drums at the Stockyards in Fort Worth. Gregory asked me to help organize an IIA powwow at Southern Methodist University (SMU) in Dallas. He was in Albuquerque, and I was in Plano, Texas, north of Dallas. To make the powwow happen, I needed someone local, who knew how to connect me with people, places, and things; this is when I met Tosawi Marshall in 2006. Some people recognize her married name, Tosawi Pena. As I was reaching out to the Native community for more volunteers, a name, "Robin," was mentioned several times. "She knows everyone." "She has a lot of experience." "You should get her to help you." "She knows how-to put-on events," etc. Finally, I asked Tosawi if she knew anyone in the Native community named Robin. Guess what? Tosawi Marshall, aka Robin. It caused a good laugh because she had not used that name for several years.

Tosawi did a lot for the DFW community. In her early years, she was a stunt woman for movies and TV; she worked as a casting agent and helped many now-famous American Indian actors get their first roles in film and TV. She helped with casting for *Walker, Texas Ranger*. I have heard stories about her getting small acting parts for Gregory Gomez and Eddie Sandoval in the show. Apparently, while on the set reenacting a "sweat lodge" scene a few harmless tricks were pulled on the lead actor, Chuck Norris. According to Greg, Chuck Norris was a very genuine, friendly person who opened doors for many Native people in our community.

Finding Tosawi was a blessing as we began all the planning for the first IIA event in DFW. Her talent and creativity were as powerful as I had heard from the community. Thinking back, I don't know how we made it happen. There was no Zoom back then for meetings, and we were all computer illiterate. I would design a flyer on my computer and send it to Greg for approval. He would open it on his computer and see pictures in all kinds of weird places, and the font and location of the words would change. We didn't even know how to do a screenshot or text message to send back and forth for corrections. Surprisingly, we coordinated between Albuquerque and Texas to pull off the event.

In 2007, our Celebration of Life Powwow was held at SMU. The powwow was possible because of the generosity of Steven Denson, a citizen of the Chickasaw Nation and a professor at SMU. This pow-wow was a tobacco, old-school powwow with our local drum, Bearclaw Singers. DFW Native community members such as Sonny and Darrell Blackbear, James and Tim Yellowfish sang at the drum. Dennis Begay, one of our well-respected Native elders, was gourd dancing, and his wife Majorie Begay danced the Southern Cloth dance style at the powwow. Peggy Larney offered informal advice on providing hospitality for the drummers. Linda Durant, a descendant of Norene Chisholm Durant (one of the first young women to come to Dallas on the Relocation program and a descendant of Jesse Chisholm, the namesake for the Chisholm Trail) helped advise me on protocol for the Head Staff.

For the first time, an Aztec dance group, Mitotiliztli Yaoyollohtli, organized by Evelio Flores, was invited and participated in the powwow. In the 2000s, the DFW American Indian people from the federally rec-ognized Tribes did not acknowledge or validate our relations with Native people south of the Rio Grande. It was unheard of to "mix" our cultural traditions. We didn't receive criticism for inviting their dancers, but there appeared to be genuine confusion about why they were invited and par-ticipated. Gregory Gomez, being the historian and knowledge keeper, has been instrumental in educating people; sometimes, it has seemed so slow to help people get past the lies they were taught in school. Being Mexican is related to political boundaries, but it is not a culture. Gregory was the person who taught me that the Spanish language is the most commonly spoken language among Indigenous people in all the Americas. Consider the political struggles in Texas during the 2020s and the Eurocentric view of the border between the United States and Mexico. Who belongs or doesn't belong in the United States is skewed by non-Indigenous people in political power.

As an organization, IIA started to form and become an educational group through individual efforts such as storytelling, consultation, confer-ence presentations, etc. The IIA powwow brought together some of our well-loved advisors, such as Dr. Patrisia Gonzales and the late Ambrose

Wiley. But since 2009, the community has associated us with an annual cultural event, formerly called Santa Fe Days, held in Carrollton, Texas. We grew the event and relocated to Cleburne, Texas, with a new name and new branding, IIAmericas Celebration, known as IIAC.

The Santa Fe Days cultural event originally reflected the Texas educational system's view of Indigenous people: Native people are extinct in Texas. In 2008–9, Tosawi and I accidentally entered the door of the "American Indian/Native American" event called Santa Fe Days on the Square. We reached out to the committee, thinking it was a Native organization. Tosawi made the first phone call and realized in five minutes that a group of well-meaning downtown merchants in Carrollton, Texas, had sponsored and organized the event. In the first years, they didn't know there were "Indians" in Dallas–Fort Worth. Founder Dave Oldfield's only experience was meeting the Santo Domingo Pueblo Indians while on vacation at Angel Fire in New Mexico. He was able to develop a historic relationship with the Santo Domingo Disabled Veterans Group.[5] He used his own money to bus them to Texas to sell their jewelry on the downtown square. It started as a replica of the downtown Santa Fe, New Mexico, sidewalks. Thus, the name Santa Fe Days. During that first phone call, they asked us to come to their meeting. They truly knew nothing about the culture that was the focus of their event. Some of our advice was confusing to people outside the culture, but they trusted us and did their best to follow our recommendations.

A simple example was the cultural protocol of gifting the drummers, dancers, etc. The non-Indian committee members were conflicted about paying an honorarium to these important people and also gifting them. "We pay them; why do we need to do gifting?" There was also a misunderstanding about the economic status of the Native artists. We would overhear the non-Native committee members' comments about "how much money the artists made in sales at the event." We had to educate them about the reality of Pueblo life. The income they worked so hard to earn probably didn't even cover the total cost of the materials to make the jewelry, and this one event might have to feed three generations of family members for several months.

In 2014, a series of events happened in downtown Carrollton that caused the event to be discontinued. We asked for the event to be transferred to our organization and we were able to relocate to Sandy

Lake Amusement Park, a privately owned park only one mile from our original event location. The Frank Rush family–owned Sandy Lake Amusement Park, coincidentally, had three generations of personal friendships with people in the Southwest Tribes in Oklahoma.[6] Another piece of Dallas–Fort Worth history was the Wild West shows at Six Flags in the 1960s.[7] Mr. Rush helped organize them. One of our elders, Mr. Dennis Begay, was a young guy at that time and performed hoop dances for these shows. Our event enjoyed four excellent years at Sandy Lake, but the Rush family decided to retire in 2019, just before the impact of COVID-19. IIA searched for a new welcoming venue and found it at the Chisholm Trail Outdoor Museum in Cleburne, Texas. It is farther away from the Metroplex but with more land and the ability to have a traditional gathering, which includes camping, outdoor cooking, and late-night socializing. Cleburne is also where Kiowa, Apache, and Comanche relatives lived and hunted for thousands of years.

In 2024, we will celebrate our seventeenth year. Our all-volunteer group has helped expand our reputation in the community through traditional knowledge education, which includes Indigenous Grocery Store, Food as Medicine, Seed Ambassador Program, and more. These initiatives are the direct result of Dr. Patrisia Gonzales's consultation and advice. The IIA Powwow has, since 2007, helped bring visibility to the Native American community, schools, corporations, and other nonprofit organizations.

DFW Native American Community and Organizations

Taking a step back, in the 1990s Indian Health Service began to distribute money for health care, even in urban areas, for the Native community. 42 Code of Federal Regulations (C.F.R.) § Part 136 had many stipulations that limited who in the Native community could be served with this money. Some people had Tribal enrollment cards issued by their Tribes. The Certificate of Degree of Indian Blood (CDIB) card was another document issued by the BIA and other government entities. It became the validating piece of paper that separated people in the Indian community. Before that law and money became involved, people were welcomed in the Native community based on traditional values such as family ties, participation in ceremonies, helping at events, and other Native ethics.

What I saw was the development of unjustified prejudice among some DFW Indian communities. The federal government has pitted us against each other for hundreds of years to get resources—Nation against Nation and family against family. Some Native community members had been adopted at birth by White families and never received any legal status from their tribes. The American Indian Urban Relocation Program in the 1950s and '60s brought many Native people to the DFW area, but it also resulted in many people marrying spouses from different tribes. Some children and grandchildren, obviously raised and identified as Native children, became ineligible to receive a CDIB card or Tribal enrollment.

It was regrettable to see these factions of people. It felt like people were gossiping about their Tribal status behind their backs. Still, when the Indian community needed donations, volunteerism, etc., many people without a Tribal card were the first to step forward. Not everyone acted that way, but there was enough of this colonizing thinking to impact and be hurtful to some people. Even the protections of the ICWA for adoptees did not protect some of the adoptees. Our organization's vice president was adopted, but her birth mother made sure she was Tribally enrolled. That is not true of most of the adoptions in the past. The whole purpose of adoption was the same as boarding schools: to get rid of the "Indianness" in these children.

In the Dallas–Fort Worth area before COVID-19, I witnessed this continued polarity of "carded vs. no card." All of it stemmed from limited financial resources. Medical services, special contracts for their businesses, jobs, scholarships, housing, or distributed discretionary income that some Tribes share with individual Tribal citizens referred to as "per cap": most of these financial resources were determined by federal policy rather than the Native community. At one time, there was no available money for Native urban centers. The community seemed more cohesive and relied on the spirit of volunteerism and generosity before the 1990s. These federal policies also eliminated services for the Tribes that Texas or the federal government never recognized, yet we live and work on their homelands. As people without Tribal enrollment or a CDIB were turned away, it seemed to create an artificial entitlement within the community. Not everyone had that view, but it was enough to make life a struggle for families who were Native but now were on the outer edge of a circle. They weren't White, and they weren't Indian.

Since the pandemic, I have seen some positive shifts in our community. People have been more exposed to national and international online conversations about Indigenous peoples. Words such as decolonization, sovereignty, land acknowledgments, rematriation, Traditional worldviews, Traditional ecological knowledge, Missing and Murdered Indigenous Relatives, Two-Spirit, and other accurate and honest representations of our history are beginning to have an impact. I will admit our young adults took a leadership role on these issues. Some college students in the Native American student associations at the University of North Texas, TCU, and the University of Texas at Arlington have been terrific advocates for inclusion and honest history. As an old fogie, I had to learn more about where I was living. Texas massacres and Mission Indians were nowhere in my cultural or formal education. I served on a volunteer task force for over four years to develop a course for Texas high school students on American Indian and Native studies. That collaboration with up to seventy elders and educators made me see how unique my cultural opportunities had been growing up. Yet I was utterly ignorant outside my own Tribes and personal bubble. The concerted efforts to bring accurate knowledge into the Texas classrooms regarding our culture may also be making some tiny footprints toward the future.

At the same time, I worry that our community continues to be torn in our political polarity. The radical right- and left-wing politics have continued in Texas. They may alienate us from our roots with Tribal Nations forced south of the Rio Grande and those who originated there but migrated thousands of years ago into the forty-eight states. We must remember that many in our Native community are third-generation relocation families who were raised on the same lies that have been taught in Texas schools for the last one hundred years. The social studies curriculum has not changed and is becoming even more conservative at this time! Many of our urban children need the benefit of an elder who was born and raised on their Traditional lands and Traditional knowledge. Formal education may be one of our children's only sources of information about their cultures, so we want it to be truthful and validating.

I have listened to this community's stories and history through the elders representing the last seventy years. There was great diversity in the Tribal cultures who relocated to Dallas and Fort Worth. Some families were from the Five Civilized Tribes, who had stomp dance traditions, but to my knowledge, there are no active ceremonial stomp dance grounds in Texas. Families from the Plains Nations might have been identified as the powwow people. Texas was some of their traditional homelands, yet they were forced out to Oklahoma and back again to Texas on the relocation program. Sadly, no one received a title to reclaim their land. Reservation and Pueblo people also relocated to DFW. Traditional lifeways were so hard to replicate in DFW; there must have been so much longing by all the people for community, food, familiar land, rivers, weather, and their own Nation's Traditional gatherings. It wasn't affordable to return home for those gatherings.

There was a strong Christian community, which overlapped with the powwow and stomp dance communities. I don't remember anyone discussing the Native American Church presence in DFW, but that was not part of my traditions and not something normally discussed in casual conversations. The Indian churches are often a focal point of Native community activities in Dallas; the churches seemed to have been the first welcoming committee for many families who came on the relocation program. The Trinity River Mission, I believe, was the name of one of the first churches that reached out to these families. Today, we have a few Indian churches, but the Dallas Indian Mission Methodist Church seems to be a place for many people, even if they aren't "church" people. It is a hub for wild onion dinners, Indian taco night, bingo, and much more.

It was always interesting that the Fort Worth Native people had to travel to Dallas for most events. I only remember going to Fort Worth a few times, and it was always for the Fort Worth Indian Education Program Powwow led by Alicia Barrientez. Alice was one of the few outdoor educators, meaning she could teach our kids archery, fire lighting, camping, plant knowledge, and more. Sadly, that program was closed after a few years, and we lost Alice's knowledge in the public schools as she went to the private sector to work. In recent years, Fort Worth Independent School District revitalized the American Indian Education Program. They have successfully developed a two-week summer indoor program where children learn crafts and Traditional knowledge. There was also a powwow north of Fort Worth at Eagle Mountain Lake. The Native community never really talked about Fort Worth as a center for the relocation program, but I am aware through our IIA resources that Indigenous people were always in the Fort Worth area but have never received the same visibility and recognition.[8]

Once Larry Larney was telling me about the relocation program, and he said the federal program people would sit the adults down and let them look at a book and decide what trade they were going to learn. It could have been that Fort Worth was the place for some of the apprentice programs, but Dallas again was the focus of the training and implementation of the trade schools and colleges. When the Indian families arrived in Dallas, they were moved into the public housing next to the Spanish-speaking families. Some elders think they put them next to people who look similar, but they didn't speak Spanish. I was told that food became the universal language because the Indian families were greeted with tamales, beans, and tortillas and felt welcomed by their new neighbors. Families that decided to stay got their training/jobs and saved money, and many moved into the Oak Cliff area of Dallas. If you weren't part of the groups who came on the relocation program and knew each other, it could take a very long time to be accepted in the Indian community. Even when there was an intertribal center, it wasn't advertised to the broader community when I first came. I can't tell you how many Native people I meet who have not figured out how to find our community.

Since 2020, social media has impacted the willingness of the Native community to open its doors to newcomers. I have also seen our people grasping the impact of Texas history on the Tribes that once hunted, traded, or lived on this land. The federal and state governments continuously challenge our Texas Tribes who remained in this area. I still observe prejudice and alienation toward people from these Nations, which is perpetuated by our public school education.

The State of Texas has a long history of failure toward the First people of this land. Some of the Tribal Nations had histories entrenched in the Catholic mission system. To survive, these Tribes were forced to identify as "Mexican." I was in Texas several years before I understood the long-term impact of this label and the racism toward the Indigenous people who had to use it to survive. Currently, the term "Mexican" is thrown around as a label for people considered "illegals" or "aliens," ironic as many of these people can trace their history to this land, the rivers, the canyons, and mountains before colonial contact and the establishment of Mexico as a nation-state.

Another Texan failure is connected to the 1965 establishment of the Commission for Indian Affairs by the Texas Legislature, renamed the

Texas Indian Commission in 1975 and dissolved in 1989 by the Texas
Sunset Commission. Conflict and dissension occurred between the commission and representatives from the federally recognized reservations in
Texas. The commission functioned as a politician-led oversight group,
but Native people wanted it restructured as a Native governance and
advocacy group driven by Native people. The Texas Sunset Advisory
Commission, however, essentially recommended dissolving the Texas
Indian Commission, on the excuse that the Texas Tribes were under the
jurisdiction of the federal government. This action cut off any opportunity for non–federally recognized Tribes in Texas to have a voice or
representation in Texas government.[9]

Today, I think about how we can show our respect, support, and
validation for the people who first lived within the boundaries of this
metroplex. Over 7.76 million people are now occupying their land. That
thought overwhelms me. How do we welcome back those Nations and
the people who once called these 15,600 square miles of the Metroplex
region home? I know only a handful of people living in the Metroplex
whose ancestors lived on this land. Most of our Native people from the
relocation program would be considered immigrants to the land we sit
on today. Imagine for a moment you were forced out of the house you
live in now by someone you don't know and without your permission.
Now, imagine how you would feel being invited back to a dinner party
at your stolen home hosted by the thief who took your home, and even
worse, the dinner party is being held in your honor! Not for the reason
of giving you back your home, but only to honor you. The Nations who
lived here used Native science to prepare an environment that could
sustain human beings and their plants and animal relatives. It's so sad to
think that the environmental practices of the foreign immigrants have
led to our water tables being contaminated, the loss of essential species,
and irreversible ecological changes to the landscapes. Their home was
not just taken but trashed in the process.

The Tribes with a history south of the Rio Grande also had a history
north of the Rio Grande. The river is not ours to use as a boundary;
Native people did not acknowledge or agree to it as a border. It was
never relinquished voluntarily to the people who colonized and stole this
land. There is an attitude among some of the Native people in the DFW
metroplex that Indigenous people living on the south side of the Rio

Grande, whether by force or survival, are people who are not entitled to be American Indian or to live in Texas. That message confuses me. I have friends from Nations on either side of the river and friends whose Nation's territory encompasses the river and both sides of the bank. I am stunned and disappointed when the Native community allows, and sometimes perpetuates, this prejudice to contaminate what we think and say about these relatives. We are replicating and supporting the historical policies that destroyed our Nations and traumatized our people since 1492.

Recently, I met with a group of Indigenous women who work with Alianza Indígena Sin Fronteras.[10] Fourteen Indigenous languages have been identified among the families currently being kept in the border camps by the Border Patrol. These languages are also spoken by Tribes in our forty-eight contiguous states. What is wrong with our thinking? It is arrogant for our elected officials in the Texas government to be more entitled to live on this land than its first land protectors.

Even though I get discouraged at times, I am also an optimist and see change and more acceptance within our Native community. I want our community to seek our own knowledge rather than passively accept the messages taught in outdated textbooks and resources in Texas schools. We should explore and question social media and news media. We must be careful and avoid tunnel vision or narrow-minded thinking; the messages and policies that separate Native people are usually perpetuated by people outside our culture whose interest in this land is for economic gain.

The Sun Is Rising

Many more nonprofits and Indigenous-led organizations have formed in the Metroplex since I came to this community in the mid-1980s. IIA was fortunate to have volunteers like Constance Hargis, who served on many Native organizations' boards. We had other volunteers like Tosawi Marshall. She became the last executive director of the American Indian Chamber of Commerce.[11] The AICCT organization started in 1988 but unfortunately closed sometime before 2012. Financial concerns led to talks of a merger with the DFW Indian Chamber of Commerce, but the merger was never completed. There has been no formal Chamber of Commerce representing Native-owned businesses for many years.

Recently, members of the Native American Business Association have been visible. It has been exciting to see them supporting a local lacrosse team that has members who are Native. It has been exciting to see these lacrosse stars attend Native events, which really supports that pride Native families feel playing the lacrosse origins game, Stickball. Since 2016 the community stickball group, Little Brothers of War, directed by Eli Hickman, has been an enjoyable recreational activity and source of pride for our Native people. Some initiatives are new to the community, like our IIA Seed Ambassador Program. Other programs are attempting to bring back cultural knowledge and activities that once were commonplace in the sixties and seventies. Elders are showing more interest in teaching arts and crafts. Powwows, stickball, and basketball are more visible. Indian Education programs in public schools and other organizations are helping bring together the youth through drumming, dance, and other cultural skills. Members of specific Nations such as the Chickasaws, Muscogees, and Cherokees meet to discuss cultural knowledge unique to their people such as stomp dance, beadwork technique, songs, and more.

Texas Native Health, formerly the Urban Intertribal Center of Texas, has been developing opportunities for activities and support across the lifespan. The staff are trying to serve more Indigenous people, including those without CDIB cards and Tribal enrollment cards who need help. This shift in policy and resources is a sign of progress happening within the community. In the 1970s, before it became a health center, it was a gathering place for all Native people.[12] I hope the new mental health services and its work in teaching cultural practices and sponsoring health education will encourage more people to feel welcome inside the agency. The more Indigenous people from all Nations are welcome, the more people will build new relationships and promote healing of the traumas done to Texas Nations.

Several organizations have brought Native American issues to the forefront of conversations in DFW. Most of the public's interest becomes visible around Thanksgiving, Native American Heritage Month, Indigenous Peoples Day, and American Indian Heritage Day in Texas. At other times, the public becomes interested in our community due to outrages, such as news in national headlines about children's graves at boarding schools, the Dakota Access Pipeline, and MMIR. Since the COVID-19 pandemic, there has been even more notice in our community. People were looking for alternative medicines to fight or prevent the symptoms of COVID-19. Even the most conservative political leaders were touting the fantastic plants that Native Americans have used to counteract sickness. Sadly, their motivation was in opposition to vaccines and antiviral drugs.

As land acknowledgments became a part of our protocols, I saw another type of awareness happen within and outside our community. People reached out for help writing them and trying to understand why we needed them. With the change from Columbus Day to Indigenous Peoples Day and changing mascots in schools and sports, these efforts may become significant shifts for the general public. Also, during the pandemic, people were stuck at home and wanted something new to learn and do. Our community seemed interested in learning more about their language, history, and arts. For the first time, we had great content on YouTube, podcasts, and Pinterest teaching cultural knowledge online. We were exposed to more discussions about Indigenous peoples throughout the Americas, who have a shared but unique history of colonization. Zoom became the conduit for new knowledge and thought.

Our community also became more visitable through public gatherings. The Intertribal Community Council of North Texas revitalized the American Indian Arts Festival in Dallas. They did a beautiful job capturing the excitement and ambiance that attracts people from many cultures. We lost one of our large powwows at Trader's Village in Grand Prairie, however. That powwow was discontinued after the pandemic. The UTA Powwow probably now draws the largest gathering of Native people to Arlington. It is an annual event sponsored by UTA and its Native American Student Association.

Since about 2018, school districts, museums, and corporations have been reaching out directly to the Native community. It is like someone finally got the message that Native people should be consulted on things related to our cultures.[13] For example, the Holocaust Museum contacted key people in the Missing and Murdered Indigenous Women movement. The Dallas Museum of Arts (DMA) hosted the elaborate Spiro Mounds exhibit "Spirit Lodge: Mississippian Art from Spiro" and directly contacted Native organizations for a special invitation night. The DMA told me they always had an Indigenous room, but I never felt specifically invited or welcomed until this exhibit.

From the higher education groups in DFW, the UTA Powwow has received the most attention over the years. Native engagement in this university probably happens mostly because of this powwow. I know that keeping a solid Native student group has required the help of local Native alums from UTA and other student groups. Our college enrollment is small, so we must help one another when planning significant events. The University of North Texas also has a student organization. They have sponsored events on their campus for the last few years. Sadly, we don't know the future of public colleges and their relationship with Native American people. What will happen due to Texas legislation banning the use of funds for diversity, equity, and inclusion?[14] Our community relies on some outside funds to pay the costs associated with these events that the public also enjoys.

One concern I have expressed to businesses, nonprofits, and universities numerous times is the suspicion and trust problems we have with outsiders. On many occasions, elders, performers, and artists have felt used or deceived regarding the agenda for those relationships. It is hard to repair the damage in any relationship once ties have been broken in our community.

It is also hard for Native organizations to navigate state and federal policies to get nonprofit status or to apply for grants. Some groups have tried to keep it simple to avoid ties with government agencies. The organizational structure required for approval as a nonprofit is designed based on Eurocentric models of democracy and hierarchy. Raising money to implement programs and activities is almost impossible today. Employer identification numbers (EIN), insurance, certifications, licenses, and 501(c)(3) status are necessary to receive grants, donations, and honorariums. Native groups and individuals get inundated with presentation requests, especially during Native American Heritage Month. Recently, IIA received a request for a one-hour cultural presentation. We agreed to travel to their location, and we agreed to develop and implement a presentation. The requesting organization contacted us about a month before the event requesting a signature on a seven-page contract, W-9 documentation, CVs, resume, headshot, topic description, and insurance. The burden was placed on us to meet the requirements of their bureaucracy so that we could provide a presentation that had no benefit to us.

From an Indigenous perspective, it is serious when someone requests you to help with something. It is part of our honor system. A handshake is more valuable than any piece of paper with a signature. We can learn a great deal about the ethics of broader culture by looking at the signatures on treaties. The signatures of many Nations were made with blood, but the European signatures were made with ink.

This lack of respect by agencies and corporations leads to a need for scarce resources: money, attorneys, and Certified Public Accountants (CPAs). We don't have many Native people who are wealthy philanthropists; we don't have many in the occupations needed to navigate state and national government systems. If you are an attorney or a CPA, you end up helping all the organizations; ask our IIA CPAs, Constance Hargis and Glynis Golden, or attorney Eric Reed. Their contributions over the many years have been essential to the formation and durability of almost every Native American organization in the DFW area. Much like the feeling of a broken treaty, the Native community still feels the need to be cautious of all organizations, sometimes within our community as well. Our Achilles' heel is our desperation for funding, which sometimes leads to mistakes, and we can only see the problems in these relationships too late.

TCU and Native Relationships

TCU is a private university. That status may allow TCU to take the lead in Native programming in the future. At the time of this writing, public colleges are in jeopardy, especially when it comes to DEI. I will admit I have always been cautious about any group that refers to themselves as "Christians." It is part of our peoples' collective memories and the Christian religion's impact on our ways of life. At the same time, all the qualities people call "Christian" were a natural part of our culture. They were not things we needed to learn. Love your neighbor, be honest, don't steal, be faithful, treat your body with respect, don't hurt others, take care of the land, honor your parents, and care for your children. These values are something I can agree with, and I have found these characteristics in the staff and faculty that I have personally interacted with on this journey at TCU.

As mentioned, trust and first impressions in the Native community are everything. There is a long history of organizations, colleges, and corporations purposely or inadvertently exploiting us. Sometimes in the name of research, and other times well-meaning but off the mark. We have paranoia and trauma based on over 530 years of experience with Eurocentric thinkers.

When I first meet an organization representative, I look for signals that the person is respectful, honest, and has good ethics. Dr. Scott Langston, TCU's former Native American Nations and Communities Liaison, passed the test from day one and has continued to fulfill the role of a trusted support person in our community. Dr. Langston is very knowledgeable about our cultures. He shows his openness to more than feathers and drums. He can look much deeper and seriously consider aspects of our cultures that many of us have never questioned or attempted to deconstruct. Dr. Langston is a listener and an absorber. I appreciate that he does not bring his own agenda to push on us. He always seems genuinely willing to implement our thoughts and ideas. This is a unique quality that is rarely seen. Our normal experience is when a person or entity outside our culture approaches us, almost always, they have a plan for what our role will be and how they want things done. Then all the interactions that take place are related to manipulating our people or organizations to cooperate with the plans that have already taken place. Dr. Langston comes to the table with thoughts but never plans. He has a gentle way of approaching people, which is genuine, thoughtful, and respectful of our culture and us as individuals, within those cultures.

By comparison, our IIA organization repeatedly gets approached by groups saying they want to learn from us, but what they really want is for us to "perform" for them. Rarely do these interactions feel genuine; they want their stereotypes fulfilled rather than learning anything about our culture. They look for a show or a performance. Sometimes, Native American Heritage Month has become a modern version of the old Wild West shows. I often get a call saying, we'd like to have someone here for Native American Heritage Month. Can you bring a drum? Can you bring people who wear a lot of feathers? Feathers are so pretty. I love your feathers. Native Americans are so wonderful because of the outfits they wear. When I begin to ask questions such as, "Can you help the drummers and dancers with transportation costs or an honorarium?" Usually there is silence. Once a person replied, "Don't they just do it because they enjoy dancing?" I have experienced plenty of requests from educational

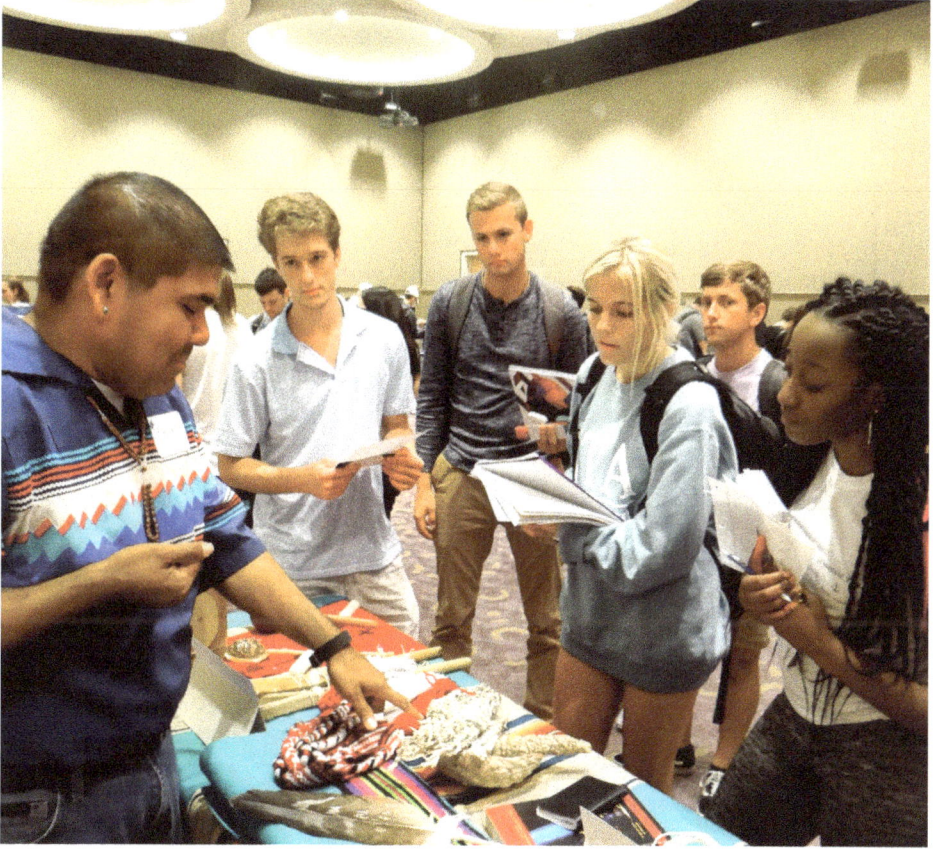

Chebon Kernell speaking with students at the Native American Health and Wellness Fair, part of TCU's fourth annual Native American and Indigenous Peoples Day Symposium, October 7, 2019. *Photo by Jaclyn Clark.*

institutions, corporations, and community gatherings, but most of the time, they are highly inappropriate. I try to gently guide them to what I believe are more meaningful experiences that don't reinforce stereotypes. Sometimes, I am not successful in swaying their minds, so I have to decline because my organization does not "own" any dancers. Everyone is an equal volunteer. We are not a performance group. Another somewhat comical experience we get several times a year is the invitation to various city and school international festivals. It is funny because people view us as outsiders even though we are the only people who actually belong to this country. The people who belong in this country are relegated as foreigners.

I never felt misused or devalued by TCU or Dr. Langston, unlike other institutions. I love the initiatives and programming. I think Dr. Langston's leadership has helped build these strong bridges in the Native community and as a result, it reflects well on the university. The events at TCU are always substantive and authentic. I can tell that Dr. Langston and the Native and Indigenous Student Association contemplated these gatherings. I was most influenced by a TCU health fair where Native people could talk with small groups of students about our cultural knowledge and values and their impact on health. Topics for the symposiums are cutting-edge and in-depth. I have never seen the NISA group or Dr. Langston refuse or shy away from an issue because it could cause controversy. Boarding schools, intergenerational trauma, Missing and Murdered Indigenous Relatives, medicine practices, and even the writing of this book, all put together, bring about a relationship of trust that hopefully will transfer to the entire TCU community.

Another positive magnet I felt with TCU is its mascot. I have always called this beautiful creature a horned toad, but at TCU, they are called the Horned Frogs. Regardless of the name, they are very sacred and endangered. Horned toads were an important part of my family history. My dad always brought me horned toad replicas and fetishes from his travels in the oil fields. People should never underestimate the value Native people place on the small things. The TCU mascot might have opened the first psychological door. We could call it a "Native Thing." Imagine my relationship with the university if the mascot was the Apache, the Indians, or the Warriors. A mascot does have meaning when you look at the context of our other experiences in this world.

For the first time, TCU recruited professors who showed their value for our culture by encouraging students to interact within our culture by volunteering at our events. In 2023, with the encouragement of Dr. Abel Gomez, IIA benefited from the help of his many students who attended and supported our IIAmericas Celebration. These TCU students were instrumental in the success of our event. There aren't enough young adults in our Native community to do all that needs to be done. We needed support for physical labor and caretaking for our elderly. I can say that each student proved to be outstanding in work ethic and attitude toward our culture. They were thrown into an unfamiliar cultural event yet found a way to fit in. Wouldn't it be amazing if, one day, TCU becomes our "go-to" volunteer pool for Native events because we can trust the students have a foundation in Native history and a level of respect for our culture through their Land Acknowledgment and other best practices?

When I look back at my relationship with TCU, the first person who pops into my head is Peggy Larney. She was the first person to invite me to a TCU campus event. Many times, we arrived at the same time in the parking lot and walked over to the student center. TCU has hosted conversations on national topics and brought in national experts on the topics, but even more exciting is the respect given to our own elders located in the DFW area. We are always involved and invited; there is never a feeling of being left out. Without the university hosting these opportunities, our community would never have been able to share and learn about these painful stories from our past and present. TCU gives us the opportunity to meet these famous people and have meaningful conversations outside of their presentations.

I will say that TCU and Dr. Langston were the first to listen to my goofy heirloom seeds stories. Dr. Langston is one of the few people I will bounce my crazy ideas to and not be embarrassed if it doesn't sound "quite right." More times than not, he would help me verbalize my thoughts and help me bring the concepts to life. I also wish I had his talent for research and writing. I can talk, but as you can see, writing is not my talent. I think I was the last writer for this book because it was so intimidating to try and edit my interview. Dr. Langston is also one of the few people whose DNA is outside our culture, but his heart understands and so he is adopted by many Native people as family. He understands my seed metaphors and the medicine ways of our plants without needing proof through some scientific method.

Supaman performing in concert during TCU's third annual Native American and Indigenous Peoples Day Symposium, October 1, 2018. *Photo by Cristian ArguetaSoto.*

One of the most exciting events was Supaman at TCU as part of the Native American and Indigenous Peoples Day Symposium in 2018. He is an amazing, inspirational Native rap artist who helped fill the room with fun and happiness. We all felt proud that night. People from every culture danced our round dance. It was a great memory and highlight for those who attended.

From a distance and financial standpoint, it was always challenging for many of our community Native events hosted by institutions. Believe it or not, the fact that we can park for free at TCU and that the campus is not too difficult to navigate makes it a positive experience for our community. With every event, someone, usually Dr. Langston, provided maps and detailed descriptions of the campus so we weren't frustrated or lost. Many times, there was water and snacks; food is a key bridge builder for Native people. These simple types of consideration are not always true with other locations and sponsoring groups. Once we were asked to bring our culture to Channel 8 news station in DFW. No one said we had to pay ten dollars for parking. Many of our people don't carry credit cards or cash, so some of our dancers got stuck in the parking lot and missed the performance time. If you don't make it easy for our community to attend an event, you must not really want us there. I've always been impressed with the number of people who have attended the TCU events, even elders come to evening events despite the struggle to drive. I also like the mixture of national figures and respected local elders at the TCU events.

My organization has developed long-lasting friendships because of TCU programming. I allied with TCU alum Albert Nungaray and his sister Laura Nungaray. They are amazing desert plant knowledge keepers. Annita Lucchesi on the Missing and Murdered Indigenous Women and MMIR emergency facing our cultures. The boarding school panels allowed our elders to talk about firsthand experiences. I remember seeing some tears in students' eyes. Dr. Patrisia Gonzales, understanding Native plants and healing practices. TCU could be an icon for understanding the Native worldview and integrating that knowledge into practice.

I genuinely value my time serving on the TCU Native American Advisory Circle. Listening to the history and knowledge of these elders and young people is another precious gift. This body of people represents the ancestors of people who lived on the land we are writing about today. I remember reviewing Dr. Langston's extensive research about the land history of TCU. Dr. Langston put into writing the context of TCU and the Native community over time. I have met many Native people who don't know about the land they are on. I found it very powerful to see our stories finally written and published on the TCU website. In May 2023, the reaction on Facebook was powerful when Dr. Langston posted the story of the land where TCU stands. Even our Native community had no idea how awful Texas history was to its first people.

I am going to sound very biased, but our culture, lifeways, and world-view have much to offer this country, especially with the chaos in this state. The climate of our world today, both the land and the psychology, could benefit from Native science and Native health practices. Incorporating those worldviews could help with the divisiveness. Our Native communities were founded on the ability to negotiate, listen, compromise, and respect other people's knowledge, equality among sexes, respect for our youth, elders, and veterans, and equality within governance patterns. These values are also TCU's opportunities to support healthy relationships using this grounded knowledge. Imagine how students and the surrounding community could benefit from a thoughtful connection with the land. How powerful that could be? As a social worker, I also feel students can be healthier if connected to the land where they go to school.

When we listen to the Earth and become observers of what the land has to offer us, we are never alone. Sitting on a park bench between classes and watching the squirrels work so hard to collect our sacred medicine, the acorn, can make us smile. Smelling the whiff of our sacred juniper and cedar medicine can help purify our thoughts. We join all the people whose footprints came before us. Students from other countries must feel so alone and miss their countries; that is how our Native students feel when their land is only two hours away. It feels like we are a continent away. Also, remembering and understanding our relations and what they experienced gives a better perspective on our own lives.

I don't want our young college students to feel any guilt over what their great-great-great-grandparents did to our people. But we can help them remember that a stolen laptop or cell phone differs from stolen land. If we lose our perspective, we will feel helpless and powerless. The intensity of grief feels equally powerful, but that grief won't help us survive and become better people. We must keep perspective. Part of our seventh-generation prophecy is remembering what our previous generations withstood and recognizing their creative resiliency under harsh conditions. Our Native students at the university, as do all the other students, need our support. What we forget when a Native student stands before us is the struggle inside their bodies and minds due to multigenerational historical trauma. Sadly, they are too young to put their finger on those experiences and feelings. The feelings of being alone and disconnected from our Native community can be improved with the spirituality of land connection. Understanding that there's a history behind where you're studying that goes back many, many, many years ago, and each person contributes to this university being either a good place or a wrong place. If they can empathize with the people who once lived here, they may become more sensitive to their impact on the world around them.

Today, TCU is uniquely positioned to recruit, support, and learn from students of our many Nations. Traditional Native teachings can move people toward healing. Native perspectives can impact every university field of study. What would happen if every professor, in every class, took it upon themselves to see what Native culture would say about the subject they were teaching or how they have contributed to the knowledge? Most of the time, this is done only in Native studies courses. It reminds me of a story about the raven having black feathers. He went up to the sun on task, but when he came back to Earth, he caught on fire, and his feathers turned black. How did Native people know that something entering the Earth's atmosphere would catch on fire? Why are some of our creation stories about a muskrat being the only animal to stay underwater long enough to bring mud from the bottom of the ocean to the turtle's back? How can the science found within the medicine wheel on Cloud Peak and Bear Butte help guide us to understand more about science? How could Native knowledge of agricultural practices save a continent from starvation? Philosophy, math, geometry, architecture, medicine, physiology, computer science, psychology, and many more.

TCU stated its contribution and opportunities through its Land Acknowledgment. The TCU Land Acknowledgment is a carefully crafted statement and a testament to the sincerity of the group that selected each word. It is more than a statement that tells us who lived on the land.

I have worked on the Grand Prairie Independent School District American Indian/Native Studies High School curriculum development since 2020. I did not realize how much Texas education had failed our students by the twelfth grade. TCU is inheriting students who think all Native people are extinct. Texas is not alone in this failure, but a freshman coming to TCU may be hearing for the first time in their lives that they are sitting in class on stolen land. One way to address misinformation, prejudice, and bias is through human-to-human interaction. I have always been taught that we change our thinking based on relationships rather than through books and lectures. Deep, long-lasting, effective change in attitudes must come through personal connections.

Formal education helps the brain make a shift, but relationships with people from other cultures can validate us as human beings. Dr. Abel Gomez made our organization's IIAmericas Celebration event both in April 2023 and 2024 an extra-credit opportunity for his students. It wasn't required, but it could help them with their grades. He invited my daughter and me to introduce ourselves to his class so they could have familiar faces and would be more relaxed about attending the event. As mentioned before, many of his students came. They made the difference between the event working and not working. It was cute, because some of them said, "This is not what I thought a Native American event would be." They experienced the usual chaos and coordination issues of any significant event. They realized we had the same problems anybody has, but that experience, in and of itself, dispelled many myths. There were a lot of funny jokes and silliness, but they expected Native people to be stoic, scary, and serious. Several of them said they were apprehensive about coming, but at the end of the event, they asked to be invited next year. The students worked very hard but still had a great time.

They couldn't truly learn from a book about boarding schools. So I sent some of them to help Dora Brought-Plenty, who was a boarding school survivor, at her artist booth. "Wow, this is a real person." They'd maybe seen her give her talk at one of the TCU presentations, but to see her in action trying to hang up her clothes and generously sponsoring the fashion show was so different. Dr. Gomez recently told me that the class we spoke to in person before the event shifted their attitude toward the Native history he was teaching. They became more positive and open, but the classes that did not attend continued to be somewhat pessimistic and negative about learning. This indicates to me that our Native community also needs to help TCU professors by being present and available as a way to connect people to people.

Just to repeat, it was TCU that sent students to our event, when no other university did. They didn't sit back and act like outsiders. They jumped in, almost like we were at a family reunion. I attribute the students' sincerity to Dr. Gomez's teaching in class and the idea of bringing our culture directly to the students in addition to learning about it in books.

The recent hiring of professors Dr. Pablo Montes and Dr. Abel Gomez increases the chance that TCU can become a major advocate for Native cultural issues. I wish every student had an opportunity to listen to their words. One of the things Dr. Langston has done is to advocate for two critical things at TCU: a permanent Native American Nations and Communities Liaison and full scholarships for two Native students each year.[15] Listening to Native college students, I realize that success for these college students will depend on the support they receive from someone willing to be there "like family" when the stress of being away from home becomes too great. The full scholarship will relieve one of the most significant educational barriers, the cost of board and tuition. Despite what people think, there are no free rides just because you are Native. When TCU recruits Native candidates, we must have good mentors for them. Given the current politics at public universities, TCU may need to be a leader for this mentorship with other students in the DFW metroplex. DEI defunding at other universities may result in Native students dropping out. Maybe TCU could incorporate the support of other students from other universities to create an even more prominent family for the TCU Native students. Growing up in a Native community usually means being familiar with a large community of people who know you. The isolation can be devastating when attending college outside your community. There is a more significant role TCU can play because its private funding is not tied to legislation. The more TCU welcomes Native people to its campus, the more we must consider support systems for those new students.

TCU might consider a one-semester credit course for all students on Native history in Texas. All the students would be on the same page and with the same knowledge base. The Land Acknowledgment would have more meaning for Native people, and for the average person who has no idea where and why an acknowledgment is so important. At a minimum, Horned Frogs' first-year orientation should include a Native history of where they are going to school, with representatives from the Native community, if possible, coming to meet them. TCU could set the tone and expectations for their students. Let's not just talk about the land; let's help students become the new stewards of this land. TCU can build a reputation built on Indigenous respect.

I would encourage department heads to look at whether they have ever invited a Native person to meet the faculty in their program or offered an opportunity for the faculty to ask questions about what they are running into with students and the Land Acknowledgment. Maybe the Native community can help provide some support. We also must expand our definitions of who is Indigenous. Using language as a research base, at least 25 percent, some say as high as 40 percent, of people who mark forms as Hispanic are Indigenous people in their countries of origin. They maintain their ceremonial ties to their land and speak the language of these Nations. We need to be sure our eyes and ears are open, so we do not miss students with an identity closer to our American Indian Tribes.

Lastly, if I were going to start with one thing to recommend to TCU leaders, it is to study your Land Acknowledgment and follow your heart with its meaning. Take it to heart; don't consider it a history lesson. I'm an optimistic person, and if you study that Land Acknowledgment and think about it and absorb it, it sensitizes you. So that's what we call "a good way" to start.

TCU Land Acknowledgment from My Heart

by Annette Anderson

As a university (everyone at TCU),
we acknowledge (validating the past even though we weren't there)
the many benefits we have of being in this place. (Reflecting on the
bounty we received from someone else's hurt.)
It is a space we share (no one has more rights than any other)
with all living beings, human and non-human. (We must give equal
standing to everything below the soil, on the soil, and up in the
atmosphere.)

It is an ancient space (so old it is sacred and beyond our human understanding)

where others have lived before us. (People cultivated the land, gave birth to their children, and died on this land; it meant everything to them.)

The monument created jointly (many long talks and building trust)

by TCU and the Wichita and Affiliated Tribes (it's a sacred agreement)

reminds us of our benefits, responsibilities, and relationships.

We pause (stop, listen, and think) to reflect on its words:

This ancient land (here before the two-legged were formed),

for all our relations. (Our brothers and sisters who live under the Earth, on the Earth, and in the sky, those we can see and those we cannot see but trust they are there)

We respectfully (we are humble and struggle to understand)

acknowledge (validate the truth)

all Native American peoples (anyone who lived and hunted on this land)

who have lived on this land since time immemorial. (Since creation)

TCU especially acknowledges (the University and all its faculty, staff, and students)

and pays respect (we thank you and are sorry about this history)

to the Wichita and Affiliated Tribes (the people who had to sacrifice their land through violence, from no fault of their own),

upon whose historical homeland (the sacred ground that carries their memories)

our university is located.

NOTES

Ediorial Notes

1. For more information about the changes taking place around the time of publication, see Eric Hoover, "In Sweeping Letter, Ed. Dept. Says SCOTUS Ruling Applies to All Race-Conscious Programs," *Chronicle of Higher Education*, Feb. 16, 2025. https://www.chronicle.com/article/in-sweeping-letter-ed-dept-says-scotus-ruling-applies-to-all-race-conscious-programs, accessed April 7, 2025.

Foreword

1. Gregory Gomez, my brother in "the Indian way," as we say, or adopted kin.
2. S. Mintz and S. McNeil, "Texas' Second President Calls for the Expulsion or Extermination of the Republic's Indians," *Digital History* 2018, https://www.digitalhistory.uh.edu/disp_textbook.cfm?smtid=3&psid=3667.
3. K. Tsianina Lomawaima and Teresa L. McCarty, *"To Remain an Indian": Lessons in Democracy from a Century of Native American Education* (New York: Teachers College Press, 2006).
4. George Klos, "American Indians," in *Handbook of Texas*, Texas State Historical Association, December 1,1995, https://www.tshaonline.org/handbook/entries/indians; C. Herndon Williams, "1800 Texas Populated with Many Indian Tribes," *Coastal Bend Chronicles*, June 15, 2021, https://www.stexasnews.com/refugio_county_press/1800-texas-populated-with-many-indian-tribes/article_99c42d7c-cd56-11eb-ba6b-93be1da4e2b3.html.
5. Robert Lee and Tristan Ahtone, "Land-Grab Universities: Expropriated Indigenous Land Is the Foundation for the Land Grant University System," *High Country News*, March 30, 2020, https://www.hcn.org/issues/52-4/indigenous-affairs-education-land-grab-universities/.
6. Holy See Press Office, "The Joint Statement of the Dicasteries for Culture and

Education and for Promoting Integral Human Development on the 'Doctrine of Discovery,' 30–03–2023," https://press.vatican.va/content/salastampa/en/bollettino/pubblico/2023/03/30/230330b.html.

7. Sandy Grande, "Un-Settling the University: Toward a Decolonial Praxis," presented at Teaching, Learning, Socio-Cultural Studies Graduate Student Colloquy: I-We:mta: Foregrounding Indigenous Epistemologies in Education, University of Arizona, February 22, 2018.

8. The Horned Frog, or horned lizard, is TCU's mascot.

9. Purple is TCU's school color.

10. Patrisia Gonzales, "Water-Womb-Land Cosmologic: Protocols for Traditional Ecological Knowledge," *Ecopsychology*, special issue on "Wisdom Traditions, Science and Care for the Earth 12," no. 2 (June 2020): 84–90.

11. Ana I. Sánchez-Rivera, Paul Jacobs, and Cody Spence, "A Look at the Largest American Indian and Alaska Native Tribes and Villages in the Nation, Tribal Areas and States," *Detailed Data for Hundreds of Native American and Alaska Native Tribes, U.S. Census*, October 3, 2023, https://www.census.gov/library/stories/2023/10/2020-census-dhc-a-aian-population.html.

12. Juanita Cabrera Lopez, Patrisia Gonzales, Rachel Starks, and Lorena Brady, "Indigenous Peoples' Rights to Exist, Self Determination, Language and Due Process in Migration," report submitted to the United Nations' Universal Periodic Review of the United States Human Rights Record, May 2020.

13. Patrisia Gonzales, *The Mud People: Chronicles, Testimonios and Remembrances* (San Jose, CA: Chusma House Press, 2003).

14. Gregory Cajete, *Native Science: Natural Laws of Interdependence* (Santa Fe, NM: Clear Light Publishers, 2000).

Introduction

1. For example, in Fall 2012 Langston began teaching an introductory religion course, "Understanding Religion: Society and Culture: Native Americans, Christians, and American Ideals." As the syllabus indicated, this course addressed "Native American experiences with and responses to Christianity, as well as European and American efforts to use Christianity to dominate Native Americans and dismantle their cultures from 1492 to the present." Other faculty taught Native American-related courses from their respective disciplinary perspectives. Yet there was nothing that knit these courses together in a broader, organized, and institutional manner.

2. See Sam Bruton, "TCU explores Indigenous People's Day at inaugural symposium," TCU 360, October 5, 2016, https://tcu360.com/2016/10/05/tcu-explores-indigenous-peoples-day-at-inaugural-symposium/.

3. "Overview," Texas Native Health, LinkedIn, https://www.linkedin.com/company/texasnativehealth/about/; Texas Native Health website, https://uitct.org/, both accessed July 16, 2023.

4. Kyle D. Dean, *The Economic Impact of Tribal Nations in Oklahoma, Fiscal Year 2019*, Oklahoma Native Impact, March 23, 2022, http://www.oknativeimpact.com/

wp-content/uploads/2022/03/All-Tribe-Impact-Report-2022-Final.pdf; "New Report Captures Economic Impact of Tribal Nations in Oklahoma," *Oklahoman*, March 24, 2022, https://www.oklahoman.com/story/news/2022/03/24/ oklahoma-native-impact-report-tribal-nation-state-economy/7133043001/.

5. The guide can be downloaded from TCU's Native American and Indigenous Peoples Initiative webpage at https://www.tcu.edu/native-american-indigenous-peoples/index.php, accessed June 25, 2023.

6. Four Directions Scholars Program, https://admissions.tcu.edu/four-directions.php, accessed October 15, 2023.

7. For a fuller explanation of the meaning and process of the monument, see the document "TCU's Native American Monument: Lessons in Diversity, Equity, and Inclusion," located on TCU's Native American and Indigenous Peoples Initiative webpage, https://web.archive.org/web/20240621170119/https://addran.tcu.edu/ files/Learning-Guide-for-NA-Monument-Lessons-in-DEI-7-09-19.pdf, accessed June 25, 2023. See also Nick Stephens, "New Monument Recognizes Native American and Indigenous Peoples," TCU 360, October 11, 2018, https://tcu360.com/2018/10/11/ new-monument-recognizes-native-american-and-indigenous-peoples/.

8. The document can be found on TCU's Native American and Indigenous Peoples Initiative webpage, https://www.tcu.edu/native-american-indigenous-peoples/index.php, accessed June 25, 2023.

9. "Artwork Creates Space to Learn, Partner with NAIP," TCU, News, April 19, 2022, https://www.tcu.edu/news/2022/artwork-creates-space-to-learn-partner-with-naip.php; Riley Knight, "Symposium Challenges Native American Stereotypes," TCU 360, October 3, 2017, https://tcu360.com/2017/10/03/ symposium-challenges-native-american-stereotypes/.

PART I: BEING IN RELATION WITH THE LAND AND INDIGENOUS PEOPLES

What the Prairies and Rivers Can Teach Us
Learning from and Being Accountable to Land at Texas Christian University

1. "Salvatierra, Guanajuato," Gobierno de México, last modified July 4, 2019, https://www.gob.mx/sectur/articulos/salvatierra-guanajuato.

2. I capitalize Land throughout this chapter intentionally to indicate "Land" as a proper noun. As many Indigenous scholars have shared, capitalizing Land is a discursive maneuver to highlight Land as a social, spiritual, and sacred relation instead of "land," which often is fixated to only a geopolitical materiality. See Sandra Styres and Dawn M. Zinga, "The Community-First Land-Centred Theoretical Framework: Bringing a 'Good Mind' to Indigenous Education Research?" *Canadian Journal of Education* 36, no. 2 (2013): 300–301.

3. Theresa Stewart-Ambo and K. Wayne Yang, "Beyond Land Acknowledgment in Settler Institutions," *Social Text* 39, no. 1 (2021): 31.

4. Stewart-Ambo and Yang, "Beyond Land Acknowledgment in Settler Institutions," 34.

5. Stewart-Ambo and Yang, "Beyond Land Acknowledgment in Settler Institutions," 34.

6. "Native American Land Acknowledgement," TCU Center for Connection Culture, https://www.tcu.edu/native-american-indigenous-peoples/about/native-american-land-acknowledgment.php, accessed August 1, 2023.

7. Eve Tuck and K. Wayne Yang, "Decolonization Is Not a Metaphor," *Tabula Rasa* 38 (2021): 10.

8. I draw on abolitionist feminism as a praxis that is politically informed and demands the destruction of violent systems of oppression through intentional movements, organizing, and transforming. See Angela Y. Davis, Gina Dent, Erica R. Meiners, and Beth E. Richie, *Abolition. Feminism. Now*, vol. 2 (Chicago: Haymarket Books, 2022), 4.

9. Futurities are best described as questions not only about the outcomes of certain futures but how futures are implicated, negotiated, and contested through various ways of understanding. Whereas Indigenous futurities are invested in uprooting and destroying settler colonialism, settler futures desire the elimination of Indigenous peoples. As Tuck and Gaztambide-Fernandez state, "Our commitments are to what might be called an Indigenous futurity, which does not foreclose the inhabitation of Indigenous land by non-Indigenous peoples, but does foreclose settler colonialism and settler epistemologies. That is to say that Indigenous futurity does not require the erasure of now-settlers in the ways that settler futurity requires of Indigenous peoples." See Eve Tuck and Rubén A. Gaztambide-Fernández, "Curriculum, Replacement, and Settler Futurity," *Journal of Curriculum Theorizing* 29, no. 1 (2013): 80.

10. Also, these minimal asks are not exhaustive and Indigenous communities might have different perceptions of what minimal asks may entail. I offer these suggestions as entryways into the conversation of reparative work that needs to be done and not as a definitive solution.

11. Leigh Patel, *Decolonizing Educational Research: From Ownership to Answerability* (New York: Routledge, 2015), 8.

12. Linda Tuhiwai Smith, Eve Tuck, and K. Wayne Yang, eds., *Indigenous and Decolonizing Studies in Education: Mapping the Long View* (New York: Routledge, 2018), 10.

TCU's Relationships with Native Americans and the Land, 1838–2014

1. When referring to TCU, I mean the institution in all its manifestations and the actions taken by its members as part of the TCU community.

2. There are great differences of opinion and preference for terminology referring to the original inhabitants of what is now called the Americas, including differences in legal, academic, and popular use. I have followed the guidelines given in the Native American Journalists Association's Reporting Guide, "Reporting and Indigenous Terminology," https://najanewsroom.com/wp-content/uploads/2018/11/NAJA_Reporting_and_ Indigenous_Terminology_Guide.pdf, accessed July 24, 2023. In short, I use specific tribal affiliations whenever possible, but when needing to refer collectively to multiple Native Nations, I primarily use the terms "Native American" and "Indigenous," recognizing that both are problematic and difficult to define. The United Nations' Office of the High Commissioner for Human Rights explains that even though "Indigenous peoples live on all continents, from the Arctic to the Pacific, via Asia, Africa and the Americas," "there is no singularly authoritative definition of Indigenous Peoples under international law and policy." When using this term, therefore, "the identification of an indigenous people is the right of the people itself—the right of self-identification." See "About Indigenous Peoples and human rights. OHCHR and Indigenous Peoples," https://www.ohchr.org/ en/indigenous-peoples/about-indigenous-peoples-and-human-rights, accessed July 24,

2023. I follow the point made by the United Nations Permanent Forum on Indigenous Issues that "the most fruitful approach is to identify, rather than define indigenous peoples." See "Indigenous Peoples, Indigenous Voices Factsheet," https://www.un.org/esa/socdev/unpfii/documents/5session_factsheet1.pdf, accessed July 24, 2023. While I use the term "Native American" to refer to the Indigenous peoples residing within the territories claimed by the United States, I also recognize the definition given by the National Congress of American Indians, "All Native people of the United States and its trust territories (i.e., American Indians, Alaska Natives, Native Hawaiians, Chamorros, and American Samoans), as well as persons from Canadian First Nations and Indigenous communities in Mexico and Central and South America who are US residents." See *Tribal Nations and the United States: An Introduction,*" February 2020, 11, https://archive.ncai.org/tribalnations/introduction/Indian_Country_101_Updated_February_2019.pdf.

3. TCU's Land Acknowledgment and supporting resources can be found at https://www.tcu.edu/native-american-indigenous-peoples/index.php, accessed June 18, 2023.

4. See, for instance, "Mission & History," on TCU's webpage, https://www.tcu.edu/about/mission-history.php, and TCU's Race and Reconciliation Initiative, https://www.tcu.edu/race-reconciliation-initiative/index.php, both accessed June 10, 2023.

5. William E. Tucker, "Muddle in the Middle: The 'C' in TCU," *TCU Magazine* (Winter 2001), https://magazine.tcu.edu/winter-2001/muddle-in-the-middle-the-c-in-tcu/, and Elizabeth H. Flowers and Darren J. N. Middleton, "The 'C' in TCU," *Horned Frog* (blog), October 28, 2014, https://tcuadmission.wordpress.com/2014/10/28/faculty-feature-the-c-in-tcu/. For examples of Euro-American Christianity's role in colonization, see Vine Deloria Jr., "An Open Letter to the Heads of the Christian Churches in America," in *For This Land: Writings on Religion in America*, ed. James Treat (New York: Routledge, 1999), 77–83; and Scott M. Langston, "'A Running Thread of Ideals': Joshua and the Israelite Conquest in American History," in *On Prophets, Warriors, and Kings: Former Prophets through the Eyes of Their Interpreters*, ed. G. J. Brooke and A. Feldman, Beihefte zur Zeitschrift für die alttestamentliche Wissenschaft 470 (Berlin: De Gruyter, 2016), 229–64.

6. Susan C. Vehik, "Wichita Ethnohistory," in *Kansas Archaeology*, ed. Robert J. Hoard and William E. Banks (Lawrence: University Press of Kansas, 2006), 206–18. See also "Gault School of Archaeological Research," https://www.gaultschool.org/ and Timothy K. Perttula, Thomas R. Hester, Stephen L. Black, Carolyn E. Boyd, Michael B. Collins, Myles R. Miller, J. Michael Quigg, Wilson W. Crook III, Bryon Schroeder, Ellen Sue Turner, Drew Sitters, Nancy Velchoff, Richard A. Weinstein, and Thomas J. Williams, "Prehistory," *Handbook of Texas Online*, https://www.tshaonline.org/handbook/entries/prehistory, both accessed July 09, 2023. For pronunciation of the Wichita terms, see the Tribe's online dictionary at https://wichitatribe.com/dictionary, accessed July 10, 2023.

7. Mirabeau B. Lamar, "Message to the Senate and House of Representatives," December 20, 1838, *Journal of the House of Representatives of the Republic of Texas*, Regular Session, Third Congress, November 5, 1838 (Houston: Intelligencer Office, 1839), 174, https://www.lrl.texas.gov/scanned/CongressJournals/03/HouseJournal3rdCon_Entire.pdf. For an extensive account of how Texas sought to exterminate Native Americans, see Gary Clayton Anderson, *The Conquest of Texas: Ethnic Cleansing in the Promised Land, 1820–1875* (Norman: University of Oklahoma Press, 2005).

8. Interview with Joseph Addison Clark in "He Worked on the News," *Galveston Daily News,*

February 15, 1892, 7; Randolph Clark, *Reminiscences Biographical and Historical* (Lee Clark: Wichita Falls, TX, 1919), 11–13, 16, 19.

9.   "History of Texas Public Lands," Texas General Land Office, 10–11, https://www. glo.texas.gov/sites/default/files/2025-01/history-of-texas-public-lands%202022.pdf, accessed June 12, 2023. While "those with African blood" were denied Texas citizenship by the 1836 constitution, bounty and donation land acts did not specifically forbid Blacks from receiving military land grants and, in fact, a few did receive them. Prior to the Republic of Texas, Spain and Mexico issued land grants in Texas, although there do not appear to have been any in what eventually became Tarrant County.

10. *Telegraph and Texas Register*, November 10, 1838. The *Telegraph and Texas Register* was founded in 1835 and became the official news outlet for the Republic of Texas. The Trinity River's four branches are the Clear, West, Elm, and East.

11. By the 1830s, diverse groups of American Indians were living in north and east Texas. On October 12, 1837, the Republic of Texas Senate's Standing Committee on Indian Affairs submitted "a list of the different tribes" residing within Texas, along with brief descriptions of them. This report identified "the Keechi, Tawakoni, Waco and Tawehash or Pawnee" as "Indians of the Prairies" who "reside mostly on the Head waters of the Trinity, Brazos, and Colorado" and who "are now at war with this Republick." "The Caddo, Ioni, Anadarko, Abadoche among whom are dispersed the Ais and Nacogdoches Indians . . . previous to their late Hostilities live in the County of Nacogdoches." (In 1837, Nacogdoches County encompassed an area that would eventually become all or part of twenty other counties in east Texas). The committee noted that currently most of them were "on the Prairies united with the Hostile tribes that dwell there." The report also identified the "Huawni [Hainai?] and Choctaw" as living in Nacogdoches and Shelby counties, and the Coushatta, Alabama, Biloxi, and Muskogee living in Nacogdoches and Liberty counties. The "Northern Indians" consisted of the Kickapoo, Shawnee, Delaware, Potawatomi, and Menominee and lived in Nacogdoches County. The Cherokee also lived in Nacogdoches County and "are now in continual communication with the Prairie Indians." Regarding the Comanche, the standing committee confessed that it "knows but little" but did note that the Comanche were "the natural enemies of the Mexicans" and "are roving Indians." The committee also described the Lipan, Karankawa, and Tonkawa "as part of the Mexican nation" who live in west Texas and are "no longer to be considered as a different people from that nation." See "Report of Standing Committee on Indian Affairs" in *The Indian Papers of Texas and the Southwest*, ed. Dorman H. Winfrey and James M. Day (Austin: Texas State Historical Association, 1995), vol. 1, 22–28. The Kickapoo Tribe of Oklahoma website explains, "By the mid-18th century the Kickapoo lived in two communities, the "Prairie Band," along Illinois's Sangamon River, and the "Vermillion Band," east of the Wabash River in Indiana. The Prairie Kickapoo band resisted acculturation and continued to migrate, going first to Missouri and then to the Spanish province of Texas before the 1821 Mexican Revolution. Spanish officials gave them land in Texas. However, after the Texas Revolution, the Republic of Texas did not want them. In 1839, they were forcibly removed, and many traveled to Mexico." See https://www. kickapootribeofoklahoma.com/, accessed July 8, 2023. The Shawnee Tribe's website indicates that its "ancestral, pre-contact homeland is the greater middle Ohio River Valley region," but they "were regularly forced to relocate their settlements beyond the ever-expanding boundary of colonial-controlled lands." After obtaining a Spanish land grant in 1793 near Cape Girardeau, Missouri, they were forced to move again in 1825 after signing a treaty with the

United States that ceded their Missouri lands for a reservation in what is now eastern Kansas. "Other Shawnees moved to Texas and Old Mexico and later to southern Oklahoma, becoming the Absentee Shawnee Tribe." See https://web.archive.org/web/20221127230025/, accessed July 8, 2023. During the 1820s–30s, the Cherokee, Muscogee/Creek, and Seminole Tribes were forcibly removed from their homelands in what is called the southeastern part of the United States and relocated to what is now Oklahoma. At the time of European contact, the Hasinai (Caddo) belonged to three confederacies, the Kadohadacho ("Caddo" being a shortened form that was eventually applied to all groups), Natchitoches, and Hasinai, with traditional homelands in what became the states of Oklahoma, Louisiana, Arkansas, and Texas. For the Hasinai, east Texas was their ancestral homeland and the Trinity River marked the western boundary of their traditional territory. Hasinai is translated as "our people." I am grateful for the assistance of Alaina Tahlate, Language Revitalizationist, Caddo Nation of Oklahoma, email, July 10, 2023. See also Cecile Elkins Carter, *Caddo Indians: Where We Come From* (Norman: University of Oklahoma Press, 1995), 4, 295.

12. There are three accounts of the attack given by participants. The first came a few weeks after the attack and was written by the militia's Acting Brigade Inspector. See, Wm. N. Porter, Acting Brigade Inspector, June 5, 1841, *Journals of the Sixth Congress of the Republic of Texas, 1841–1842*, vol. 3, Journals called session, 416–19, found at https://www.lrl.texas. gov/scanned/CongressJournals/06/6thCongressExtra.pdf. The other two were given decades after the attack. Henry Stout gave an interview to the *Fort Worth Weekly Gazette* on July 1, 1887, under the title "The Long Ago. A Half Hour's Chat with Mr. Henry Stout of Wood County, one of the Texas Veterans," 7. Rev. Andrew Davis wrote an account that appeared in the *Dallas Morning News* on October 7, 1900, titled "Story of Denton's Death," 15. There also have been many popular retellings, as well as a few academic accounts. For the latter, see, Rex Wallace Strickland, "History of Fannin County, 1836–1843, II," *Southwestern Historical Quarterly* 34, no. 1 (July 1930): 38–68, and Janet Suzanne Claeys-Shahmiri, *Ethnohistorical Investigation of the Battle of Village Creek, Tarrant County, Texas, in 1841* (MA thesis, University of Texas, Arlington, 1989). See also Stephen Lee Maxwell, "An Analysis of the Lithic Artifacts and Debitage from the Village Creek Sites of North Central Texas" (MA thesis, University of Texas, Arlington, 2002). Gary Clayton Anderson gives a good rendering in his book, *The Conquest of Texas* (Norman: University of Oklahoma Press, 2019), 192–93. It is briefly mentioned in Randolph B. Campbell, *Gone to Texas: A History of the Lone Star State* (New York: Oxford University Press, 2003), 172.

13. For Stout's account, see "The Long Ago." For the return of the captured child, see "Late From The Frontier—Indian Treaty," *Northern Standard* (Clarksville), October 14, 1843, 2. José Maria, or Aasch (Iesh), was *caddi* (leader) of the Nadako, or Anadarko, Tribe (see Carter, *Caddo Indians*, 295). In addition to Henry Stout's account of the two women and baby, a report of the attack published a month after it occurred refers to a "squaw" who had been captured. See "Another Indian Horde Routed," *Telegraph and Texas Register*, June 23, 1841, 2. According to Gerard Gerdes ("Scout Who Missed Mier by Fraction Lives at Ranger," *Fort Worth Star-Telegram*, May 17, 1914), "a squaw and a boy" were captured, but the "squaw" soon escaped. Gerdes claimed that he "often saw the Indian boy, who was kept by Mrs. Tarrant till prisoners were exchanged." In 1988, Tarrant's keeping of the boy was given as evidence that though he was an "Indian fighter," he was not an "Indian hater." See Jerry Coffey, "To Honor the General," *Fort Worth Star-Telegram*, May 27, 1988.

14. Porter, *Journals of the Sixth Congress of the Republic of Texas, 1841–1842*, vol. 3, Journals called

session, 418–19.

15. "Expedition against the Trinity Indians," *Telegraph and Texas Register*, September 1, 1841, 3; Omer C. Stewart, *Forgotten Fires: Native Americans and the Transient Wilderness* (Norman: University of Oklahoma Press, 2002), 114; Carolyn Merchant, *American Environmental History: An Introduction* (New York: Columbia University Press, 2007), 15–22; "Report of Secretary of State," *Weekly Texian* (Austin), December 8, 1841, 1; "National Anniversary," *Telegraph and Texas Register*, March 2, 1842, 2; "Many of the Indians," *Telegraph and Texas Register*, November 22, 1843, 3. The latter article explained that many of the various tribes that signed the treaty at Bird's Fort had been "attacked by fevers, and a large number of them died. The Indians were ill provided with provisions or clothing, and appeared very poor and dejected." On the same page, the article "Colony in the Cross Timbers" explained that twenty-five families had settled in Peters Colony "near the mouth of Elm Creek," from "Bird's Fort to Dallas, a distance of 17 miles."

16. For Denton as the Warrior Preacher, see "Letter from Mr. Harrison Reporting on General Rusk's El Paso Exploring Party," *Gonzales Inquirer*, November 12, 1853, 1. See also Cecil Harper Jr., "Bryan, John Neely," *Handbook of Texas Online*, Texas State Historical Association, https://www.tshaonline.org/handbook/entries/bryan-john-neely, accessed May 27, 2021. Overall, Peters Colony brought 2,205 families to Texas and dispersed 879,920 acres of land. For a succinct overview of Peters Colony, see the Texas General Land Office's summary and biographical note at https://www.glo.texas.gov/archive-collections/peters-colony-records, accessed June 7, 2023. See also Seymour V. Connor, *The Peters Colony of Texas* (Austin: Texas State Historical Association, 1959). For the two Texas reservations, see F. Todd Smith, *The Caddos, the Wichitas, and the United States, 1846–1901* (College Station: Texas A&M University Press, 1996), 39–69.

17. Randolph Clark explained that the Clarks sold their families' lands in various parts of the state and gave that money to the college to help Add-Ran College survive financially. See *Reminiscences*, 52–53.

18. "Teacher's Guide: An Introduction to the Land History of Texas," Teacher Resources, Texas History Lesson Plans, Additional Resources, Texas General Land Office, 2–3, https://www.glo.texas.gov/sites/default/files/20241018/texas-land-history-teachers-guide.pdf, accessed June 12, 2023 (first quote); "History of Texas Public Lands," Texas General Land Office, 11, https://www.glo.texas.gov/sites/default/files/2025-01/history-of-texas-public-lands%202022.pdf, accessed June 12, 2023 (second quote). A headright was a land grant intended to induce settlement in Texas.

19. "Teacher's Guide," 2–3.

20. The history of this land claim and survey is complicated. The delay between the 1859 survey and the 1868 patent is likely due to challenges regarding the validity of the headright certificate, which was eventually verified. The 640-acre certificate was also subdivided into three parts, two for 160 acres each and one for 320 acres, and sold multiple times before being surveyed. Ultimately, the lands claimed were the 160 acres in which TCU is located, and 160-acre and 320-acre surveys located ironically near Village Creek. I am grateful to the staff in the General Land Office for their assistance in making sense of this file. See also Contract Fairmount Land Co. with Texas Christian University, November 20, 1910, Minutes, 1889–1922, box 1, Records of the TCU Board of Trustees, RU 01, Archives and Special Collections, Mary Couts Burnett Library (hereafter cited as TCU Special Collections), 233–38; Colby D. Hall, *The History of Texas Christian University: A College of the Cattle Frontier* (Fort Worth: TCU Press, 1947, repr. 2014), 136–37; Texas

Christian University to Texas Building Company, Mechanics Lien, Tarrant County, Texas Clerk, October 16, 1911, vol. 28, 478, and Wade H. Hudson, Robertson 3rd class, abstracts 716, 717, and 718, file 004988, Texas General Land Office, https:// s3.glo.texas.gov/ncu/SCANDOCS/archives_webfiles/arcmaps/webfiles/landgrants/ PDFs/3/4/9/349003.pdf, accessed June 6, 2023. Hudson qualified to receive these lands under section ten of "An Act Relating to Lands in Peters Colony," passed by the Texas Legislature on February 10, 1852 (Hans Peter Gammel and Mareus Neilsen, *The Laws of Texas, 1822–1897*, vol. 3, 1898 (Austin, Texas), 77–78, available at https://texashistory. unt.edu/ark:/67531/metapth6728/.) Hudson's survey first appears on an 1867 Tarrant County map. See 1867 Tarrant County, Texas map, Map/Doc 4066, General Map Collection, Texas General Land Office (Publisher) George J. Thielepape (Compiler), https://historictexasmaps.com/collection/search-results/4066-map-of-tarrant-county- general-map-collection. TCU's location on the Hudson and other surveys can be viewed at the General Land Office's GIS land and lease mapping viewer, https://gisweb.glo. texas.gov/glomapjs/index.html, accessed June 13, 2023.

21. "Trustees Select Site at Forest Park," *Fort Worth Star-Telegram*, June 5, 1910, 8; "Forest Park Will Be Chosen as T. C. U. Site," *Fort Worth Star-Telegram*, June 2, 1910, 1; "T.C.U. Will Erect Eleven Handsome Big Buildings Here," *Fort Worth Star-Telegram*, October 16, 1910, 25; "T.C.U. Returns after 38 Years," *Fort Worth Star-Telegram*, September 3, 1911, 7; and *A Catalog of the Officers and Students of Texas Christian University* 7, no. 3 (May 1910): 13, TCU Digital Repository. Unless otherwise indicated, all TCU publications referenced in this essay can be found at TCU Digital Repository, https://repository.tcu. edu/, accessed June 5, 2023.

22. *Catalog of the Officers and Students of Texas Christian University*, 13; "Add Ran College Was a Pioneering School in This Section of Texas," *Stephenville Empire-Tribune*, September 8, 1933, 2. See also "Thorp Springs A Beauty Spot; 40 Miles Ft. Worth!" *Fort Worth Star-Telegram*, May 23, 1909, 20.

23. "Our Campus," TCU website, https://www.tcu.edu/about/our-campus.php, accessed June 5, 2023.

24. "Add-Ran Open Session," *Skiff* 3, no. 16 (December 21, 1904): 1, 4; see also *The Horned Frog 1905* (Waco: Texas Christian University, 1904), unnumbered page.

25. "These Fifty Years," Golden Jubilee Celebration Pageant program booklet, Texas Christian University (June 5, 1923), 7, 23–24.

26. For a brief overview of the meaning and background of *Tejas*, see Phillip L. Fry, "Texas, Origin of Name," *Handbook of Texas Online*, https://www.tshaonline.org/handbook/entries/ texas-origin-of-name, accessed June 14, 2023.

27. "Centennial Celebration to Provide Views of Past, Present, Future," *Daily Skiff* 70, no. 73 (February 17, 1972): 2; Centennial Convocation, Texas Christian University (January 25, 1973), 6.

28. For a brief overview of the Adobe Walls battle, see "Adobe Walls, Second Battle of," *Handbook of Texas Online*, https://www.tshaonline.org/handbook/entries/adobe- walls-second-battle-of, and Michael D. Pierce, "Red River War (1874–1875)," *Encyclopedia of Oklahoma History and Culture*, https://www.okhistory.org/publications/enc/entry. php?entry=RE010, both accessed June 14, 2023.

29. Edward McShane Waits, *The Report of the Texas Christian University to the State Convention of the*

Christian Church, Houston, Texas (April 26–29, 1927), 7–8; Colby D. Hall, "To the Youth of T.C.U.," *Horned Frog 1931*, 21; Hall, *History of Texas Christian University: The Meaning of Gifts*, Texas Christian University and the Building Program Committee (1946), 5; *Seventy-Fifth Anniversary Program* (September 20, 1948), 3; and "Clarks Persevered to Create Add-Ran," *Daily Skiff* 96, no. 59 (January 22, 1999): 1.

30. Ed. S. McKinney, "The Legend of Lover's Leap," *Skiff* 1, no. 33 (May 16, 1903): 4. See also Decca Lamar West, *The Legend of Lovers' Leap and an Historical Sketch of Waco, Texas* (Waco: Knight Printing, 1912), https://babel.hathitrust.org/cgi/pt?id=loc.ark:/13960/t5v69s89v&view=1up&seq=3 and Prisca Bird, "Lover's Leap," Institute for Oral History and the Texas Collection, Baylor University, https://wacohistory.org/items/show/38, accessed June 15, 2023.

31. *Skiff* 20, no. 8 (November 14, 1921): 1. Haskell defeated TCU, 14–0; "Superior Football Fails to Score; Indians Rally and Defeat Christians," *Skiff* 20, no. 9 (November 21, 1921): 1; "Indians, Broncos Trounce Frogs," *Daily Skiff* 74, no. 50 (December 3, 1975): 4. Haskell was founded in 1884 in Lawrence, Kansas, as a Native American boarding school operated by the federal government. It is now Haskell Indian Nations University.

32. "Commencement Week Opens Wednesday Eve with May Festival" and "Rehearsals for May Fete Promise Great Success for Affair," *Skiff* 20, no. 31 (May 29, 1922): 1 and *The Horned Frog 1923*, 224 (for May Fete) and 236 (for Shirley-Walton banquet).

33. "Hulbert Smith's Heap Big Hobby Indian Collection," *Skiff* 34, no. 16 (January 17, 1936): 2; "Editorial Comment," *Skiff* 55, no. 22 (March 8, 1957): 6; "Sports Talk," *Daily Skiff* 79, no. 29 (October 22, 1980): 4.

34. *The Horned Frog 1925*, unnumbered page. "Football Men Have Nick-names Varying from Trustee to Popeye" *Skiff* 31, no. 8 (November 11, 1932): 6; "Football Champions of 1938," booklet (Fort Worth: T.C.U. Ex-Letterman's Association, 1938), unnumbered page; *The Horned Frog 1943*, unnumbered page.

35. "Little Stories with Big Morals," *Skiff* 58, no. 26 (January 8, 1960): 5.

36. "Chemist Catalogues Cactus Compounds," *Skiff* 65, no. 7 (October 7, 1966): 11. There is a long history of non-Natives misunderstanding and villainizing peyote and its ceremonial use. For a brief explanation, see Omer C. Stewart, *Peyote Religion: A History* (Norman: University of Oklahoma Press, 1987), 3–14. In short, "Peyote is not habit forming, and in the controlled ambience of a peyote meeting it is in no way harmful" (pg. 3).

37. "Campus Security should 'hoof it' when patrolling," *Daily Skiff* 76, no. 8 (September 14, 1977): 2.

38. "TCU Professor's Book Nominated for Pulitzer Prize," *Daily Skiff* 82, no. 12 (September 21, 1983): 1; Todd Camp, "The Campus Underground," *Au Courant*, February 18, 1985, 4.

39. "Cast Is Named for Indian Pageant at T.C.U.," *Fort Worth Star-Telegram*, May 6, 1928, 9; "Indian Pageant Given at TCU Stadium," *Fort Worth Star-Telegram*, May 13, 1928, 46; *Texas Christian University Interpreter* 2, no. 6–7 (April–May 1928): 8; *The Horned Frog 1928*, 191; "Practice on Annual P.T. Pageant Is Started," *Skiff* 26, no. 18 (February 22, 1928): 3; "Annual Indian Pageant on May 12," *Skiff* 26, no. 28 (May 9, 1928): 1; and *1928 May Fete* program.

40. *Horned Frog 1913*, 153.

41. Texas Christian University Glee Club program, 1915–16 season, 4.

42. *Horned Frog 1928*, 184, and *1927 May Fete* program.

43. "Early Religious Life of Texas Portrayed," *Skiff* 29, no. 2 (September 26, 1930): 1; "350 Girls to be Guests of W.A.A.," *Skiff* 29, no. 24 (March 20, 1931): 1; "Water Pageant to Be Seen Monday," *Skiff* 31, no. 13 (January 12, 1933): 1; "Pageant Draws Crowd," *Skiff* 31, no. 14 (January 20, 1933): 1; "Jack Murphy Dreams, Composes Masterpiece on Texas Centennial," *Skiff* 34, no. 21 (February 21, 1936): 2.

44. "700 Participants to Give Cantata Tomorrow Night," *Skiff* 29, no. 30 (May 8, 1931): 1; "16,000 Laud Presentation of 'The Sunset Trail," Charles W. Cadman's Famous Operatic Cantata," *Skiff* 29, no. 31 (May 15, 1931): 1. Regarding Dietzel, see "Parts Are Given in Pageant Work," *Skiff* 29, no. 28 (April 24, 1931): 1. While he was described as an "Indian chief" in a subsequent article, I can find no evidence suggesting that he was Native American. Federal census information indicates that his family was from Germany. See "Gold Dust Twins," *Skiff* 29, no. 33 (May 29, 1931): 3.

45. "Musical Numbers Are Announced for 'Daze of '29'," *Skiff* 33, no. 15 (January 25, 1935): 3; "N.R.A. Is Motif Underlying Plot of 'Daze of '29'," *Skiff* 33, no. 21 (March 8, 1935): 1.

46. "Annual Pageant Will Be at 7:45 Tomorrow Night," *Skiff* 34, no. 31 (May 8, 1936): 1; "4000 See History Enacted in Pageant," *Skiff* 34, no. 33 (May 22, 1936): 1.

47. "Tunes, Old and New, Are Featured in May Pageant Tomorrow Night," *Skiff* 37, no. 30 (May 12, 1939): 1.

48. "Pageant Almost Ready; Coeds Working Fast," *Skiff* 38, no. 32 (May 3, 1940): 1; "TCU's Pageant Will Rival the Varsity Show or Casa Manana in Spectacle and Scenery," *Skiff* 38, no. 33 (May 10, 1940): 1.

49. "Texas' Romance to Be Depicted in Spring Pageant," *Skiff* 40, no. 25 (March 20, 1942): 1.

50. "Scientists Make Western Tour in Furnished House on Wheels," *Skiff* 31, no. 9 (November 18, 1932): 1; "Mrs. Cahoon Speaks on Indian Music," *Skiff* 31, no. 14 (January 20, 1933): 3; "Mrs. Winton Speaks to Literature Class," *Skiff* 31, no. 19 (March 3, 1933): 1; "Mrs. Winton to Speak," *Skiff* 32, no. 19 (February 23, 1934): 3; "Mrs. Winton Speaks to Literature Class," *Skiff* 32, no. 21 (March 9, 1934): 3; "Pictures of Indians to Be Shown April 6," *Skiff* 32, no. 23 (March 23, 1934): 1; "Wintons' Films Will Be Shown," *Skiff* 32, no. 24 (April 6, 1934): 1; "Sigma Tau Deltas to Meet Tuesday," *Skiff* 33, no. 8 (November 9, 1934): 3; "New Smith-Major Book Southwest Interpretation," *Skiff* 37, no. 17 (February 10, 1939): 1.

51. "Indians Alive and Well at TCU," *Daily Skiff* 75, no. 95 (April 26, 1977): 2; "'Indians': Vietnam in the Old West," *Daily Skiff* 71, no. 28 (October 20, 1972): 3; Maurice Boyd, "Peyotism: The Kiowas' Religion and a Memory of Tribal Dignity," *Daily Skiff* 79, no. 38 (November 6, 1980): 2; "Author Chronicles Kiowa Heritage," *Daily Skiff* 80, no. 43 (November 17, 1981): 1; "Addenda. Kiowa Voices," *Dallas Morning News*, April 3, 1983: 183; "Book Preserves Kiowas' Legacy," *Fort Worth Star-Telegram*, April 6, 1983: 1; "'Indians' Review by Larry Bouchard," *Daily Skiff* 71, no. 32 (October 27, 1972): 3; "Events," *TCU This Week* 5.22 (February 14, 2000): 1.

52. "Oklahoma Indian, Son of Pawnee Chief, At T.C.U.," *Skiff* 27, no. 21 (February 27, 1929): 1; "Indian's Voice Puts Him through Texas College," *Pawnee Courier-Dispatch*, July 25, 1929, 9; "Bert Peters All-Around Man at O.B.U.," *Pawnee Courier-Dispatch*, July 7, 1932, 1. See also "Pawnee Indian News," *Pawnee Courier-Dispatch*, March 14, 1929, 3.

53. *Horned Frog 1938*, 174; "Allie White, Tackle," *Football Champions of 1938 Texas Christian University* booklet, TCU's ex-Lettermen's Association, 1938, unnumbered page; *Horned Frog 1939*, 186; "Allie White," Texas Sports Hall of Fame, https://www.tshof.org/

store/p366/Allie_White.html, accessed June 19, 2023. See also "'38 Froggies Frolic to Championship," *Skiff* 57, no. 7 (October 31, 1958): 4.

54. "'Cherokee' Jack Is 'Bull' Fiddler, Guitar Strummer," *Skiff* 38, no. 10 (November 17, 1939): 4; "'Sa Fact," *Skiff* 38, no. 26 (March 21, 1941): 2.

55. *Horned Frog 1943*, unnumbered page.

56. "Names 'n Notes," *Skiff* 46, no. 36 (June 18, 1948): 2.

57. "Calm Down, Men, It Ain't Injuns: That's Ole 'Gatorfoot' Harris," *Skiff* 51, no. 6 (October 24, 1952): 7.

58. "Rattlesnake Eggs and Nursing Interest Three Arizona Coeds," *Skiff* 51, no. 7 (October 31, 1952): 11.

59. "Cherokee Lassie Ah-Neu-Et Finds Happy Stomping Ground at TCU," *Skiff* 52, no. 9 (November 13, 1953): 5.

60. Devon Abbott, "Ancestry Sacrificed to Greed," *Daily Skiff* 85, no. 46 (April 24, 1985): 2; "Indians against Display of Remains," *Daily Skiff* 85, no. 55 (December 3, 1987): 2; "Ancestors Defended by Indians," *Fort Worth Star-Telegram*, May 21, 1986. See also "Devon A. Mihesuah," American Indian Health and Diet Project, https://aihd.ku.edu/exercise/AboutMeMihesuah.html, accessed June 20, 2023.

61. "Foreign—Native Students Meet in Friendship Club," *Horned Frog 1965*, 314; "Committee Deems Diversity Important for University's Future," *Daily Skiff* 87, no. 31 (October 18, 1989): 1; "Organizations Still Face Diversity Issues," *Daily Skiff* 101, no. 94 (March 26, 2004): 1; "History Professor Leaves over Lack of Ethnic Courses," *Daily Skiff* 91, no. 43 (November 10, 1993): 1; TCU Factbook, Institutional Research, Students, https://ir.tcu.edu/facts-data/students/, accessed June 20, 2023.

62. "Native American Cultural Awareness Goal for New Campus Organization," *Daily Skiff* 89, no. 39 (November 5, 1991): 1; "Native Americans to Apply for Official Recognition on Campus," *Daily Skiff* 89, no. 67 (February 6, 1992): 1; "Student Group Celebrates Native American Month," *Daily Skiff* 93, no. 48 (November 16, 1995): 1; interview with Larry Adams, part 2, TCU Oral History Project, Spring 2012, https://tcu.digication.com/the_tcu_oral_history_project/Larry_Adams_Second_interview.

63. "Second Discrimination Charge Filed," *Daily Skiff* 72, no. 103 (May 2, 1974): 1; "Indian Art Is Specialty of New Faculty Member," *Daily Skiff* 73, no. 8 (September 17, 1974): 6; "HEW Finds Discrimination, NAACP Says," *Daily Skiff* 74, no. 13 (September 24, 1975): 1; "Minority Hiring Hard," *Daily Skiff* 85, no. 105 (April 20, 1988): 1; TCU Factbook, Institutional Research, Faculty & Staff, https://ir.tcu.edu/facts-data/faculty-staff/, accessed June 20, 2023.

64. The Kiowa Five were actually six artists: Spencer Asah (1905 or 1910–1954), Jack Hokeah (1902–1969), Stephen Mopope (1898–1974), Monroe Tsatoke (1904–1937), Lois (Bougetah) Smoky (1907–1981), and James Auchiah (1906–1974). "Two Kiowa Indians Visit Campus," *Skiff* 32, no. 7 (November 3, 1933): 4; "Next Forums Showing: Mohawks Pro Peace," *Daily Skiff* 70, no. 74 (February 18, 1972): 1; "Pictures Loaned to Library," *Skiff* 32, no. 18 (February 16, 1934): 5; "Students Dance to Different Drum," *Daily Skiff* 70, no. 77 (February 24, 1972): 1; "Time to Heal Wounded Knee," *Daily Skiff* 73, no. 51 (December 5, 1974): 1; "Novelist to Join Honors Fest," *Daily Skiff* 71, no. 90 (March 23, 1973): 1; "Author Stresses Imagination," *Daily Skiff* 71, no. 94 (March 30, 1973): 1; "Come to Church—but Bring Your Loincloth," *Daily Skiff* 75, no. 22 (October 8, 1976): 5;

"Creative Writing Week to Feature Novelists," *Daily Skiff* 81, no. 81 (March 29, 1983): 3; "Poets' Readings to End Creative Writing Week," *Daily Skiff* 81, no. 82 (March 30, 1983): 3; "Divinity Student Befriends Kickapoo Indian Tribe," *Daily Skiff* 81, no. 75 (February 23, 1983): 1; "House Reaches Out to Help Shunned Indians," *Daily Skiff* 83, no. 85 (March 15, 1984): 3; "Praise Due TCU Community for Labor of Love," *Daily Skiff* 83, no. 91 (April 3, 1984): 2; "Kickapoos: Tribe with No Homeland," *Daily Skiff* 85, no. 51 (May 2, 1985): 3; "Food Drive," *Fort Worth Star-Telegram*, May 14, 1986, 29; Larry J. Crocker, "The Plight of the Kickapoo Indians: An Appeal for Assistance," March 10, 1983, TCU Special Collections; "Mankiller Looks to Bright Future," *Daily Skiff* 84, no. 101 (April 23, 1987): 1; "About Brite," Brite Divinity School, https://brite.edu/aboutbrite, accessed July 24, 2023. For Sakokwenonkwas's background, see https://concord-ium.us/programs/degree-offering/collegium/tom-porter-sakikwenionkwas/, accessed June 21, 2023.

Part III: Being in Relation with Native Community Partners

How to Talk about MMIW:
Pedagogy and Partnerships between Indigenous Organizers and University Faculty

1. See Sarah Deer, *The Beginning and End of Rape: Confronting Sexual Violence in Native America* (Minneapolis: University of Minnesota Press, 2015) and Sabina E. Vaught, Bryan McKinley Jones Brayboy, and Chin Jeremiah, *The School-Prison Trust* (Summertown: University of Minnesota Press, 2022).

2. MMIW Texas was founded under the umbrella of the organization American Indian Heritage Day in Texas in 2018. In 2022, the organization was renamed MMIW Texas Rematriate and became independent of AIHD. Though the organization operated under two different names during the period described in this essay, we will refer to it by its current name for consistency. A note on terminology: MMIW was the first acronym used in the broader movement, though over the years, the mission of many organizers doing MMIW work has expanded to include a focus on missing girls, Two Spirit people, and Native people/relatives more broadly. Organizers in the movement and particular organizations will sometimes use different acronyms to reflect this expansive work. MMIW Texas Rematriate uses the history of its name to narrate the evolving breadth of its work. In particular, the addition of "Rematriate" was an effort to emphasize the importance of land, the larger context of Native ways of knowing and being in the world, and the significance of matrilineality in this work. In Voice Yellowfish's words, "What happens to the land, happens to the people."

3. "Missing and Murdered Indigenous Women, Girls, and Two-Spirit People," TCU Women and Gender Studies, AddRan College of Liberal Arts, Texas Christian University, n.d., https://addran.tcu.edu/wgst/community/missing-indigenous-women.php#accd23e114-mmiw-scholarship, accessed September 15, 2023. We intentionally use the term "responsibility" to invoke and to act upon the commitment made in the TCU Land Acknowledgement, which "reminds us of our benefits, responsibilities, and relationships." TCU's "responsibility" in this context is toward our local Native organizers and all of those impacted by MMIW, with whom the TCU community exists in relation.

4. "Missing and Murdered Indigenous Women, Girls, and Two-Spirit People."

5. "Missing and Murdered Indigenous Women, Girls, and Two-Spirit People."

6. By tokenized, we mean the extractive use of a Native person's or community's identity,

knowledge, culture, or experience to benefit a non-Native person or community without reciprocity.

7. See, for example, NFB Education, "MMIWG: Breaking the Silence, Starting the Conversation in Classrooms," NFB Blog, November 16, 2020, https://blog.nfb.ca/blog/2020/11/16/edu-mmiwg-breaking-the-silence-starting-the-conversation-in-classrooms/; Shauneen Peet, "Troubling Curricula: Teaching and Learning about MMIW," Opentextbooks.uregina.ca, October 2021, https://opentextbooks.uregina.ca/femicide/chapter/15-troubling-curricula-teaching-and-learning-about-mmiw46/; "Their Voices Will Guide Us," n.d., https://www.mmiwg-ffada.ca/wp-content/uploads/2018/11/NIMMIWG-THEIR-VOICES-WILL-GUIDE-US.pdf, accessed September 15, 2023; Roopika Risam, "Indigenizing Decolonial Media Theory: The Extractive and Redistributive Currencies of Media Activism," *Feminist Media Histories* 8, no. 1 (Winter 2022): 134–164; and Vaught, Brayboy, and Jeremiah, *School-Prison Trust*.

8. "Intake" refers to the formal process of ascertaining the facts of a particular missing person's situation, which precedes the organization's formal work with the relatives of the missing person.

Building Trust:
The Dallas–Fort Worth Native Community and Texas Christian University

1. Whenever I use the word Traditional, I am referring to a way of life, behavioral practices, or worldview that is distinctive and related to common threads among Native families who try to put into practice our historical knowledge.

2. "Understanding the ICWA," the ICWA Law Center website, 2014, https://www.icwlc.org/education-hub/understanding-the-icwa/.

3. "Larry Larney Obituary," *Dallas Morning News*, December 2012, https://obits.dallasnews.com/us/obituaries/dallasmorningnews/name/larry-larney-obituary?id=7179356.

4. "Indian Boy Suspended from School for Wearing Long Hair," UPI Archives, September 26, 1992, https://www.upi.com/Archives/1992/09/26/Indian-boy-suspended-from-school-for-wearing-long-hair/2426717480000.

5. At the time of the first Santa Fe Days event in 2004, the Santo Domingo Pueblo was not as open to outsiders as other Pueblos. Handmade jewelry by the Tribal members was usually sold through traders. When Mr. Oldfield met the Disabled Veterans Groups at the Vietnam Memorial in Angel Fire, New Mexico, it was reportedly one of the first times the Pueblo government allowed them to go outside the Pueblo to sell. When Mr. Oldfield approached them about coming to Texas, it required a meeting with the full Pueblo council. He complained about the amount of tobacco smoke in the air and how they passed around a cigarette as they spoke. He was not aware that they were smoking tobacco at this meeting as a way to make a ceremonial decision about allowing these Tribal members to go outside the state. Ultimately, the council and the lieutenant governor of the State of New Mexico had to officially approve their participation in the event. Since 2004, when this agreement was approved, our annual event honors this agreement with the Santo Domingo Pueblo.

6. "Frank Rush," the Gateway to Oklahoma History, Oklahoma Historical Society, https://gateway.okhistory.org/ark:/67531/metadc1622911/, accessed August 31, 2023.

7. "Past Attractions," SFOT Source, https://www.sfotsource.com/past-attractions?itemId=iu5c79cic4h5tjxvjtu4f1imozpf2d, accessed August 31, 2023.

8. Patrisia Gonzales, "Last Caretakers of the Trinity River," Indigenous Institute of the Americas, https://iiamericas.org/last-caretakers-of-the-trinity-river/, accessed August 31, 2023.

9. Vivian Elizabeth Smyrl, "Texas Sunset Advisory Commission," Texas State Historical Association, https://www.tshaonline.org/handbook/entries/texas-sunset-advisory-commission, John R. Wunder, "Texas Indian Commission," Texas State Historical Association, https://www.tshaonline.org/handbook/entries/texas-indian-commission, accessed August 31, 2023.

10. Haury Program, "Faculty Fellow Patrisia Gonzales Connects People with Resources and across Indigenous Experiences and Histories," Agnese Nelms Haury Program in Environment and Social Justice, The University of Arizona, August 20, 2020, https://www.haury.arizona.edu/news/faculty-fellow-patrisia-gonzales-connects-people-resources-and-across-indigenous-experiences.

11. "Women in Business: Tosawi Pena, American Indian Chamber of Commerce of Texas," *Dallas Business Journal,* June 14, 2013, https://www.bizjournals.com/dallas/print-edition/2013/06/14/tosawi-pen-american-indian-chamber-of.html.

12. Martin Frost, "Urban Inter-Tribal Center of Texas," Local Legacies, Library of Congress, https://memory.loc.gov/diglib/legacies/loc.afc.afc-legacies.200003564/index.html, accessed August 31, 2023.

13. See, for example, the document produced by the Native American Center for Excellence: Substance Abuse Prevention titled "Executive Summary: Steps for Conducting Research and Evaluation in Native Communities," Substance Abuse and Mental Health Services Administration, 2020, https://www.samhsa.gov/sites/default/files/nace-steps-conducting-research-evaluation-native-communities.pdf.

14. Audra D. S. Burch, "In Texas, Lawmakers Ban D.E.I. at Colleges: [National Desk]," *New York Times*, May 30, 2023.

15. "New First-Year Scholarship Aims to Develop Leaders for Tribal Nations," *TCU News*, September 6, 2023, https://www.tcu.edu/news/2023/new-first-year-scholarship-aims-to-develop-leaders-for-tribal-nations.php.

INDEX

ABOUT THE EDITORS

Theresa Strouth Gaul is professor of English and director of the Core Curriculum at Texas Christian University. She has published numerous books and articles in nineteenth-century American literature, Native and Indigenous Studies, US women's writing, and epistolary writings. She helped to found the TCU Native American and Indigenous Peoples Initative.

Scott M. Langston works in the fields of Native American studies, reception history of the Bible, and Southern Jewish History. He recently retired from Texas Christian University where he taught in the Religion Department and helped to found the university's Native American and Indigenous Peoples Initiative, including serving as the inaugural Native American Nations and Communities Liaison.

C. Annette Anderson, LCSW, is a forty-plus-year Licensed Clinical Social Worker/Supervisor. She is on the Council for the Indigenous Institute of the Americas and the Native American Advisory Circle at Texas Christian University. She is Chair for the IIA 2-day Native American Celebration (IIAC). Ms. Anderson is a Chickasaw and Cherokee descendant.

www.ingramcontent.com/pod-product-compliance
Lightning Source LLC
Chambersburg PA
CBHW040142270326
41928CB00023B/3301